Between Nationalism and Europeanisation
Narratives of National Identity in Bulgaria and Macedonia

Nevena Nancheva

Copyright © Nevena Nancheva 2015

First published by the ECPR Press in 2015

The ECPR Press is the publishing imprint of the European Consortium for Political Research (ECPR), a scholarly association, which supports and encourages the training, research and cross-national co-operation of political scientists in institutions throughout Europe and beyond.

ECPR Press
Harbour House
Hythe Quay
Colchester
CO2 8JF
United Kingdom

All rights reserved. No part of this book may be reprinted or reproduced or utilised in any form or by any electronic, mechanical, or other means, now known or hereafter invented, including photocopying and recording, or in any information storage or retrieval system, without permission in writing from the publishers.

Typeset by Lapiz Digital Services

Printed and bound by Lightning Source

British Library Cataloguing in Publication Data

A catalogue record for this book is available from the British Library

ISBN 978-1-785-521-43-0

PDF ISBN 978-1-785-521-84-3

EPUB ISBN 978-1-785-521-85-0

KINDLE ISBN 978-1-785-521-86-7

ECPR Press Series Editors
Peter Kennealy (European University Institute)
Alexandra Segerberg (Stockholm University)
Ian O'Flynn (Newcastle University)

More on the European Union and International Relations from ECPR Press

Consultative Committees in the European Union: No Vote, No Influence?
Diana Panke, Christoph Hönnige and Julia Gollub
How, and under which conditions, can the EU's consultative committees exert influence if they have access to legislators (voice) but no formal veto power (vote)?
ISBN 9781910259429

Integrating Indifference: A Comparative, Qualitative and Quantitative Approach to the Legitimacy of European Integration
Virginie Van Ingelgom
The author explores the various faces of indifference to European integration, from fatalism, to detachment and distance, via sheer indecision.
ISBN 9781907301483

Democratic Institutions and Authoritarian Rule in Southeast Europe
Danijela Dolenec
Why did post-communist democratisation in this region disappoint initial expectations? The author argues that progress was hindered by the nondemocratic practices of dominant authoritarian parties, which continue to subvert the rule of law today.
ISBN 1781907301438

To my parents

Contents

List of Figures and Tables	ix
List of Abbreviations	xi
Chapter One – Introduction: External Europeanisation, Conflict and the Boundaries of National Community	1
Chapter Two – National Identity and Political Community in Europe	15
Chapter Three – Which Narratives? Studying the Europeanisation of National Identities	35
Chapter Four – Identity without Europe: Bulgaria and Macedonia before Europeanisation	47
Chapter Five – From Conflict to Reconciliation: The European Ways	79
Chapter Six – Narrating National Identity within the Realm of Europe	151
Chapter Seven – Conclusion: Legitimacy and the Europeanisation of National Identities	173
Bibliography	187
Index	201

List of Figures and Tables

Figure

Figure 7.1: Discursive logic of the Europeanisation of national identity narratives   180

Tables

Table 3.1: Units of analysis   40

Table 3.2: Analytical timeline and salience of identity narratives   43

Table 3.3: Identity narratives of Self with examples of established modifications   45

Table 3.4: Identity narratives of Other: examples of established modifications   46

Table 4.1: Discursive patterns of national identity before Europeanisation: Bulgaria and Macedonia   77

Table 5.1: Identity narratives of recognition and post-recognition in Bulgaria and Macedonia   105

Table 5.2: Narratives of the language dispute in Bulgaria and Macedonia   125

Table 5.3: Narratives on national minorities in Bulgaria and Macedonia   147

Table 6.1: Changed patterns of national identity: Bulgaria and Macedonia   171

List of Abbreviations

BTA	Bulgarian Telegraph Agency
FYRoM	Former Yugoslav Republic of Macedonia
PHARE	Poland and Hungary Assistance for the Restructuring of the Economy
UDF	United Democratic Forces
UMO Ilinden	United Macedonian Organisation Ilinden
UMO Ilinden–PIRIN	United Macedonian Organisation Ilinden – Party for Economic Development and Integration of the Peoples
VMRO	Internal Macedonian Revolutionary Organisation
VMRO–DPMNE	Internal Macedonian Revolutionary Organisation – Democratic Party for Macedonian National Unity
VMRO–SMD	Internal Macedonian Revolutionary Organisation – Union of the Macedonian Associations
VMRO–Tatkovinsko	Internal Macedonian Revolutionary Organisation – Tatkovisnko
VMRO–TMO	Internal Macedonian Revolutionary Organisation – Traditional Macedonian Organisation

Chapter One

Introduction: External Europeanisation, Conflict and the Boundaries of National Community

This book explores the impact of Europeanisation on the narration of national identity in the context of the European Union (EU) enlargement agenda. The goal is to assess any modifications in demarcating the boundaries of national political community within the dynamics of Europeanisation and what their effects are on the perceived legitimacy of both national politics and integration. The theoretical background against which this research goal has been formulated covers several central issues in the study of European politics: the challenged legitimacy and relevance of European integration to national politics; the role of nationalism and the phenomena associated with it in antagonistic polities, policies and politics; the place of national identity in legitimising the political community of the state. The empirical reference point of the analysis is the identity-based conflict that governed Bulgarian–Macedonian relations in the years following the break-up of communism, and the reconciliation efforts that both states made in view of their preparation for EU membership negotiations. This book is therefore about nationalism in Bulgarian–Macedonian relations as much as it is about Europeanisation and its complex links to national identity. This might seem disconcerting to those accustomed to the habitual Orientalist undertones found in studies of Balkan conflicts, and to those socialised into analysing the external dimension of Europeanisation through the conditionality framework and the debate between benefits-focused rationalists and norm-oriented constructivists. The book hopes to challenge both.

I attempt to demonstrate that, beyond the specific historical contexts, there is nothing too peculiar in the way national identities in Bulgaria and Macedonia have been constructed and maintained. National identity is being narrated with reference to discursive elements common to all national identity constructions. There is nothing essentially region-specific in the way Bulgarian and Macedonian leaderships have strived to engage with national identity narration as a vehicle to popular mobilisation, influence in the public sphere, and, ultimately, power. There is nothing unusual in the antagonisms engendered by national identities narrated in contradictory and mutually exclusive terms. And there is nothing surprising in the reconciliatory effects of narrating such identity stories with consideration for the other and their own national stories, as well as with consideration of a common future. But the inertia of studying identity-based conflict in the Balkans as a phenomenon alien to Europe has framed the Balkans as the European exception when it comes to nationalism (Rutar, 2014). Identity-based struggles within the EU (such as demands for devolution and autonomy) have not been systematically approached through the framework of the study of nationalism. Within the Western part of the European continent, the liberal democratic tradition had locked nationalist ideas in the clockwork of 'client politics' (Freeman, 1995), legal constitutional constraints and moral obligations towards 'historically particular groups' (Joppke, 1998: 266) – that is, until the non-antagonistic façade of liberal democracy (Mouffe, 2000, 2007) was challenged by the stronger and more diverse migration flows of the past couple of decades. Globalisation, enlargement to post-communist Europe, the transformed visibility of local Muslim communities in view of the 'War on Terror', economic and humanitarian migrants and refugees from troubled spots in Africa and the Middle East, all reminded Europe of its internal Others: xenophobia, racism and nationalism (Risse, 2010; Delanty *et al.*, 2011). Identity-based antagonisms at the level of national politics have thus become an integral element in shaping political contestation in Europe (Hooghe and Marks, 2009: 2). In this sense, there is nothing essentially different in nationalism and identity-based conflictuality in the Balkans, as compared to the rest of Europe. This is the first key message that this book hopes to send across: one that is meant both as an academic challenge and a political warning.

In just the same way, I hope to show that Europeanisation in its external dimension (that which refers to EU candidate states) is much more about identity politics than it is about conditionality and norm transfer. More than a decade ago, in a work that is now a cornerstone in the study of external Europeanisation, Frank Schimmelfennig (2001) pointed to the identity arguments (the 'rhetorical entrapment') that governed the EU in its seemingly perplexing decision to enlarge to post-communist Europe. I argue that the commitment of candidate states to the process of Europeanisation and the successful completion of this process is also a matter of identity politics, and one that goes beyond the 'rhetorical entrapment' described by Schimmelfennig. This is not an original argument in itself: Lene Hansen and Ole Wæver (2002) have analysed the accession of the Nordic states (and the dissent of Norway) along these lines. But the Balkans have never been studied in the same way as the Nord! It is often axiomatically presumed that, because of the economic and socio-political tribulations in the region, Balkan states see the mere benefit of membership as 'the main rationale [...] for adopting the *acquis*' (Sedelmeier, 2011: 6), never mind identity politics (compare Ingebritsen and Larson, 1997). This book points to the limitations of such claims. It argues that European leverage in the Balkans is conditional upon the Europeanisation of national identities, not the other way around. Failure to successfully incorporate Europe *and* its states as an element of the national story, as Macedonia's case demonstrates, can halt and perhaps cancel the progress of Europeanisation, despite the allure of membership and the adoption of European norms. This is the second key message of this book.

Because of its explicit double focus on the complex antagonistic relationship between two Balkan states and their engagement with Europeanisation as EU candidate members, this book is also about the project of European integration and its relationship with nationalism. Studies of European integration and nationalism usually take one of two courses. They often conceptualise Europeanisation as the antidote to nationalism and point to an emerging European identity that can, over time, become the basis of a post-national 'community of Europeans' (in Thomas Risse's powerful vocabulary) transcending the borders of the nation-states and the limits of nationalism. Alternatively, they demonstrate the 'apparent exclusionary [and boundary-making] aspects of the EU' (Karolewski and Suszycki, 2011: 196) to claim that the best European integration can hope for in terms of political community is to replicate nationalism at the supranational level (also, Billig, 1995: 141). This book cannot side with either of these strands of research. National identity may, indeed, be 'historically non-coincidental', as Karolewski and Suszycki suggest (2010: 74). But this means that it may not be possible for national identity to be replaced or superseded at the supranational level by either a cosmopolitan or a nationalist European identity. On the one hand, the supranational polity created by the process of integration lacks some of the constitutive elements that established the nation-state as the norm. Primarily, it lacks the self-sacrificial, pre-given allegiance that nationalism has been able to ascribe to identification with the nation-state (Bloom, 1990). Thus, identification with the supranational polity cannot be meaningfully compared with national identity and the negative consequences of nationalism. On the other hand, thinking of European integration as a *sui generis* nationalist project at the supranational level overlooks the normative foundation of integration as a vehicle to non-nationalist politics, as well as the fact that the basis of exclusion and boundary-making in the EU is much more complex than in the nation-state. Thus simply extrapolating the same dynamics of identity building at the supranational level tells us nothing of the interaction between integration and nationalism proper.

Research on European integration and nationalism that is interested in the themes of identity, legitimacy and conflict should therefore focus not on the supranational level, where analyses are sometimes forced to operate in the realm of the theoretically possible, but on the level of national politics, where actual observations can be made. By studying the domestic discursive struggles over the meaning of national stories in a political context dominated by nationalist politics but engaged in the process of Europeanisation, this book sets out to do just that. It demonstrates that, albeit displaying some exclusionary aspects, Europeanisation does clash with nationalism in its interpretations of national identity stories. The consequences of this clash are relevant not so much to the supranational but to the level of national politics because that is where the meaning of belonging in Europe is being contested and negotiated (e.g. Hooghe and Marks, 2009).

Studying the impact of Europeanisation on the narration of national identities from the perspective of national politics, this book explores two propositions. The first one is that the Europeanisation of national identities debilitates the structuring logic of nationalism in governing state behaviour, official rhetoric and national policies. As a result, identity-based conflictuality may be managed and reconciled. The second proposition this book explores is that re-narrating national identity within the logic of Europeanisation includes European integration as a discursive element in national identity constructions. As a result, the relevance of integration to national politics appears much more immediate. This outcome, unlike identification with 'Europe' (Hooghe and Marks, 2009), can have direct consequences for maintaining support for integration by bridging the gulf between political contestation and European politics.

These propositions are being explored within the dynamics of external Europeanisation and the specific context of the EU's post-communist enlargement. In this sense they should not be uncritically divorced from the historical circumstances that shaped the studied processes. But the problems that the analysis investigates – the discursive clash between nationalism and Europeanisation in determining the limit of political community and the basis of belonging, and the re-narration of national identity to incorporate the meanings of Europe – by far transcend the specific historical circumstances of the studied cases. The analytical avenues for understanding and analysing these problems, which this book hopes to open, can be followed both within the dynamics of internal Europeanisation, and in external Europeanisation contexts beyond the specific regional enlargement.

Nationalism, elites and political community in Europe

Studying the impact of Europeanisation on the narration of national identity thus implies understanding the discursive struggles that shape the meaning of national identity and the discursive mechanisms that translate this meaning to the language of national politics. It is impossible to understand the former without acknowledging the structuring logic of nationalism, and it is impossible to understand the latter without examining the role of elites.

In different historical ages, people have had different ideas about how far their political communities extended (Deutsch, 1954: 13–14). Historical circumstances in Europe established the sovereign nation-state as the legitimate form of political community: the idea of *popular* sovereignty gradually aligned state jurisdictions (Hooghe and Marks, 2009: 22–3) with nations as personifying the *populi*. Nationalism played a key role in this process. Even in liberal democratic communities the limits of the social contract were marked by national institutions (Rousseau, 1895 [1762]), which in turn had been established on the basis of commonality of culture, language (Fichte, 2009; Herder, 1913, quoted by Barnard, 1967), and people's desire to live together (Renan, 1982). In the absence of a different institutional arrangement for exercising sovereignty, the overlap between the notions of political community, sovereign nation-state, and nation remained unchallenged as the norm (even though, outside the ideal of a national state, these notions never fully overlapped).

European integration changed that. By pooling national sovereignty, it established an alternative centre of power that over the years led scholars to imagine a supranational 'community of Europeans'. In the wake of the first Iraq war and popular protests against it across Europe, Habermas and Derrida saw 'a feeling of common political belonging' (2003: 293) among European citizens. But the majority of analysts now list evidence of decreasing popular support for integration (Karolewski and Kaina, 2012) and citizens' growing distance from the

EU (Hix, 2005: 151; Deutsch, 2006; Hooghe, 2007; Taylor, 2008; Kaina, 2009). The most common claim made on the basis of such evidence is that European citizens want less Europe. Another claim, usually in dissent, argues that European citizens simply want a different kind of Europe (e.g. Bruter, 2008; Hooghe and Marks, 2009) and more say in deciding its course. In any case, there is a strong indication that debates about integration are increasingly being taken down to the level of national politics, where they are meeting resistance to the visions of supranational political community claimed by Habermas.

It may therefore be premature to project and theorise at the supranational level the consequences of European integration for re-imagining the notion of political community outside the boundaries of national sovereignty. As the sovereign nation-state has remained the locus of political contestation, political community 'happens' within the realm of national politics and the consequences of European integration for re-imagining its meaning are to be sought there. Given the structuring role of nationalism in determining the limit of the national political community as personified by the state and described by national identity narratives, the impact of Europeanisation should depend on its ability to displace and marginalise nationalist visions of political community and belonging.

Europeanisation, however, cannot tell its own stories: people can. This means that the impact of Europeanisation on the narration of the political community personified by the state is bound by the willingness of political elites representing the state to tell European stories about national identity and belonging. But while political elites are 'almost constantly in the business of identity constructions', only some of these constructions are consensual at any given point in time (Cowles, Caporaso and Risse-Kappen, 2001: 201). This means that elites are constrained in their interpretations of collective identity by the possibility of summoning popular support for their projects. There are various explanations for these constraints, which usually refer to the compatibility of ideas of Europe with national identities (Marcussen *et al.*, 1999), to electoral calculations (Risse, 2001: 203), or to the elite's ability to appropriate the language of the masses (Deutsch, 1942: 533). Analysts point to the dynamics of norm diffusion and internalisation to demonstrate why certain ideas gain acceptance and begin to be taken for granted (Finnemore and Sikkink, 1998). In any case, such explanations refer to a communicative interaction that happens at the levels and sub-levels of national politics and within the political community contained in the state.

Exploring the discursive mechanisms of this interaction in the re-narration of national identity highlights the central role of political elites in demarcating political community and belonging within the context of Europeanisation. Europeanisation cannot happen on its own. Without the political will to advance the integration project, change in the re-imagining of political community cannot be produced. At the same time, it cannot be 'imposed' from the top: national identity needs to reflect adequately the political community it refers to. This locks elites and their publics into a complex dynamic of renegotiation whose purpose is bifurcated. On the one hand, it aims to secure popular engagement with politics for the purposes of political mobilisation. On the other hand, the renegotiation of national identity needs to secure legitimacy for the agents of sovereign power and governance claiming to represent the political community. It is the mechanisms of this complex dynamic that are the object of investigation of this book.

Europe and the Balkans

This dynamic has been very visible in the process of EU enlargement to post-communist Europe. As soon as EU membership became the key strategic goal of the transition, Europeanisation turned into a visible object of political contestation at the level of national politics in the post-communist states. As they had not participated in the making of the integration project, they had to negotiate anew the rationale behind integration and its inherent good. In many ways this created a historical context similar to the first years of integration, when the added value of the European project to European politics was visible, despite concerns about giving up sovereignty. Traditional EU member states have been separated from this context by many years of participating in the dynamics of integration, which has become a habitual item in the political landscape (and a regular point of debate in the other European democracies). Of course, political elites in traditional EU member states have also had to constantly negotiate the rationale behind EU policies. But the role of the EU polity has long been normalised as a fact of political life. So, even when integration is being criticised within EU member states, it is difficult to draw the line between 'outside Euroscepticism' (which is against integration as a project) and 'inside Euroscepticism' (which is only against certain features of integration), as per Bruter's apt distinction (2008: 275–6). This makes it difficult to study the impact of Europeanisation on political community as there is no clarity on what is cause and what is effect. In this sense, the context of EU enlargement to post-communist Europe offers the unique opportunity of a 'clean slate' in the negotiation of belonging with respect to Europe.

At the same time, no region of Europe's has been so strongly associated with nationalism and its negative consequences for political community as the Balkans (Breuilly, 2014). Among all post-communist states, states in the Balkans have most often been analysed within the frame of nationalism, both in view of their economic and socio-political 'backwardness' (Todorova, 2005), and in view of their antagonistic international and inter-group relations. Taking account of the specific regional context, I endorse Breuilly's argument (2014) that nationalism in the Balkans follows similar lines of formation as nationalism elsewhere in Europe. As an 'elite response' to shifts in global politics (Breuilly, 2014: 45), it is politically contextual and not essentially distinct. By untangling some of the key narratives sustaining nationalist political agendas in two Balkan states, and by tracing their re-narration in view of Europeanisation, I hope to make a contribution to the literature on re-imagining the Balkans in an inclusive manner (Todorova, 1997; Rutar, 2014). But pointing to the highly contextual and contingent nature of the European re-narration, I would also like to draw attention to the political relevance of negotiating the meaning of Europe in the process of external Europeanisation. This concerns especially the states that still firmly carry the 'Balkans' label

(Breuilly, 2014: 45): Bosnia and Herzegovina, Kosovo, Macedonia, Albania, Serbia, Montenegro, as they are lined up for EU membership. Internal EU squabbles about the boundaries of political community have a direct impact on the external role of Europeanisation as an agent of change and on the future of integration as an all-European project. Analysing the process of translating and inscribing the meaning of political community in Europe into the national stories of two Balkan states that currently stand in rather different positions with regard to the EU serves to illustrate this point.

Bulgaria and Macedonia

This book studies Bulgaria and Macedonia in the awareness that both states are considered outliers in Balkan politics in general, and in the respective groups within which they have traditionally been studied. Bulgaria is usually paired with Romania and added to the group of the 2004 EU joiners as the 'laggard' of the group (e.g. Noutcheva and Bechev, 2008; Gati, 1996), only admitted to membership in 2007. Macedonia is usually studied with the so-called 'Western Balkans' group and praised for preserving the peace during the turbulent 1990s when other former Yugoslav republics resorted to violent conflict (Glenny, 2000: 634ff). In the early 2000s, however, Macedonia also succumbed to a brief period of violent inter-ethnic tension (Daskalovski, 2004; Ragaru, 2008), while Bulgaria accelerated the pace of its pre-accession reforms. Taking the two states as the basis of the empirical analysis, this book aims to challenge some of the mental maps used to label the states in groups. It also aims to enhance understanding of the intrinsic peculiarities of recent Bulgarian and Macedonian history, and their similarities with states in the rest of Europe.

But beyond that, Bulgaria and Macedonia offer a good context for a study of the Europeanisation of national identities and its consequences for the boundaries of political community, because of the complex bilateral relations between the two states. From the late nineteenth century, when the political paths of what are now Bulgaria and Macedonia split (Bulgaria embarked on independent statehood while Macedonia remained within the borders of the Ottoman empire), the relationship between Bulgarians, Macedonians and their respective elites has been torn by revolution, political frustration, policy contradictions and propaganda (for historical overviews, Perry, 1988; Tröbst, 1983). Despite their apparent similarities and the long-shared history, the two states plunged into a peculiar bilateral dispute as soon as they emerged out of totalitarianism. For the best part of the 1990s Bulgaria and Macedonia could not establish official bilateral relations or communicate at state level because of a disagreement over language. Bulgarian officials would not recognise Macedonian as a language in its own right (claiming, instead, that it was a dialect of Bulgarian), while Macedonian officials would refuse to speak to their Bulgarian counterparts without an interpreter (despite the great proximity in the two languages). Despite the trivial technicality of such objections, they did prevent official communication between the two states in a crucial period for both. Furthermore, Bulgaria refused to 'recognise' Macedonian nationhood, refused to talk about Macedonian minorities and minority rights within its borders, and refused to allow any political representation to groups identifying themselves with the name 'Macedonian'. Likewise, Macedonia denied any historical commonality with Bulgaria, maintained strong anti-Bulgarian rhetoric in its public sphere, refused to discuss commemorating jointly with Bulgaria common elements of the regional history, and strongly opposed Bulgaria's own commemorations of these. The result was a freeze in bilateral relations and a rise in antagonistic identity politics on both sides of the shared border, hate speech in the media and among the political leadership, mistrust and missed regional opportunities, and the gradual build-up of identity-based conflict.

It is precisely this conflict that makes Bulgaria and Macedonia good cases for a book interested in the external Europeanisation of national identities. After the break-up of communism, the two states joined the 'return to Europe' chorus of the other post-communist states (Risse, 2010) and framed the strategic long-term goal of EU membership as expected evidence of their Europeanisation. In the course of their application and preparation for negotiation and accession, bilateral relations between Bulgaria and Macedonia changed. The two states managed to solve their language dispute diplomatically, to leave their historical controversies gradually behind (at least at state level and in the official public sphere), they consistently worked together to address hate speech and claims of institutional abuse, and to improve and deepen bilateral cooperation in a number of previously unexplored areas, including preparation for EU membership.

The Europeanisation of national identity

How did this happen? What enabled the move from conflict to reconciliation? How was this move employed in the deliberative public spheres of national politics? These are the questions this book sets out to answer. Putting to work a methodological hybrid of discourse and content analysis of textual data from public rhetoric deployed by state actors, combined with historical and foreign policy analysis, I argue that managing the conflict and overcoming the antagonistic rules of the relationship was made possible by a change in the narration of national identity in both states. This change has had both a horizontal and a vertical dimension. Along the horizontal dimension, the change allowed for the reconciliatory re-narration of the immediate regional Other(s) engaged in the Europeanisation dynamic. This debilitated some of the central aspects of the nationalist vision of political community. Along the vertical dimension, the change allowed for the successful inclusion of Europe in the narration of the national stories. This brought integration closer to the dynamics of national politics and increased its political relevance. Both dimensions of the change therefore refer to a political community with different boundaries: one resting upon the foundation of the national stories but engaged with the supranational political order.

This book looks into a very narrow caveat of European politics – of Balkan politics, really. It is a modest attempt to tell a 'small story' about a small part of Europe. But telling this small story against the themes of Europeanisation, legitimacy and identity-based conflict links it to other, 'bigger stories' about European politics. One of these 'bigger stories' is of national identity and its relationship to Europeanisation. The investigation of the identity conflict between Bulgaria and Macedonia points to national identity as the key referent in narrating political community in the two states. The conflict arises from mutually exclusive interpretations and antagonistic narration of the national stories. Examining the gradual reconciliation that followed when the two states joined the Europeanisation dynamic, the analysis identifies changes in the national identity narratives that include European references *and* enable a non-antagonistic narration of the Other. These observations sustain the central argument of this book that the Europeanisation of national identity facilitates the imagining of a political community with different boundaries: in the vertical dimension these boundaries refer to Europe as the EU, while in the horizontal dimension they refer to those national Others that are also engaged with the process of Europeanisation. These changes in the imagining of the political community are important for two reasons. One, they make integration immediately relevant to national politics by inscribing it into the national stories. Two, they can prevent conflict by narrating the national Other(s) in an inclusive and non-antagonistic manner (provided these Others, too, are engaged with Europeanisation).

Obviously, this argument refers to the external strand of Europeanisation (the EU's enlargement agenda) and the regional context in the Balkans (where the legacies of recent identity-based conflict and nationalist politics remain present). However, in view of the renegotiation of the role of European integration in EU member states (internal Europeanisation) and elsewhere, and the ever greater salience of identity-based conflict in Europe (dressed in the language of xenophobia, racism and nationalism against non-EU foreigners, internal EU migrants, religious minorities, asylum seekers and refugees) the key tenet of the argument retains its relevance. Europeanisation changes the dynamics of exclusion and inclusion within the political community and has the potential to redress legitimacy shortfalls in contemporary European politics, if the mechanisms of this change are fully understood and employed. What happens to the notion of political community in the context of Europeanisation and how integration relates to identity-based antagonisms remain central problems in the study of Europeanisation, and ones that invite further research.

Contribution

One of the key messages of this book concerns precisely the role of integration in renegotiating political antagonisms and the basis of inclusion and exclusion in political communities in Europe. Pushing the boundary of Otherness beyond the national through supranational governance and including national Others into a shared communicative space has created a unique opportunity for renegotiating political belonging. Taking advantage of this opportunity or interpreting it as a risk is a political choice that is made individually in each national context and its subcontexts. But understanding the consequences of both routes is a task for academic research, not least because of the centrality of the themes of belonging, community and identity in both national and supranational politics. The correlation between the impact of Europeanisation and reconciliatory policies may contain the potential to alleviate some of the identity-based controversies that Europe is currently struggling with. Rejecting the modifications introduced by Europeanisation in the national discursive spaces, in turn, does not bode well for the future relevance of integration as a central feature of European politics. The logic of nationalism that is inherent in exclusively national governance suggests that national political communities detached from the realm of integration cannot but perpetuate international antagonisms and exclusion of non-members (e.g. Aykaç, 2011: 124–6). Through the specific cases it examines and beyond them, this book aims to highlight the central role of the integration project in renegotiating the basis of belonging in contemporary Europe. The EU's significance in European politics is to be found in its potential to foster commonality on the basis of national differences and to prevent the sedimentation of such differences as a basis for exclusion through engaging its participants in a narrative of common governance. Reconciliation in Bulgarian–Macedonian relations in view of Europeanisation comes to demonstrate how this happens in the practice of the political narration of belonging.

The discursive dynamics generated by the relationship between European integration and national identity narration has two directions. It concerns not only the impact of integration on renegotiating belonging in Europe. Another task this book takes up is to emphasise the impact of the modalities of identity narration upon the course of Europeanisation. This is particularly relevant to the external strand of Europeanisation literature, which has tended to compartmentalise the role of identity and to focus more on conditionality and norm socialisation. The overplayed focus of dominant approaches on rational agency, cost–benefit calculations and predictability omits key features of international and inter-group relations in the Balkans in the context of Europeanisation (such as intractable 'cold' conflicts). By failing to address satisfactorily central tenets of Balkan politics, such approaches construct the Balkans as inherently irrational, thus sustaining the 'orientalisation' of the region. In contrast, this book aims to demonstrate that a reflectivist framework focusing on identity and its implications is much better suited to explain the success and failure of Europeanisation in the Balkans. By exploring the mechanisms of identity re-narration within the dynamics of Europeanisation, the analysis also hopes to highlight the relevance of this process to the process of identity re-narration within the EU proper (Hoffmann, 1966). Demonstrating how the relevance of integration increases with the successful engagement of European meanings with national identity narratives, the book hopes to point to a novel way of studying the modalities of political and popular support for integration, which is one of the central problems facing the European project. From this perspective, the book is in an attempt to dissipate the assumption of peculiarity of the Balkans in terms of national identity and nationalism, as much as it is an attempt to enhance understanding of the process of (external but also indirectly internal) Europeanisation.

Bringing the themes of national identity and nationalism from the periphery to the core of the study of Europeanisation suggests the applicability of a multidisciplinary framework to understanding European integration. The third contribution this book hopes to offer is a multidisciplinary framework for the study of national identity and nationalism in view of Europeanisation, drawing on theories and explanations from regional and area studies, international relations theory, cultural-political geography, Europeanisation literature and the study of nationalism. This multiplicity permits to overcome the somewhat fragmented study of national identity and nationalism within the dynamics of Europeanisation and to position the themes against the key debates in the Europeanisation literature.

Methodologically, this book also strives to make a modest contribution towards conceptualising and understanding identity change. It applies discourse and content analysis in combination with historical and foreign policy analysis to trace the mechanisms of narrating and re-narrating national identity within a changing discursive environment. Taking as an object of analysis selected narrative units, the book examines the modifications in them in order to establish the links between particular patterns within the national identity construction and antagonistic or reconciliatory state behaviour. Placing this examination within the discursive context of Europeanisation provides an insight into the multi-layered debates about national identity and integration, particularly in view of legitimising political community.

Finally, the specific area focus of this book – bilateral relations between Bulgaria and Macedonia – is a contribution to an understudied but highly relevant caveat of Balkan politics that has received relatively little academic attention outside the dominant historical narratives in the two countries (Gotsev, 1981). The analysis investigates the axes of conflictuality that have shaped bilateral relations and it traces the mechanisms that have enabled reconciliation. Such an object of analysis is relevant not only to the specific regional context but to the wider theoretical issues around identity-based conflict and the potential of Europeanisation in harnessing it. Bulgarian–Macedonian relations, in the context of joining the Europeanisation dynamic, are thus investigated not only in view of understanding the concrete regional pattern of politics, but also in view of understanding identity-based conflicts in the course of Europeanisation.

Structure of the book

Having thus sketched in the introductory chapter what it does and does not do, the book proceeds as follows. Chapter Two highlights the relevance of reflectivist approaches to conceptualising the central themes of this book: national identity, nationalism, Europeanisation and identity change. After reviewing the literature relevant to these themes and highlighting where further research is needed, Chapter Two sketches the main reference points that sustain the conceptual scaffolding of the argument.

Chapter Three concerns itself with operationalising a research model of identity change and the impact of Europeanisation. It introduces the methodology of the comparative case study and the method of data collection and selection, as well as the multidisciplinary angle. It presents the research design and explains the structure of the empirical investigation.

Chapters Four, Five and Six contain the empirical investigation itself. Chapter Four begins with a section mapping out the discursive contexts which shape the meaning of identity at the beginning of the analysed period. The section discusses specific historical constellations that reactivated nationalism as hegemonic discourse, and points to the political conditions that challenged this hegemony and opened its discursive space to alternative (European) interpretations. The second section of this chapter presents the first group of narratives. Under study are six narrative units from each of the two cases and their modifications over the specified timeframe. The analysis conditionally 'splits' the dynamics of identity maintenance into two narrative streams: narratives predominantly occupied with determining the discursive position of the Self, and narratives predominantly focused on determining the discursive position of the Other. The interactions between these two narrative streams produce the Self–Other dialectic, which upholds national identities. The analysis selects three narratives of the first type and three narratives of the second type. Narratives of Self are thought of as more stable and less prone to modification, which is why they are studied over a longer period of time. They are investigated in Chapter Four – at the beginning of transition – and in Chapter Six, after the empowerment of Europeanisation had gained speed and until Bulgaria joined the EU. A comparative analysis of the two cases helps highlight and explain the identified modifications within the narrative units. Narratives of Other are more dependent on the political factors that condition state behaviour – such as intensified relations with a particular state or group of states. This is why they are analysed in the context of bilateral relations and in the chronological sequence in which they gain prominence. The analysis traces modification within and across the unit, before moving on to the next narrative group. Since they follow the chronological evolution of bilateral relations, these narratives have been grouped together in one chapter: Chapter Five.

Chapter Seven: Conclusion. Having identified modifications in the studied narratives, the analysis summarises and synthesises them in order to draw conclusions. Applying the analytical frame of the investigation to the findings, the concluding Chapter Seven aims to demonstrate how these findings relate to the central argument: the Europeanisation of national identities – the changes in national identity narration within the discursive realm of European integration – transforms the boundaries of national political communities and affects their legitimacy. By expanding the boundaries of political community horizontally to include national Others, Europeanisation can transform the basis of inclusion and exclusion, and can – if consistently employed to this end – reduce identity-based conflictuality. Such an outcome can have significant consequences for the legitimacy of national political communities. By extending the boundaries of political community vertically to include notions of Europe and European-ness into the national stories, the Europeanisation of national identities can increase the immediate relevance of European integration to national politics. This outcome can address many of the EU's own issues with legitimacy and the crisis of popular confidence. The book concludes by pointing to the new analytical avenues that it opens.

Chapter Two

National Identity and Political Community in Europe

National identity is the pivot around which the sovereign nation-state has been established as the modern norm of political community. It transcends other forms of identification in scope and in power (Smith, 1992: 58). The historical particularities of nationalism and its inseparable links to 'a world of nations' have elevated national identity above other loyalties as a structuring feature of modern politics and an overarching link between the personal and the political (Billig, 1995: 60–5). National identity also links the present to a story of shared past, positioning the individual as a participant in a meaningful plot spanning through history and time. Attached to particular political and historical contexts, social subjects find themselves 'entrapped' within stories of national identity that cannot be renounced individually (Miller, 1995: 22–7). This is how national identity narratives appear sedimented and begin to be taken for granted. Their intertwinement with the division of the political world into nation-states justifies this condition.

But the meaning of national identity has been constructed on the basis of boundary-making, exclusion and the maintenance of difference (e.g. the review of Neumann, 1992 of various perspectives on the theme). Identities in the modern nation-state system have rested on the construction of clear and unambiguous inside/outside and Self/Other distinctions (Rumelili, 2004: 27). The antagonistic politics engendered by such dynamics of identity construction has uncovered the legitimacy shortfalls of nationalism as system-structuring logic and as a political project (e.g. Delanty *et al.*, 2011). European integration has offered an alternative arrangement for the exercise of sovereignty in Europe that has meant to transcend such antagonisms; but it could not compete with the historical precedence of nationalism. In the face of economic austerity and fast-paced social change, the 'permissive consensus' (Lindberg and Scheingold, 1970) that enabled the steady progress of integration gradually dissolved. With it went predictions of a supranational community of Europeans governed by common institutions and an 'ever closer union' between the states of Europe. In the ensuing crisis of confidence in the EU (Thomassen, 2009; Risse, 2014, etc.), nationalist narratives re-emerged within the discursive space of European politics, gradually refocusing political agendas back to the national spaces and questioning the logic, impact and benefits of integration. The conflictual potential of politics following the restated logic of nationalism became evident once more in responses to new challenges: austerity and the Euro crisis, migration and asylum, welfare and redistribution policies, etc. (Fligstein *et al.*, 2012).

This book points to the dynamics and mechanisms of the Europeanisation of national identities as containing the potential to harness identity-based conflictuality and enhance the challenged legitimacy of European integration. On the one hand, it demonstrates how the re-narration of national identities within the logic of Europeanisation destabilises the discursive hegemony of nationalist interpretations in the practice of national politics. Challenging and marginalising the central meanings of identity narrated within nationalism, the Europeanisation of national identity can depoliticise antagonisms and enable cooperation. The implications of this potential have been studied from the perspective of securitisation theory and minority/majority conflictuality (e.g. Galbreath and McEvoy, 2012). This book takes up the case of bilateral relations and explores the logic of desecuritisation and depoliticisation of antagonistic national identities in foreign and regional policies to study the normative power of Europeanisation over nationalism.

On the other hand, the book analyses the Europeanisation of national identities as a potential bridge between integration and the dynamic of political contestation and participation that lends legitimacy to politics at the national level. Understanding the logic and discursive mechanisms of this process can provide a political tool that increases the relevance of integration to national politics and the level of political support for integration in view of widely established claims of democratic and ultimately legitimacy deficits in the EU (a survey of the literature by Føllesdal, 2006; see also Kaina, 2009). This does not refer only to maintaining the progress of external Europeanisation as a political process with a clear end objective. It can be very relevant also to maintaining the pace of Europeanisation after membership and within older EU member states. Of course, focused empirical work will be needed to explore the implications of the Europeanisation of national identities in view of boosting the relevance, legitimacy and support for integration in each of these political contexts. The purpose of this book is to identify the logic and mechanisms of Europeanisation in the specific context of Bulgarian–Macedonian relations and to point to the implications and ramifications of the argument.

The case of Bulgarian–Macedonian relations and the identity-based conflictuality that strains them demonstrates two things. One is that the re-narration of national identities within the context of Europeanisation prompted and facilitated reconciliation. The second is that the process of Europeanisation engaged national identity narratives with European meanings that brought integration closer to the level of national politics, made it immediately relevant to visions of national purpose and interest and ultimately facilitated the progress of Europeanisation itself. Where the re-narration faltered and nationalist interpretations retained their salience, conflictuality persisted, challenging the normative power of Europeanisation to invoke change. Chapters Four, Five and Six will investigate these processes in detail. At this stage, it is important to note the central role of the narrating agents – the people acting on behalf of the national community and claiming to represent it. It is through the stories told by them in the discursive spaces of the national public sphere that the meanings of national identity are being debated and negotiated. In the national identity narratives told by state actors the political community emerges as a collectivity that exists, has vital needs and follows a grand purpose. The separate people (and peoples) living under the sovereignty of the state become one community that acts together and chooses one course of action over another collectively on the basis of these stories, told at the commanding end of governance, of who the recipients of governance are and what they want. In their claims to represent the national political community and in their capacity to act on its behalf, the actors vested in state power play a central role in narrating the national stories as stories of the state. How credibly and successfully they do this determines the perceived legitimacy of the course the state embarks upon under their leadership. It is this legitimising role of national identity narratives told *by the state* that determines their centrality in the national political community and turns them into the object of this investigation.

Within the dynamics of Europeanisation, national identity narratives are modified to reflect the formal requirements, the normative foundation and the policy logic of integration. These modifications have important consequences for the perceived legitimacy of national policies but also for the perceived legitimacy of integration itself. The Europeanisation of national identities marginalises some of the most exclusionary and antagonistic aspects of nationalist interpretations of community and can facilitate reconciliation of identity-based conflict. It also incorporates European meanings into the national stories and increases the immediate relevance of integration to national politics. The rest of this chapter lays out the theoretical reference points that sustain this argument. Separate sections define the central concepts: political community, nation, national identity, nationalism and Europeanisation. The chapter maps out the established approaches to studying the central themes of this book and where the present analysis stands with regard to them. It also restates the argument in view of the methodological advantages of studying the above *problématique* within the external strand of the Europeanisation literature. Within the structure of the book, the purpose of this chapter is to build the conceptual backbone of the empirical analysis.

Political community

The launch of the integration project challenged the norm of explicitly national organisation of political community by institutionalising an alternative polity for the exercise of sovereignty. Supranational institutions were created whose constitutional practices inspired Habermas (1998) to speak of 'transnational democracy' and the possibility of a post-national, civic European identity. The identity-building 'technologies' employed by EU elites (Kaina and Karolewski, 2006; Karolewski and Suszycki, 2010; also Foret, 2009, 2010) have highlighted the commonality of culture and the linguistic diversity in Europe as a value in themselves. In fact, the acknowledgement of difference, 'the reciprocal acknowledgment of the Other in his otherness' (Habermas and Derrida, 2003: 294) has become a key normative feature of commonality within the realm of the EU and an expression of the will to a common destiny, necessary for establishing the boundaries of political community. Supranational governance and its consequences during the past decades have enabled the imagining of a supranational political community that includes many nations, and whose legitimacy can be conjured up on the basis of both civic, cultural and, to a certain degree, affective identification (Burgess, 2002; Caporaso and Kim, 2009; Risse, 2014, etc.).

The vision of a truly post-Westphalian European order (Habermas, 1998; Cox, 1993) has not come true, as the EU has hit the legitimacy limits of its current form. But its transformative impact on the notions of political community in Europe cannot be ignored, as integration has affected key elements in the construction of political community in very direct ways. In his critique of the sovereign state system and defence of its widening moral boundaries, Andrew Linklater (1998: 203) confirms that 'Europe remains the most encouraging site for the development of new forms of political community'. By breaking the Westphalian arrangement, the project of European integration has set out to rearrange 'sovereignty, territoriality, citizenship and nationality [in an effort to] provide a more effective means of reconciling the claims of universality and difference' (ibid.). Diez, Manners and Whitman (2011: 117) speak of an intertwinement of domestic and international elements into a 'multiperspectival society' sustained by the new institutions of the EU: a pooling of sovereignty, the acquis communautaire, multi-managerialism, pacific democracy, member state coalitions and multiperspectivity. The EU has established a European citizenship involving a new set of legal and political rights guaranteed by supranational institutions and superseding national arrangements. The EU has attempted to employ different interpretations of solidarity and redistribution policies at the supranational level (albeit in an arguably successful manner, as attempts at solving the Euro currency crisis have indicated). The EU has introduced significant changes in the accommodation of difference in Europe by incorporating the notion of commonality (the 'common good') into the justification of all of its policies. The notion of a shared space, the institution of citizenship and the membership and rights it implies (e.g. Hanauer, 2011: 198), ideas of solidarity and trust, the claim of commonality and common interests are discursive elements traditionally employed in the legitimation of national political communities and contained in the construction of national identity. The modifications in their meaning introduced by the process of integration suggest an enormous transformative potential of Europeanisation.

At the same time, however, all-European political discussions about exclusion and inclusion that seem to have taken over the discursive space of European politics also point to national identity as their common reference point. Delanty, Wodak and Jones (2011) link these discussions to a phenomenon they describe as 'post-liberal nationalism', 'xeno-racism' or 'syncretic racism' (Delanty *et al.*, 2011: 3). The authors suggest that this exclusionary phenomenon lacks a specific object of discrimination: it can refer to anything from foreigners, migrants, ethnic and religious minorities, to race (Delanty *et al.*, 2011: 6–9). But what unites the varied referents of exclusionary rhetoric and attitudes, described by Delanty *et al.*, is the aspect of intrusion into the discursive space demarcated by national identity as the unifying centre of political community. Despite the numerous aberrations from the structuring rule of nationalism (an overlap between political community, nation and state), which nationalism has always had to address in one way or another, the discursive space of the national political community has been constructed as relatively homogeneous. The opposed dynamics of globalisation and fragmentation that have characterised the end of the twentieth and the beginning of the twenty-first centuries has challenged this homogeneity in very visible ways (Baylis *et al.*, 2011). 'Post-liberal' exclusionary rhetoric and attitudes emerge from the discursive struggle to redress the incursions into national homogeneity and, ultimately, to renationalise European politics.

It is obvious then that European integration cannot provide an immediate antidote to post-liberal nationalism and the phenomena associated with it, as it is itself struggling to redefine the basis of inclusion and exclusion and the notion of collective belonging at the supranational level. Moreover, when employed from the top, strategies of cultivating a sense of belonging are more often than not interpreted as 'elite manipulation' (Kopper, 2006: 297) and can have adverse effects on the shared sense of community because of the 'gulf' already identified between elites and publics (Buecker, 2006: 298). Besides, the 'commanding heights' of the EU are comparatively detached from political contestation and are much busier with the distribution of power (Foret and Rittelmeyer, 2014).

These valid objections to the transformative record of Europeanisation, however, do not cancel out its potential to invoke change if its true transformative effects are understood and streamlined politically. The EU remains by far the most radical and significant alternative to the logic of nationalism in the organisation of European politics. The project of European integration has challenged (although not displaced) the hegemonic norm of nation-state sovereignty as the only legitimate form of political community in Europe. This challenge can be interpreted as an opportunity or as a risk, and both routes imply important consequences. But in any case, there is a choice of interpretation that the people who speak on behalf of the national political communities, summoning support for their political projects, can make and have made in the past decades (see Wodak, 2011 on UK public discourse). It is of vital importance, then, to understand the implications of these choices. The paragraphs above point to the narratives of national identity and their discursive elements (membership, rights, solidarity, common purpose, etc.) as the link in the construction of political community both within the context of Europeanisation, and within the context of traditional and post-liberal nationalism. This invites further attention to the ways Europeanisation and nationalism differ in their interpretations of national identity and what the consequences of the divergent interpretations are for the national political community and for integration. A further thought follows from the above observations: Europeanisation has been ambivalent about lifting the centre of collective belonging to the supranational level. Political community continues to be negotiated at the level of national politics where new forms of exclusion sustain the political relevance of nationalism and challenge the relevance of integration.

If Europeanisation can have any impact on the negotiation of collective belonging, it should be sought at the level of national politics and not at the supranational level, where proponents of post-national politics have been inspired to look. These notes point to the object of study of this book – the effect of Europeanisation on the narration of national identity; to the level of analysis – national politics and state behaviour; and to the aim of the investigation – identifying the consequences of the Europeanisation of national identities for the meanings of political community in Europe.

Studying identity: between Europe and the nation

The multifaceted use of the framework of identity – the 'hard work' that identity has been made to do in the social sciences – has led Rogers Brubaker and Frederick Cooper (2000: 6–8) to famously question its usefulness as a category of analysis. Their argument suggests that just because 'identity' is a category of practice (as is 'nation'), it does not follow that 'identity' (or 'nation') should necessarily be used as an analytical category in order to understand the consequences of the practice. This makes sense, given the 'multivalent and contradictory burden' and the reifying connotations that riddle the concept (Brubaker and Cooper, 2000: 8; see also Stråth, 2002, 2011). At the same time, however, just because it is difficult to analytically operationalise the concept of identity (and 'nation'?), it does not follow that it is useless to attempt it. The reason for such perseverance is that although we can learn about identity through the frameworks of say, belonging, narrativity, identification, categorisation, social location or groupness, each of these frameworks selects only one aspect of the 'hard work' that identity does *in practice*. Further, the concept of identity cannot be done away with because almost everything we know about legitimacy and political community in Europe comes from studies of European identity, national identity and their interactions.[1]

European identity

The most common route of research exploring these themes has been studying the Europeanisation of national identity as a process, presumably leading to the emergence of a common European identity. The possibility of a European identity has then been explored in direct comparison with national identity (Schlesinger, 1999; Eriksen, 2005; also Sifft *et al.*, 2007; Pichler, 2008; Deflem and Pampel, 1996; etc.), as a sense of belonging legitimising the existence of the political community and its institutional arrangements. It seems logical that, if the EU is to establish a legitimate political community, it needs to rely on a 'shared sense

---

1. Another extensive strand of research deals with the problems of democracy and political community in Europe, but this is a much narrower focus than the one I am interested in (see also Risse, 2010: 15). As Kaina (2009: 151) observes, the problem of 'democratic deficit' in Europe (referring to the insulation of EU policy making from popular politics) must be distinguished from the problem of 'legitimacy deficit' (referring to the sense of community).

of belonging' (Kaina, 2006: 15; see also Hermann and Brewer, 2004; Bruter, 2005; Bach *et al.*, 2006, etc.). This has led scholars to explore the paths towards a supranational European identity, its substantive contents, the obstacles to its formation, and the degree to which it already exists (Kaina and Karolewski, 2009: 16ff for a succinct overview of the literature). This literature is relevant to our study in so far as it deals with the emergence of a supranational European *political* identity, conceptualised along the lines of 'a set of narratives by which political actors categorize and recognize themselves as constituents of the political entity EU' (Suszycki, 2006). Despite the sheer volume and scale of this strand of research, it has perhaps received more criticism than praise. One of the key lines of attack points to the poor quality of the instruments used to measure European identity (Bruter, 2008: 277–9; Karolewski and Kaina, 2012: 9). Peter Burgess (quoted by Bruter, 2004) calls this the 'language prison': the fact that identity is not naturally thought of in analytical terms but is lived and expressed contextually through language makes it hard to devise methodologies for measuring it (Burke, 1980). These objections are also applicable to measuring national identity. Another key line of attack against this literature points to the incompleteness of European identity as a project (purposeful, actor-led) and as a process (open-ended structural context) (Checkel and Katzenstein, 2009: 3). These objections usually refer to the sedimented and taken-for-granted quality of national identity, which European identity cannot compete with. Both lines of critique make valid points, but they cannot cancel out the analytical achievements of the literature on European identity that have nevertheless been gradually recognised. It has been acknowledged, for example, that a type of shared European identity is in the making (Kaina, 2009: 16). It has been recognised that its construction spans the levels of individual identification, national public spheres and transnational communities of communication (e.g. Risse, 2010). It has been confirmed that its relation to national identities is not a zero-sum proposition (Risse, 2012: 88). It has also been suggested that European identity 'starts at home' (Hopf, 2002): that is, the claimed constitutive effects of supranational institutions may have been over-theorised but the identities of the actors involved in the supranational dynamics (both elites and masses) have certainly been affected by integration (Risse, 2010: 102).

Despite these achievements, however, the literature exploring a supranational European identity may have taken the quest for renewed legitimacy and a shared political community in Europe off course. The suggestion that the legitimacy deficit that students of European integration have been interrogating (Kaina, 2009: 7ff) can be redressed through a common European identity can be misleading (Cerutti and Lucarelli, 2008). In a comparison between European identity and national identity, the latter is bound to 'win out' (Hansen and Wæver, 2002: 25), thus making European identity seem irrelevant. At the same time, it is unreasonable to argue that a common sense of collective belonging at the European level can be completely disregarded: even explicitly rationalist accounts confirm its emergence (Checkel and Katzenstein, 2009) and relevance (Risse, 2010). This is what suggests that a more productive route of research on legitimacy and integration would be to explore the effects of Europeanisation on the narration of *national* identity as the traditional source of legitimacy of political community in Europe.

The fact that this book's interest in political community takes an external angle (Europeanisation outside the EU) also suggests national identity as a more promising starting point for the study of legitimacy. Candidate states have had no long-term exposure to the constitutive effects of EU institutions. Established explanations of change in the post-communist space do borrow analytical frames from the internal strand of the study of Europeanisation (e.g. Moravcsik, 1998; Schimmelfennig, 2000; Checkel, 2005; Risse, 2010): gradual changes of preference under pressure from institutions (e.g. Schimmelfennig and Sedelmeier, 2005a) and incremental socialisation into a community of Europeans (e.g. Flockhart, 2006; Checkel, 2001). But in the much narrower scope and much shorter timeline of these processes in candidate states, explanations of identity change based on them lack convincing power. This becomes particularly obvious when we factor in the struggles over defining the existence and content of a common European identity within the realm of the EU proper. The conceptualisation of 'critical junctures' (Cowles *et al.*, 2001) as a mechanism of identity change seems somewhat more suited to capture the changing preferences and the persuasive socialisation in a fast-changing crisis environment (such as regime change) that could account for the renegotiation of belonging along the lines of Europeanisation. This approach acknowledges the central role of political elites in 'making sense' of the crisis and interpreting it publicly for the purposes of popular mobilisation in view of one political agenda or another. Hooghe and Marks have reported findings that corroborate this approach in their studies on mobilising support for European integration (2005) or against it (2007). In any case, national identity has been reaffirmed as the pivot of European politics and as the locus of all discussions on Europe.

National identity

In their timely introduction to the contemporary study of nation and nationalism in Europe, Karolewski and Suszycki define the nation as a political community endowed with a collective identity (2011: 37). National identity therefore carries the integrative aspect of political community, the one that preserves the balance between commonality and difference, outlines the ethical argument for belonging, and justifies a shared political arrangement. Conceptualising identity is complex and defining national identity in a consensual manner is even more daunting. There are at least three ideas, aptly summarised by Viktoria Kaina (2006: 12), that carry the meanings of national identity: identity as something individuals or collectivities have, identity as something a person or a group is, and identity in the sense of personal resources, as something people do. A great deal of intellectual effort has gone into establishing whether national identity is 'real' or not (Motyl, 2002): that is, whether it refers to a group of people or a set of ideas about people. The debate demarcates the major frontline in the contemporary study of nationalism, that between modernists and post-modernists (Karolewski and Suszycki, 2011: 41). It confirms that changing the meta-theoretical standpoint can produce rather incompatible conceptualisations of national identity.

For the purposes of this study, however, I am more interested in what national identity *does* for the legitimacy of political community than in what it actually *is*. The literature identifies three key political functions of national identity (Karolewski and Suszycki, 2011: 38–40). First, national identity maintains the internal cohesion of the nation by highlighting commonality and constructing similarities thus it creates the illusion of continuity and purpose that justify the existence of the nation as a political community. Second, national identity separates the nation from the rest of the political world (the dynamics of 'Othering') by internal assimilation ('bonding') and exclusion of non-members ('bounding'). Establishing state borders (the frontier of the dynamics of Othering) as dividing lines between nations, this function of national identity enables the practical operation of the institutional arrangement that has been set up. Third, national identity maintains the 'we–I' balance in individuals' conflicting social needs in a way no other source of collective identification can match. It permits a very high degree of individual differentiation and distinctness without negating the claim of commonality. In this way, national identity sustains the ethical dimension of nations as inherent and natural. In performing these functions, national identity has significant consequences for the political world and for the engagement of human individuals with it. Karolewski and Suszycki (2011) summarise these consequences in four groups: cognitive effects, self-esteem boosting, lending legitimacy and enabling collective action.

To begin with, national identity helps make sense of the world. Its element of territoriality (the fact that it links individuals to designated geographical locations) and the institutional aspect (the fact that these geographical locations are governed by different institutional arrangements) is particularly important in sustaining the cognitive effects of national identity. In his study of everyday nationalism, Michael Billig (1995: 60ff) speaks of national identity as a 'shorthand description' for ways of thinking and ways of talking about the self and the community (also, Bhavnani and Phoenix, 1994; Shotter and Gergen, 1989). Students of social psychology and sociology speak of socio-cognitive processes of identification and categorisation (Tajfel, 1981; Hogg and Abrams, 1988; Taylor and Moghaddam, 1994). Students of national identity leaning towards reflectivism emphasise the relational aspect of national identity's cognitive effects: the distinction between who we think we are with regard to others and who others think we are (Mole, 2007: 3). In any case, it is clear that national identity profoundly affects the way we see ourselves and the world, and the way the world sees us, by structuring and organising our cognitive frames of reference. Several decades of European integration have not been able to supplant the cognitive role of national identity, which has been reaffirmed by the organisation of politics for much longer. This is to suggest that European integration simply cannot afford to ignore national identity.

At the same time, national identity has a self-esteem boosting effect on individuals and the national community they belong to. It is in this sense that national identity can be seen as a social resource: individuals derive a sense of uniqueness, continuity and purpose from the collective memory perpetuating their national identity (Correll and Park, 2005). This is interpreted as central to maintaining the personal relevance of national identity, as it makes individual participants into something that surpasses individual human life (Castano and Dechesne, 2005). Analysts have even suggested that there is a link between lower class and lower level of education, on the one hand, and higher allegiance to national identity, on the other, in order to explain the salience of national identity against European identity and support for integration (e.g. Favell, 2008; Fuchs *et al.*, 2009; Franklin and Van der Eijk, 1996).

Another significant consequence of national identity is the legitimacy it endows upon the political community to exist and to govern. The unique legitimacy that the nation-state enjoys in modern politics is sustained by the unique characteristics of national identity as a form of identification. David Miller (1995) points out that nations are communities constituted by a shared belief that they exist. This means that national identity is not based on individual contacts or choices: it depends upon the community it signifies and choices are to a large extent pre-given. Furthermore, Miller explains, identification is binding: it cannot be renounced by considerations of the current generation because nations are communities that are not defined by the present situation. Rather, they stretch back and forth across time and link individuals with the past, present and future members of the group in ways that demand moral responsibility. These unique characteristics of identification with the national political community suggest that it may not be possible to recreate such identification with a community other than the nation, at least not in the short term, which makes national identity a unique source of legitimacy. From the perspective of political theory, analysts speak of the legitimacy derived from the positive output of governing the community, and of the legitimacy derived from citizen participation in the process of governance. Both sources of legitimacy need to be present to make a political community legitimate (Karolewski and Suszycki, 2011: 47), thus suggesting a model for understanding the impact of Europeanisation on the legitimacy of national political communities. This will be taken up again later in the book with the conceptualisation of identity change.

Last but not least, national identity has significant consequences for the possibility of collective action in the community. Because of the way national identity links individuals with the land they live in, with the institutions that govern their land, with each other and their own personal identity, with the past, present and future, it can have a powerful and immediate interpellation effect. This is crucial for the operation of politics, because of the imperatives of popular engagement and mobilisation. This is what makes national identity a preferred object of interpretation for political elites in Europe, struggling against popular disenchantment with governance and the crisis of party politics (Mastropaolo, 2012). Moreover, interpellation on the basis of national identity has an advantage over identification with a political party or programme in that it can claim moral superiority by presumably representing the whole political community, and not just fragments of it. It is this consequence of national identity that increases its salience in times of crisis and change, and that motivates political elites to engage with national identity interpretations. As the analysis will demonstrate below, identity politics in Bulgaria and Macedonia during the period of regime change and transition closely followed this pattern.

Beside these consequences for the organisation of the political, however, and on this basis, national identity also contains a powerful antagonistic potential. The organisation of the world in separate 'national' entities with their own unique claims on territory and power, the personal gratification derived from belonging to such a 'unique' community, the cognitive impulse to maintain this uniqueness by excluding Otherness, the significance of the past (with its traumas and conflicts), and the powerful force of interpellation of national identity, occur within the dynamic of maintaining national identity as the unique source of legitimacy of the nation-state. This dynamic of identity maintenance is necessarily exclusionary, as all identity maintenance is (Howarth and Torfing, 2005). But the basis for exclusion here falls along national borders and on the basis of identification with the nation, which positions national Otherness as the object of the exclusionary practices that sit at the heart of maintaining identity. This makes national politics inherently divisive and intolerant towards national, ethnic, religious, linguistic and other differences that sustain the national identity construction as unique. It also makes national identity perpetually relevant to politics, which in turn sustains its politicisation. Positioning Otherness along national borders prevents lasting international cooperation by interpreting other nations and nation-states as necessarily different and foreign. The links that national identity establishes between the individual and the nation-state enable political elites to interpret popular mobilisation against such difference as natural, binding and morally imperative. In this sense the antagonistic potential of national identity, usually addressed through the perspective of nationalism, is an indispensable aspect of national and international politics organised around nation-state sovereignty as the only legitimate form of political community.

Given the complex political functions and politically relevant consequences of national identity, it has remained central in the organisation of European politics even after the launch of European integration (Billig, 1995; Roller and Sloat, 2002; Díez Medrano and Gutiérrez, 2001, etc.). Particularly in post-communist Europe, where newly acquired national independence, sovereignty or electoral freedom have been the key markers of breaking with the totalitarian past, the relevance of national identity as the pivot of political community – sustaining the normative aspects of belonging – has been highly visible. The increased political relevance of national identity, especially in the early years of the transition, is linked as much with the regime change and the imperative of making sense of it, as with the imperatives of bringing the community together and mobilising it for political action. At the same time, however, the increased relevance of national identity as the pivot of political community has brought forth, in the face of nationalism, the negative political consequences of national identity: highly antagonised inter-ethnic relations, conflictual international relations, exclusionary polities, policies and politics, political narratives focused on the past and recalling its traumas as a vehicle to maintaining collective memory, responsibility and readiness for action. Understanding nationalism and its role in European politics has been one of the big tasks of modern political theory. But in Europe, studying nationalism has consistently been approached from the distance of time and space: as a phenomenon buried in Europe's past and only applicable to the European periphery (Özkırımlı, 2000). It was precisely in view of nationalist conflict on the periphery and only with the EU's decision to enlarge into the post-communist space that nationalism has become relevant to the study of integration.

Studying nationalism

Embodied by German romanticism and French naturalism, nationalism is first theorised as an *integrative* movement, identifying the nation as a cultural community and unifying it as a territory (in the philosophical work of Fichte, Herder, Michelet, Renan). Constructing the link between nation and territory as pre-given is a key tenet of nationalism and one that sits in the heart of its recurring significance to modern politics. The factual discrepancy between the 'natural' political community of the nation and existing state borders was addressed by mobilising movements of *disruptive* nationalism, which characterised the best part of the nineteenth century in Europe. The period marked by the two world wars prompted a new conceptualisation of nationalism as an ideology of aggression. Building on the idea of the constructive, state-building function of nationalism in the previous century, twentieth-century scholars contrasted it with the destructive, aggressive nationalism that caused the wars. This dual perspective on nationalism characterises key academic work from the period. Carlton Hayes (1931) speaks of patriotism and nationalism. Hans Kohn (1955) differentiates between civilised and barbarian nationalism. Louis Snyder (1968) contrasts 'old' nationalism and 'new' nationalism.

Conceptualising this dichotomy of nationalisms, which retains its academic and political relevance to this day, placed historical and geographical limits on the phenomenon that are largely arbitrary (Özkırımlı, 2005; Delanty and O'Mahony, 2002). The implied ethical superiority of one type of nationalism over the other establishes clear hierarchies between different nations, justifying politics of 'legitimate' domination. Moreover, the dichotomy suggests that one type of nationalism is peaceful and liberating, while another is aggressive and subjugating. This is problematic because it overlooks the fact that nationalism's antagonistic potential comes from the necessary dynamic of exclusion, without which identifying the contours of the nation and demarcating the limit of belonging would be impossible. From this point of view, all types of nationalism are antagonistic. These conceptualisations are also problematic because of their assumption of national identity types that are pre-given. This assumption reifies nations and ignores the constitutive effect over the notion of instituting sovereign nation-states as the organising rule of modern politics.

Prompted by the decline of communism, the 1980s ushered in new scholarship on nationalism that differed in method, scale and quantity (Anderson, 1991: Preface). Referenced prominently by the work of John Breuilly (1982), Ernest Gellner (1983), Benedict Anderson (1983) and Eric Hobsbawm (1990), it outlined the modernist view of nationalism, which to a large extent made previous scholarship obsolete (Anderson, 1991: xii). Most significantly, it problematised the link between nationalism and modernity and challenged the assumption of nations as pre-given and natural (Delanty and O'Mahony, 2002). But centring the analysis on the Western hemisphere, modernist scholars were largely unable to transcend the normative implication of 'failed' modernity when theorising nationalism in the developing world (Choueiri, 2000) and do not offer a convincing explication of what the key similarity is between 'good' and 'bad' nationalisms (Brubaker, 1999). Entrapped within their analytical frameworks of rationality, modernists were also puzzled by the recurrent relevance of 'bad' nationalism not only to the periphery but to the very core of the 'West'. Thinking of nationalism simply as a political project, they failed to factor in the consequences of national identity, linking the individual in a manner that is binding and non-renounceable to the political community aligned with the nation-state.

Within the wider criticism of modernity raised by critical theory and poststructuralist and postmodernist approaches in the social sciences, the study of nationalism was dramatically challenged. Uncovering the constraining effects of dominant discourses over political reality and our knowledge of it (Foucault, 2002; Lyotard, 1984; Fairclough, 1992), these approaches suggest new ways of theorising the role of the state, power relations and social control (Agger, 1991). They point to the central role of language in the process of identity building, and to the contingent nature of the identity construction (Bhabha, 1990; Kedourie, 1993; Billig, 1995; Calhoun, 1997; Özkırımlı, 2000, etc.). Reflectivist accounts of nationalism completely reverse the logic of modernist conceptualisations, which start by studying the material dimensions of nationhood and attempt to work out its meaning upon this basis (Brubaker, 1994). Despite their epistemological fragmentism, reflectivists offer ways of transcending the many limitations of modernism: its Westo-centrism, its preoccupation with typologies, its inability to account in a convincing manner for the recurring salience of national identity and its intimidation by the mobilising power of nationalist rhetoric.

By examining the mechanisms of establishing political hierarchies through appropriating control over the meaning of statehood, nationhood, belonging, responsibility and Otherness, reflectivist insights into the study of nationalism reveal its hegemonic role in maintaining the central place of national identity in the structure and organisation of modern politics. They are able to explain the antagonistic nature of this hegemony, its immediate relevance to the political process, its increased salience in the era of globalisation and fragmentation (Breuilly, 2014), as well as its conflictual potential for inter-group relations. This book sources generously from reflectivist perspectives on nationalism and national identity. The conceptualisation of the discursive dynamics of meaning-making as excluding competing interpretations (Howarth and Torfing, 2005), for example, sits at the heart of our understanding of the process of national identity construction and maintenance. This will be dealt with in greater detail in the next chapter. The conceptualisation of interpretative practices as directly linked to the legitimation of power structures is another way in which the reflectivist persuasion has been presented in this book, for instance in theorising the hegemonic place of nationalist discourse in the organisation of politics in Europe, and in understanding the radical role of Europeanisation in introducing new meanings to the notion of sovereignty. It is the reflectivist persuasion that has suggested the applicability of national identity analyses beyond the study of nationalism, to international relations theory (Campbell, 1998a and 1998b) and studies of European integration.

Studying Europeanisation and national identity change

The main branch of Europeanisation literature (on Europeanisation in member states) turned to studying national identity in Europe as a result of its grappling with issues of legitimacy, the feasibility of multi-level governance and arguments about the level of political deliberation (Checkel and Katzenstein, 2009: 7–9). Originally, proponents of Europeanisation sought to emphasise the advantages of integration over politics organised around national identity: fostering commonality among European nation-states, overcoming the limitations of national governance in view of increasingly transnational problems and processes, establishing an intricate supranational institutional framework claiming to represent both the national states and the supranational community in a balanced manner (Mitrany, 1966). This rationalist argumentative frame was soon challenged. Rational institutionalists claimed that the functioning of the integration project affected preferences in a way that left little room for identity. The implication of such claims was that national identity was largely irrelevant but in fact neofunctionalists and intergovernmentalists said little about identity at all. In the meantime, the practice of European politics, increasingly referring to national identity, began to prove them wrong. Rational institutionalists also failed to provide a convincing account of enlargement to post-communist Europe and the external impact of Europeanisation. Constructivists were conceptually better equipped to address these issues and the link between integration and national identity in Europe. Their key contribution was theorising the dependency of the formulation of preferences upon identity and changes in it. Offering impressive conceptualisations of identity change (Finnemore and Sikkink, 1998; Fierke and Wiener, 1999; Cowles *et al.*, 2001; Flockhart, 2006; Risse, 2010, etc.), they explained many of the domestic changes in European states as a result of EU membership, including the emergence of EU-wide solidarity, trust, mutual recognition, similarities in the frames of reference of national identity interpretations and the beginnings of a common European identity. They also gave a convincing explanation of the key rationalist puzzle: the decision to enlarge. But they could not overcome the theoretical contradictions generated by conceptualising a duality of interest-driven behaviour and identity-driven behaviour (e.g. Schimmelfennig, 2000), thus undermining their own arguments. In addition, constructivist expectations of cause-and-effect identity change, both in member states and in candidate members, often did not conform to the real political outcomes in the course of Europeanisation (Sedelmeier, 2012).

In the external strand of the Europeanisation literature – studying the effects of integration in candidate and new member states (Sedelmeier, 2011: 6) – the theoretical weaknesses in rationalist accounts of the link between integration and national identity became particularly visible. Even though institutionalists were convincing in arguing that the far-reaching institutional transformations in the post-communist states were driven by the appeal of EU membership as a benefit in itself, the high interference of identity politics remained unexplained within these accounts (Schimmelfennig and Sedelmeier, 2005b). Constructivists went a long way in theorising the gradual Europeanisation of post-communist Europe as dependent upon domestic structures and veto players, the persuasive power of political elites, the resonance of their arguments with collective identities at home, as well as the external 'adaptational' pressures (Cowles *et al*., 2001) and the normative and pragmatic motivation for change (Risse, 2010). But their accounts struggled with resistance to Europeanisation in certain areas (notably patterns of majority–minority relations, long-term identity-based antagonism in regional configurations and inter-group relations), which raised questions about the logic of their arguments. One of the most visible weaknesses in constructivist accounts of Europeanisation is the assumption of the central role of elites as an engine of change, which tends to disregard the deep-seated nature of the identity narratives that elites are engaging with (Karolewski and Suszycki, 2011: 98). Another weakness is the assumption of the power of rhetorical persuasion and learning against discursive frames of reference in the narration of identity, which remained largely unaltered. Yet another weakness is the one-sided approach to conceptualising the effects of Europeanisation (from Community to candidate states), thus underestimating the wide-ranging impact on the EU itself of enlargement to the post-communist states. A fourth line of critique challenges the expectation of Europeanisation in policy areas that are themselves a 'moving target' (Lavenex, 2002) in the realm of integration proper. They include, again, minority rights, asylum and migration, and the emerging European identity (Nancheva and Koneska, 2015). All this suggests that the link between Europeanisation and national identity change has not been fully understood by the constructivist mainstream.

This is what makes room for the insights of reflectivist approaches to the study of national identity and its relationship to European integration (Wodak *et al*., 1999; Hansen and Wæver, 2002; Howarth and Torfing, 2005; Mole, 2007; Delanty, Wodak and Jones, 2011; Triandafyllidou *et al*., 2009, etc.). What empowers such accounts to compete with the rationalist mainstream is their explicit focus on meaning-making and contingency, contextuality and relativity in the construction of identity (Torfing, 2005). They study national identity as a discursive construction that is contingent upon the historical context and the relations within which it is studied and upon which it is constructed. This framework allows a fuller understanding of the role of nationalism as a hegemonic structuring context within which European integration was conceived. It also offers unique insights into the embeddedness of the integration project into discourses centred upon national identity narratives. These analytical achievements have asserted the central relevance of studies of national identity to the Europeanisation discipline.

Europeanisation as change

Before we go on to outline the central claim of this book – that Europeanisation boosts the legitimacy of national political communities – it is necessary to clarify exactly how the concept of Europeanisation is being used here. I speak of Europeanisation as the *change* in polities, policies and politics invoked by the process of European integration. Most definitions of Europeanisation do make reference to the notion of change (Featherstone and Kazamias, 2001; Olsen, 2002; Schimmelfennig and Sedelmeier, 2005a; Featherstone and Radaelli, 2003; etc.). But they also raise a series of problems. One of them concerns the dynamics of the definition: whether we should define Europeanisation as the process of change or the causal result thereof. The implications of each variant are different. In the former case any response to the forces of change constitutes Europeanisation, while in the latter we can speak of Europeanisation when we observe convergence. A further specification is needed here concerning the quality of the invoked change: whether the results are reversible or not. Some analysts add the adjective 'structural' to qualify it (Featherstone and Kazamias, 2001; Featherstone and Radaelli, 2003). Another problem is the level of analysis: whether we discuss phenomena at the supranational level or at the level of national politics. A fourth problem is the scope of the definition. One aspect of it is whether we treat Europeanisation as a phenomenon internal to the EU or as concerning the states that are linked in one way or another to it (candidate members, associated members, neighbouring states, etc.). Although some analysts do include non-member states in their studies of Europeanisation (e.g. the third dimension of Europeanisation in Featherstone and Kazamias, 2001), most authors exclude states that are not closely linked to the EU as prospective candidates for membership. Another aspect of the definitional scope problem is where we look for the sources of Europeanisation: are we just talking about the effects of EU integration and EU enlargement, or do we also consider the potential of European international organisations such as the Council of Europe and the Organisation for Security and Cooperation in Europe for invoking change.

Despite the numerous intricacies of formulating a good definition of Europeanisation as change, it is what best describes the notion. Change is also the unifying notion between the two best established definitions of Europeanisation in the internal and the external strands of the literature. In the context of internal Europeanisation the concept has been defined as the emergence of distinct structures of governance at the supranational level (Cowles *et al.*, 2001: 13). In external contexts Europeanisation is usually defined as the extent of the EU's domestic impact and influence (Sedelmeier, 2011: 5, 17ff). In both cases, however, the essence of the process is change. This book understands Europeanisation as a process of change that does not necessarily lead to convergence but that reproduces commonality and similarities among and within the participating actors. These changes are not irreversible as they are ultimately contingent upon the political contexts and supranational structures that shape them. This is precisely why understanding their mechanisms is imperative for the study and politics of integration. In as much as the integration project defines itself as an all-European project, Europeanisation is relevant to all European states. In as much as the EU has come to signify Europe (Risse, 2010: 102–3), the source of Europeanisation is the integration dynamic.

Having established these limitations to the definition of Europeanisation as change, one final note needs to be made about the Europeanisation of national identities in particular. Thinking of Europeanisation as change in specific policy areas is rarely contested as we have a clear idea of what we are comparing. This is not the case with the Europeanisation of national identities (Nancheva and Koneska, 2015). The problem of operationalising national identity for the purposes of academic enquiry aside, we do not really have a supranational consensus on what European national identity is. Quite to the contrary, the meaning of European identity has never been as contested. This suggests that studying national identity change within the dynamics of integration should always be contextual and careful in identifying the contingent and relative aspects of Europeanisation. What this book hopes to do is reveal the mechanisms of incorporating Europe into the national stories and understand the implications of the change in a specific political context. But determining what Europe means beyond this context is a task in which all European elites and publics continually participate. In this sense, the Europeanisation of national identities cannot be solved in one volume. What a book can do, though, is highlight the significance of the Europeanisation of national identity for the future of Europe.

European integration and national political communities

Demarcating the limit of belonging on the basis of national identity and along the boundaries of the national community has proven an inadequate inclusion criterion in an increasingly transnational world (e.g. Linklater, 1998). The presence of numerous Others, such as national, ethnic and religious minorities, foreigners, migrants, asylum seekers and refugees, has challenged the legitimacy of *national* political communities. Evidence for this is dissolving trust and solidarity within the state (Di Palma, 2013), reflected in low voter turnouts across Europe and in the crisis of the welfare state. At the same time, attempts to 'transnationalise' the state have caused profound 'uncertainties about who constitutes the political community and where the limits of its membership lie' (Delanty *et al.*, 2011: 12–13). As a result, post-liberal nationalism has taken hold of European politics, feeding on anxieties and fears about the securities associated with the nation-state (ibid.). According to Delanty, Wodak and Jones (2011: 13), 'it is undoubtedly the case' that such anxieties were responsible for the popular rejection of projects consolidating the EU as a supranational polity (such as the 'no' votes against the planned Constitutional Treaty).

It is obvious then that a complex renegotiation of collective identities is currently forming a major challenge to the role of European integration as a response to the deficiencies of nation-state sovereignty. The outcome of this renegotiation looks likely to be able to determine not only the future of the European project but also the future of the European nation-state, because its chief objective is to re-establish the boundaries of a legitimate political community in Europe. This book argues that European integration has the potential to address the crisis of legitimacy that has befallen traditional notions of political community. The lack of an alternative arrangement for Europe and the recurring conflictuality of politics refocusing on the logic of nationalism call for renewed attention to be given to the transformative potential of integration on notions of collective belonging. Studies of the Europeanisation of national identities in EU member states, and increasingly in new member states, point to the emergence of similar frames of references and a similar degree of salience of European issues (Kaina, 2009: 16ff). This dynamic, studied both in view of individual self-identification (European identity as a process) and elite-led identity discourses (European identity as a project), has been interpreted as a basis of identification with Europe and fellow Europeans. The consequences of this dynamic for the legitimisation of the EU polity as a *supranational* political community have been found insufficient. But its consequences for the legitimacy of *national* political communities within the realm of Europeanisation have largely been overlooked. How the emergence of commonality at the European level affects the narration of identity at the national level must be properly understood, as national identity remains the unifying centre of political community in Europe.

This book takes a particular angle in exploring the renegotiation of collective belonging in Europe: it is interested in the significance of Europeanisation in destabilising and marginalising nationalist political agendas and engaging the national stories with European meanings as integral elements of the discursive construction of identity. I say 'significance' because my argument is that integration ultimately adds to the legitimacy of both national political communities and integration itself. In order to highlight this added value, I take a historical context external to the EU itself: enlargement to post-communist Europe. This analytical choice is based on a quest for contextual clarity. In the post-communist states that decided to join the dynamic of Europeanisation, negotiation over collective belonging and the relevance of European integration to national politics occurred anew, as a yes-or-no proposition that was being openly debated within the discursive realm of national politics and the public sphere. Such contexts of open debate on the relevance of integration cannot be identified within traditional EU members because of the structuring effects of long-term membership. They cannot be clearly identified in the European states that have chosen against EU membership either, as European integration has been part of the official public debate for as long as it has existed. This was not the case in post-communist Europe, which emerged out of totalitarianism with its close grip on the public sphere. In this sense, the historical context of the Eastern Enlargement offers a 'clean slate' for the renegotiation of collective belonging in the context of Europeanisation. It can therefore showcase the changes in the narration of national identity that relate to the theme of this investigation.

National identity as the pivot of legitimacy of political community and integration is a theme that has not been widely explored in research on external Europeanisation. One of the reasons is that the field has been dominated by explanations that have taken for granted the appeal of joining the integration project as a legitimisation strategy and a benefit in itself. Such explanations omit participation and deliberation as a key source of legitimacy, and provide a rather one-sided account of the appeal of integration. They undermine the normative power of Europeanisation (Manners, 2002, 2011), reducing the integration project to its tangible benefits and the appeal of joining the process to a simple cost–benefit calculation. Furthermore, thinking of Europeanisation in the context of enlargement simply as an external transfer to a recipient state omits the institutional and normative impact that candidate states have had on the EU itself. Studying the Europeanisation of national identities within the context of external Europeanisation should address these omissions in the literature. By highlighting the impact of the process on overcoming the exclusionary aspects of nationalist politics in a historical context external to the EU, this book is also a reminder of the significance of integration to politics within EU proper: significance that the current EU crisis of confidence has begun to overlook.

EU enlargement to post-communist Europe is a good analytical starting point for a study on negotiating collective belonging precisely because it showcases the salience of the conflictual narration of national identities and antagonistic international relations in the absence of integration. The post-communist transitions were marked by an increased salience of nationalist rhetoric and nationalist political agendas (Schöpflin, 2000), both as a strategy of dissent against totalitarian ideology and as a nation- and state-building strategy. Among the states that emerged out of communism and joined the Europeanisation dynamic, almost all can offer contexts of identity-based conflictuality, whether implicit or explicit (e.g. Deets, 2006; Craiutu, 1995). But in the Balkans, antagonistic inter-group relations escalated to inter-ethnic violence, ethnic cleansing and nationalist war. It was from the Balkans that Europe's claims for having tamed conflictual nationalisms were unequivocally challenged. The study of European politics has generally made sense of these antagonisms by 'orientalising' nationalism in the Balkans and absolutising the role of Europeanisation as an agent of change. By choosing to study the discursive struggle of Europeanisation and nationalism in the Balkans, this book hopes to disperse some of the misconceptions that such frames of analysis have sustained. More specifically, these misconceptions concern the qualitative difference of nationalism in the Balkans and the taken-for-granted power of Europeanisation there. Particularly in view of the exclusionary aspects of national identity narration everywhere in Europe and the rise of post-liberal nationalism, the differences between the Balkans and traditional Europe begin to fade. The legitimacy of nationalism and its relevance to the organisation of European politics had not been as visible outside the former communist space because of the specific historical background to the two world wars and the role of nationalism in them. Nevertheless, nationalism had remained highly relevant to the organisation of European politics because of the centrality of nations and national identity in legitimising political community. In this sense, the discourse of nationalism is the 'normative adversary' (Karolewski and Suszycki, 2011: 70) of Europeanisation, interpreting national identity as the pivot of collective belonging. Exploring the consequences of their competing interpretations is central to understanding the legitimacy of political community in the context of integration and the legitimacy of integration itself.

Conclusion

This book takes as its central theme national identity within the discursive realm of European integration. The main question the book seeks to answer is how Europeanisation affects the narration of national identity. The reference point that prompted this question is the exclusionary and conflictual aspects of national identity narration within the political community of the sovereign nation-state and the potential of Europeanisation to address them. The proposition that the book explores is that the Europeanisation of national identities transforms the boundaries of the national political community. The empirical analysis indicates that this transformation has at least two important dimensions. First, it extends the boundaries of the political community horizontally, thus reducing inter-group conflictuality. Second, it expands the boundaries of the political community vertically, thus making integration a part of the collective identity construction and immediately increasing its relevance to national politics. The shifted boundary of belonging has the potential to enhance the legitimacy of the national political community, thus making it better suited to cope with the challenges of both transnational politics and post-liberal nationalism as a reaction to it. The current analysis is a contribution to understanding the mechanisms of this change.

This chapter mapped out the role of European integration in transforming the notion of political community in Europe. It framed national identity as the unifying concept of this book, because of its function as a central source of legitimacy for political community in Europe and the main vehicle for negotiating commitment to integration. The chapter also presented mainstream approaches to problems of legitimacy and European integration, conceptualising a supranational European identity. It laid out key questions raised by studies of European identity and national identity. It clarified the relevance of the study of nationalism, and the problems raised by mainstream approaches in the study of Europeanisation. The chapter concluded by pointing to the rationale behind studying the Europeanisation of national identities within the external strand of the literature. The following chapter will take up the methodological considerations raised by such an analytical choice and will detail the steps that enabled the empirical analysis.

Chapter Three

Which Narratives? Studying the Europeanisation of National Identities

Struggling to re-establish the limits of inclusion and exclusion and to strike the right balance between the conflicting claims of commonality and difference, the European project has been challenged to redefine its relevance as an alternative vision of political community in Europe. European identity as a source of legitimacy for the supranational polity has widely been found deficient. This book argues that the Europeanisation of national identities can address the legitimacy shortfall within both the supranational polity and the national political communities comprising it, if there is political will for Europeanisation. Interpreting political community as more inclusive, less antagonistic, better focused on common interests and opportunities for cooperation, the dynamic of the Europeanisation of national identity transforms the boundaries of political community in Europe. This transformation has two important consequences that can significantly enhance the legitimacy of national political communities within the context of Europeanisation: it can reduce conflictuality in inter-group relations, and it can increase the immediate relevance of integration to national politics. This transformative potential of Europeanisation has sometimes been overlooked, as the extensive search for supranationalisation of political community in Europe suggests. And it has more often than not been interpreted as a risk rather than an opportunity, as the securitising trend across the EU against intra-EU migration confirms. This book sets out to examine the logic and mechanisms of the transformation that the Europeanisation of national identities invokes within national communities in order to highlight their significance for the relevance of both national and European politics. One of the key messages that the analysis conveys is that this transformation is actor-driven and is a matter of political choice. Europeanisation cannot happen if the people representing states in Europe do not manage to convince their national publics of why it should. Taking for granted the appeal of integration for those who are to still join the EU does not tell us much about how Europeanisation becomes part of national politics and produces an impact, and what the consequences of this are. To this end, neither do calls against the 'meddling from Brussels' employed in populist rhetoric as an argument against Europeanisation (both internally and externally). But understanding how the benefits of integration are translated into the language of national politics and how concerns about sovereignty are overridden by the rhetoric of benefits *can* enhance our knowledge of Europeanisation's transformative potential and political relevance. The way political elites engage with national identity narration in order to secure popular support and mobilisation for their projects in view of European integration plays a central part in this process.

The identity-based conflict between Bulgaria and Macedonia, which this book takes as its case study, offers an excellent context for investigating the logic and mechanisms of the Europeanisation of national identities and its consequences in a particular tenet of Balkan politics. Politics in Bulgaria and Macedonia in the immediate years following the break-up of communism were visibly marked by the logic of nationalism. The public salience of nationalist stories as the basis for collective belonging confirmed that nation and nationalism visibly sustained the legitimacy of political communities in the two states. At the same time, in both Bulgaria and Macedonia the normative power of the discourse of nationalism had been somewhat compromised. In Bulgaria, this was due to the instrumentalisation of nationalism within the identity politics of the totalitarian regime, while in Macedonia it was linked to inter-ethnic relations and the threat of war. This is what opened the public space for alternative visions of political legitimacy which, in the aftermath of the Cold War, came from the prospect of 'rejoining' Europe.

Both Bulgaria and Macedonia, not unlike the rest of the post-communist states, framed their transitions within the call for a 'return to Europe', and saw EU membership as the ultimate evidence for success. Their bid for EU membership engaged them with the Europeanisation dynamic and reinforced the normative power of Europe empowered as hegemonic in the communicative space and public sphere of national politics. The peculiar conflict that governed bilateral relations between the two states, however, soon began to obstruct progress towards Europeanisation. Bulgaria's and Macedonia's visibly nationalist foreign policies towards each other, and their nationalist positions in view of regional and domestic issues concerning the other state, stood in stark contrast with otherwise consistently European ambitions. The prolonged language dispute that blocked official bilateral relations, and the claims each of the states made against the other for minority rights abuses and historical identity 'theft', began to interfere in the second half of the 1990s with the pre-accession requirement for good neighbourly relations and non-antagonistic minority/majority accommodation (pursuant to the criteria formulated by the European Council in Copenhagen in 1993). It soon became obvious that some of the key national identity narratives and frames of reference that sustained the antagonistic relationship between the two states were incompatible with the logic of Europeanisation and the strategic goal of EU membership. It is this political contradiction that predicated a discursive struggle over the interpretation of national identity, and prompted a change in the narration of the national stories. The purpose of this change was to re-narrate the national stories and make them compatible with the normative logic and formal requirements of EU membership, which is why we can speak of the Europeanisation of national identities. At the same time, the attempted change in the narration of the national stories was constrained by the imperative of maintaining continuity, uniqueness and credibility as sources of personal and popular identification with the political community. This is why we can speak of a change in the basis of the political community's legitimacy. Examining the change in the narration of the national stories, prompted by the incompatibility between nationalist conflict and EU membership preparation, promises therefore to offer insights into the central problem this book is investigating: the impact of Europeanisation on the legitimacy of political community in Europe and on the legitimacy of integration itself. The present chapter contains the methodological framework that enabled the study.

Discourse and identity change

As discussed in Chapter Two, this study takes up a conceptualisation of national identity as a discursive construction. National identity performs central functions in the organisation of politics and has far-reaching consequences for the way human individuals see themselves and the world, for the way they are seen in the political order, for the way they act in it and for the way they want to change it. But it is impossible to think about national identity, its functions and its effects, outside language and the narratives employed in its construction (compare Anderson, 1983: 36–7 and Billig, 1995: 46, 105; also Derrida, 1982, etc.). This is an epistemological claim that transcends the dominant theoretical debates in the study of identity in European politics: even staunch opponents of the relevance of identity would find it hard to speak of it without the stories that sustain its existence. It is through these stories, therefore, that we set out to study identity change.

Approaching national identity as a collection of stories that sustain the discursive construction of difference and belonging, we should be able to identify the key discursive elements that carry the stories. The contents and salience of discursive elements change over time, as different interpretations of their meaning take precedence. The particular pattern of the discursive elements that sustain the narrative at one point in time is indicative of an aspect of the state's national identity at that point. So in order to study change in national identity narratives, we can start by identifying modifications in the content and patterns of the discursive elements employed in the national identity construction. Modifications can vary. Some interpretations of the meaning of a discursive element may appear or disappear over time. Some interpretations may increase or decrease in salience, but remain present. The correlation between certain elements may change. In any case, the changed interpretations will produce different content and patterns of identity, leading to the exclusion of certain stories and the inclusion of Others. It is precisely this narrative reconstruction that allows transcending antagonisms based in identity.

Our unit of analysis is therefore a narrative identified through the discursive elements carrying its story. We select narratives that seem to be important for the performance of the main functions of national identity: maintaining continuity, ensuring the distinctness of the political community, and providing a credible source for personal and collective identification. National identity narratives are stories that contain the established meaning of political community (sovereign national statehood in modern Europe) and its uniqueness in the world of nation-states. Thus, visible importance seems to be attached almost universally to the discursive elements sustaining the meaning of the nation-state as containing the political community that national identity refers to. Among them are the attachment of the national community to a clearly designated territory (homeland); selected historical events marking the struggle for independence and the road to sovereignty (statehood); the elements that sustain the ethical meaning of belonging (the bond of nationhood); the unique features of the national community (captured by the specificity of language and culture); the various historical aspirations that have steered the community through times of crisis (mission and purpose); and the attitude of the community to non-members (foreigners and minorities). Interpretations of these discursive elements can describe any nation 'parsimoniously' (Karolewski and Suszycki, 2011: 41). Apparently, then, they are central in performing the functions of national identity as the pivot of political community and the limit of belonging.

The boundaries of the community and the limit of belonging determine the balance between commonality and difference/inclusion and exclusion that underlie the notion of legitimacy: the *raison d'être* of the community as an entity. The discursive dialectic distinguishing the community from Other(s) is maintained by national identity narratives that determine who is Self and who is Other. Each identity narrative must perform that function as discursive identity is constructed against Otherness and in relation to it (Torfing, 2005). This means that each narrative determines simultaneously the discursive positions of Self and Other in the stories that it tells and the meanings that it sustains. Admittedly, though, some stories and meanings are meant to demarcate explicitly the boundaries of the national space, while others are directed exclusively at mapping the realm of Otherness. The methodological implications of the executive focus of each narrative are discussed in the next section, where the selection of units of analysis is explained.

A discursive conceptualisation of national identity as relational and contingent upon the meaning of Otherness also means that national identity cannot be studied in isolation from its Other(s). Obviously, it is not methodologically feasible to identify all possible articulations of Otherness that maintain the meaning of national identity. Their number is infinite and neither of them can be fully understood in isolation. But for the purposes of the inquiry, we can select one dimension of the Self–Other dialectic and untangle the key narratives that sustain the meaning of political community in it. In Bulgaria and in Macedonia, Bulgarian–Macedonian relations delineate one particularly salient dimension of 'Othering' in the national identity construction because of the peculiar historical circumstances that determined the two states' positions in the region. The high degree of conflictuality in the relationship confirms the salience of the narratives that maintain it. This is the methodological reasoning behind selecting Bulgarian–Macedonian relations as one of the central dimensions of identity construction in the two states.

In the dialectic constructing the national Self against its constitutive Others, and in relation to them, we can attempt to identify the changing contours of national identity. This methodological frame enables us to trace change as modifications in the narratives that structure Bulgarian–Macedonian relations. What we are interested in, of course, is the change that happened in the context of joining the Europeanisation dynamic. An empirical indication of the trajectory of change during the period under study is from conflict to reconciliation. What the analysis sets out to do is establish how Europeanisation affected this change and what consequences it has for the legitimacy of the national political community, and for the legitimacy of integration. To this end, the investigation seeks to identify transformations in the key narratives, the way they relate to Europe, and the way they change the meaning of political community. This is necessarily a simplified model of identity change, as it isolates only one dimension of the Self–Other dialectic. But at the expense of empirical comprehensiveness, this model promises a methodologically reasonable approach to understanding the logic and discursive mechanisms of identity change in the context of Europeanisation. At the same time, studying national identity in the framework of bilateral relations offers an insight into the correlation of identity narratives with state behaviour, both domestically and externally. This is indispensable to understanding the functions of national identity in establishing the legitimacy of political action and demarcating the ethical boundaries of political community. Furthermore, such a methodological model contains the advantages of the comparative perspective as it includes two states. A comparison of the outcomes of identity change in the context of Europeanisation in the two states enables transcending the peculiarities of the single case and offers a basis for inference.

Which narratives?

The collection of narratives that determine the subject positions of Self and Other in the dialectic of Bulgarian–Macedonian relations occupies many discursive planes that are linked to the key functions of national identity. They ensure continuity between past, present and future. They link the individual with the social and vice versa. They draw the limit between Self and Other as the border of political community. While exploring all of these planes as we go, I use the last one as an organising criterion. This is because my starting point is conflictuality in bilateral relations, and because my goal is to explore the changing border of the national political community in the context of Europeanisation. On the basis of this organising criterion, I conditionally split the narratives I have selected into two groups. The first narrative group is predominantly concerned with determining the discursive position of Self (the boundaries of the national space), while the second narrative group is predominantly concerned with determining the discursive position of Other (the realm of Otherness). The discursive position of Self is traditionally fixed through particular interpretations of history, territory, borders, nationhood, political culture, language, religion, traditions, etc. The discursive position of Other is fixed through elements establishing the limits of the Self. In bilateral relations they are often contentious issues that highlight difference. Several elements in Bulgarian–Macedonian relations can be seen to serve this purpose: divergent interpretations of shared past, nationhood, statehood, church autocephaly, language, minorities.

Table 3.1: Units of analysis

Identity narratives of Self	Identity narratives of Other
Territory	Recognition of statehood
Nationhood	The language dispute
National purpose	National minority rights

I have chosen to study six discursive elements: three from each narrative group. In the first narrative group, concerned with positioning the national Self, I study interpretations of the discursive elements of national territory, the contents of nationhood, and national purpose. In the second narrative group, predominantly concerned with positioning the Other, I study the stories around three contentious issues in Bulgarian–Macedonian relations: recognition of statehood, the language dispute and acknowledging the status of national minorities (Table 3.1). The selection was originally based on the visibility of these discursive elements and the narratives they sustained in public rhetoric in the two states, both domestically and externally. Unsurprisingly, however, narratives referring to the discursive elements of territory, nationhood, collective purpose, sovereignty, language and minorities can be identified in any given national identity construction. As discussed above, the significance of these discursive elements is linked to the type and functions of the political community established as the norm in modern politics: the sovereign nation-state.

Level of analysis

Modifications in narratives sustaining the meaning of the six discursive elements during the process of joining the Europeanisation dynamic can be studied at all levels of political interaction in the public sphere. This analysis operates at the level of elites and their engagement with the public. This methodological choice has been prompted by an awareness of the leading role of elites in interpreting national identity for the purposes of political mobilisation. Without disregarding the significance of popular interpretations of the meaning of national identity, I chose not to focus on them explicitly in order to preserve the key focus of the book as a study of national politics in the context of Europeanisation. Besides, as pointed out above, elites are bound in their interpretations of identity by the credible prospect of engaging their audiences. This means that they must take into account popular identity narratives and work with them, if they are to expect mobilisation. This study thus sets out to establish what can legitimately be said about national identity by representatives of the political community of the state, and how this changes over time. Choosing to study national identity change at the level of elite rhetoric has also been justified by the research goal of this analysis: to explore the changing boundaries of national political community.

As national political community in Europe has historically been aligned with the sovereign nation-state, while Europeanisation challenges that alignment, the fault line of discursive tension is ultimately the limit of the national space. A micro-perspective would therefore fail to capture the integrative aspects of the political renegotiation.

The selected narratives in this study are produced by subjects acting on behalf of the state or in their capacity as representing the political community of the state: the president, the prime minister, the speaker and members of parliament, relevant ministers, heads of national research institutes, but also speakers from the leading national media and concerned local authorities, as well as national party leaders. Furthermore, the identity narratives studied here are contained in officially produced texts meant to reach the widest possible national audiences. Only in this form could they represent identity-constituting and identity-articulating acts at the macro-level. They include, among other things, official statements of heads of states and prime ministers at key domestic occasions and crucial points in bilateral relations and foreign policy developments, statements of the speakers of parliament, press conferences; press releases of resource ministers and ambassadors on matters of disagreement, bulletins of foreign ministries; speeches and statements during exchanged formal and informal visits between the two states; official interviews in the leading media: the major party mouthpieces, national radio and television, etc. The aim has been to select textual data representative of what can legitimately be said about national identity. What is legitimate more often than not operates on the basis of what is legal, so a logical point for orientation is also interpretation of state legislation. Empirical data have not been taken from pieces of legislation per se but from official state interpretations of it. Possible sources are interpretations of constitutional provisions and their amendments (particularly in their texts on sovereignty, borders, territory, citizenship, minorities, nationhood, state symbols), domestic and international laws regulating the respective regimes (laws on national minorities, ratifications of the European Convention of Human Rights and the jurisdiction of the Court, the Framework Convention for the Protection of National Minorities, etc.), as well as official positions on European Court of Human Rights rulings, and cases of non-ratification of international legislation.

Achieving complete parity in the collected data has not been possible because of the mutually independent public behaviour of state actors in the two states. For example, the Bulgarian prime minister's statement on the political will to make progress in the language dispute because of the necessity to improve cross-border transport infrastructure has not been matched by a statement on the issue by the Macedonian prime minister. But more often than not comparable data on certain issues of interest can be collected around key points in bilateral relations. The ban on registering a political party representing the Macedonian minority in Bulgaria, for example, prompts articulations on the issue at various levels on both sides. The same applies to the Macedonian ban on registering a Bulgarian political party. At the same time, silence on certain issues can also be indicative of the content of identity narratives. Bulgarian recognition of Macedonian statehood, for example, became a central discursive element of Bulgarian politics at the time, but in Macedonia it hardly received anything other than formal acknowledgement. The discrepancy is analysed in view of the position and function of the Other in the two national identity narratives.

Disparities in the collectable data on issues like this are addressed by attempting to establish what else is being said on the topic and when. In the case of Bulgarian recognition of Macedonian independent statehood, for example, occurrences of articulations appear only on several formal occasions around the time of the event. Only later does rhetoric on the issue begin to normalise and then both positive and critical interpretations can be found. Certain issues are consistently not tackled at state level. In Bulgaria, for example, references to the ban on registration of the pro-Macedonian party are generally not contained in the rhetoric of the president. If they do appear, it is as a confirmation of the judiciary's competence to rule on the issue. In Macedonia, on the other hand, concern for the status of Macedonian communities in Bulgaria frequently appears as a central issue in identity politics at all levels. The discrepancy is analysed in terms of the different interpretations of the nation's integrity and the place of national minorities in its discursive construction.

Timeframe

The chronological timeline that the analysis covers begins with the break-up of the communist regimes. Formally this is linked to the first multi-party elections of 1990 in both Bulgaria and Macedonia, even though the symbolic marker of the end of communism is customarily placed elsewhere in the two states. In Bulgaria it is seen in the date 10 November 1989, when Bulgaria's totalitarian head of state was ousted from power in a party coup. In Macedonia, special symbolic meaning is carried by the Declaration of Independence of 8 September 1991, marking the break with the Yugoslav federation and the beginning of Macedonia's independent statehood. Despite the significant symbolism of these dates, a formal criterion has been preferred for selecting the beginning of the analysed period. First, formality enables chronological parity. Second, and more importantly, it prevents the analysis from missing out on key moments in the articulation of Macedonia's national identity narratives (which already revolved around independence) should the later date be preferred. Also, dismantling the communist regime in Bulgaria was negotiated largely by the communist party leadership (e.g. Elster, 1996: Chapter 5), so the opposition needed time to organise and mobilise before decommunisation could begin. In this sense, not much is lost in terms of official public debate on national identity if the last quarter of 1989 is not included in the analysed timeframe.

The end point of the chronological timeline covered by this book is the first day of 2007, set by Bulgaria's joining the EU as a symbolic threshold in the process of Europeanisation. Obviously, the process of Europeanisation did not end there for either of the studied states. While Bulgaria, as a new member, joined the internal Europeanisation dynamic and everything that it implies, Macedonia continued

Table 3.2: Analytical timeline and salience of identity narratives

National identity narrative groups	1990–3	1994–9	2000–6
Self	Territory	Nationhood	Purpose
Other	Recognition	Language	Minorities

to prepare for membership negotiations. But the basis of comparability changed after one of the states had achieved membership. Participating in the process of Europeanisation as a candidate and as a member state produces very dissimilar strategies of identity articulation in view of different subject positions of the state towards the supranational community and towards the participating Others. As the case of Bulgarian–Macedonian relations demonstrates, these differences produced a new type of Othering that has not been fully understood and addressed politically by EU policy-makers (Nancheva and Koneska, 2015). But they lie outside the scope of this analysis.

Such a chronological timeline is short enough to enable a feasible research design for tracking change in the narration of national identity, including meaningful understanding of key actor positions and comparability of the textual data across the two cases in terms of sources, form, and targeted audiences. At the same time, this chronological period was extremely dynamic in terms of structural change and fits the conceptualisation of a 'critical juncture': i.e. this is a period in which meaning-making and interpretation take a political forefront. This is what makes it a good context for understanding the mechanisms of identity change.

Identity narratives articulating the discursive position of Self were captured towards both the beginning and the end of the period under study. These narratives are generally more static because of their function (to stabilise the subject position). Unless their salience notably increases in view of particular political events (e.g. the inter-ethnic tension in Macedonia in 2001), it is safe to assume that the dynamic of change across these narratives requires more time to unfold. Identity narratives articulating the discursive position of the Other are much more susceptible to changing political contexts because they are more dependent on inter-state relations. Therefore, their narration is captured around significant events of bilateral concern. Narratives of the recognition of statehood were most salient around the time of Bulgaria's recognition of Macedonian independence (1991). Narratives of language are mostly linked to the period of the language dispute and its resolution (1994–9). Narratives of minorities are visible at various points during the period under study but their salience increases significantly with the involvement of the European Court of Human Rights after 1999. The analysis of narratives of Other is chronologically oriented towards these points (Table 3.2).

Research design

In order to understand the mechanisms of narrative identity change within the context of Europeanisation, the investigation traces the modifications in national identity interpretations in the course of joining the Europeanisation dynamic in Bulgaria and in Macedonia. Conceptualising national identity as a discursive construction made possible through the exclusion of Otherness, the analysis selects one central dimension of the Self–Other dialectic that sustains the identity constitution – Bulgarian–Macedonian relations – and follows its evolution during the process of Europeanisation. The investigation attempts to identify modifications in the discursive positions of Self and the Other across the selected dimension of Othering. It follows identity narratives that rearticulated towards the domestic and external discursive spaces. Empirically, this implies studying co-variations diachronically within the narrative units and synchronically across the units (Gerring, 2004: 343).

Domestic articulations of identity narratives are being traced around three discursive elements of the identity construction, which have been identified in both cases. Their meaning is sustained by interpretations of national territory, national community and national purpose. The substantive contents of these discursive elements notably changed over time during the process of Europeanisation. Some of the interpretations increased or decreased in salience, others disappeared completely, yet other new interpretations gained discursive prominence. The modifications are established in a within-unit comparison of the discursive pattern of national identity before joining the Europeanisation dynamic, when national identity is articulated within the discourse of nationalism, and during the course of Europeanisation (Table 3.3).

As visible from the table, different interpretations occupy similar discursive positions before Europeanisation has begun and during its course. They make up for different discursive patterns of national identity. The empirical analysis establishes that narratives of Self generally tend to display more divisive potential when interpreted within the logic of nationalism and be more inclusive within the dynamic of Europeanisation, irrespective of the precise content of the discursive element and the specific dynamic of conflictuality.

External articulations of identity narratives are being traced around three discursive elements whose interpretations in both states are visibly antagonistic. They are detectable around the issue of recognition of statehood, in the language dispute and on the status of national minorities The transformations of these narratives are followed in an across-unit comparison of modifications in the interpretations during the course of Europeanisation (Table 3.4).

Table 3.4 suggests that there have been visible shifts towards reconciliation in interpretations of conflictual issues. A detailed analysis of the narrative modifications suggests that what enabled transcending antagonisms was expanding the field of commonality between the two states through mutual participation in the process of Europeanisation and the new requirement and responsibilities it determined.

Table 3.3: Identity narratives of Self with examples of established modifications

National identity narratives of Self	1990		2006	
	Bulgaria	Macedonia	Bulgaria	Macedonia
Territory	Integrity	Belonging	Openness	Integrity
Nationhood	Unity	Ambiguity	Tolerance	Tolerance
Purpose	Centrality	Statehood	Contribution	Predictability

Comparing the modifications in the domestic and external narrations of national identity in the two states during the course of Europeanisation gives rise to two observations. First, participation in the dynamic of Europeanisation visibly reduces conflictuality in the interpretations of national identity narratives. It makes national identity constructions more open, more inclusive, and more focused on the possibilities for cooperation in the present at the expense of past antagonisms and traumas. Second, participation in the dynamic of Europeanisation upholds a reading of national identity that contains references to Europe as discursive elements of the identity construction itself. This ensures the relevance of integration to national politics and enables the marginalisation of exclusively nationalist agendas. Modifications in the narration of national identity, identified in the empirical analysis, immediately affect the boundaries of the national political communities. They make them more inclusive and more flexible as they allow for the inclusion of national Others along the horizontal and vertical dimensions of the dynamics of Othering. This has important consequences for the legitimacy of national political communities, whose main shortfall has been sustaining exclusionary and antagonistic politics, and for the legitimacy of integration, whose key omission has been detachment from the political process. From this perspective the Europeanisation of national identities stands out as a central problem of European politics, and one that concerns both the sovereign nation-state and European integration as a project.

Conclusion

The first three chapters of the book laid down the conceptual framework of the analysis and the methodological steps in studying identity change. The introductory chapter explained the applicability of a study of Bulgarian–Macedonian relations within the external dynamic of Europeanisation to the problem of the changing role of national identity as a source of the political community's legitimacy in Europe. It listed the aim, the structure and the main messages of the book. Chapter Two mapped out the definitional limits and the problems in the literature engaged with studying the themes of the book, and determined the stance of the current book against the achievements of the literature. Chapter Three presented the

Table 3.4: Identity narratives of Other: examples of established modifications

National identity narratives of Other	Bulgaria		Macedonia	
Recognition	1991	1993	1991	1993
	Macedonia is part of Bulgaria	First state to officially recognise the independent republic	Bulgaria as a threat to Macedonian statehood	Bulgaria as a neighbour
Language	1994	1999	1994	1999
	Macedonian is Bulgarian	Macedonia has a right to its own constitutionally defined language	Bulgarian and Macedonian have nothing in common	Despite commonality, Bulgarian and Macedonian are now different languages
Minorities	1999	2006	1999	2006
	Macedonian nation and national minorities are non-existent	Macedonians in Bulgaria have their rights guaranteed on a par with the rest of individual citizens	Bulgaria's only role in Macedonian nationhood has been as an occupant force	Occasional recognition of a Bulgarian element in the construction of the state

methodological framework and the research design. It explained in detail how the analysis went about studying narratives, which narratives it selected and why, and how it operationalised a model of tracing identity change. The following three chapters of the book presented the case study and the empirical investigation.

Chapter Four

Identity without Europe: Bulgaria and Macedonia before Europeanisation

Chapter Four consists of two sections. The first ('Contexts of identity before Europeanisation') sketches the key features of the discursive contexts and the historical circumstances shaping politics and bilateral relations at the beginning of the period under study. The second ('Patterns of identity before Europeanisation') looks at the contents of national identity narratives of Self in Bulgaria and in Macedonia before the two states joined the dynamics of Europeanisation. Both states witnessed a visible surge in nationalist rhetoric and increased popularity of their nationalist political agendas. But the specific national contexts that facilitated these outcomes are quite different. The opening section describes these differences. Mapping out a vision of political community that is constructed within the logic of nationalism, the section points to the problems of legitimacy that nationalist politics engendered in the immediate aftermath of regime change in both states. The following section presents the specific patterns of national identity constructions in the two states before they joined the process of Europeanisation. It follows the meanings contained in the key discursive elements in the selected narrative groups and their links to foreign policy behaviour and inter-group conflictuality domestically. The aim is to identify the boundaries of political communities and their sources of legitimacy before Europeanisation in order to assess the problems and deficiencies of national identity narrated within the logic of nationalism in the specific regional context, as well as the intrinsic value that joining the process of Europeanisation implied.

Contexts of identity before Europeanisation

The end of the Cold War was marked by a surge of nationalist politics in the former communist space. The reasons for this are diverse. Nationalism as an ideology of the state, publicly had to give way to a peculiar blend of Marxist–Leninist party ideology empowered, largely coercively, to uphold the project of 'people's' or 'socialist' republics. But despite concerted attempts to substitute loyalties to the national state with loyalty to the communist party and thus, symbolically, to the international communist proletariat, party ideology inevitably operated within the framework of the nation-state even when it comprised a federation, as in the Soviet or Yugoslav cases (e.g. Paleshtuski, 1983). This means that nationalism continued to structure the organisation of politics during totalitarianism. At the same time, when faced with the task of (re-)building democratic statehood from the rubble of the totalitarian regimes, the former communist states could not take recourse to other narratives representing the entirety of the population as a political community, and thus providing the legitimacy to undertake necessary, often taxing, reforms. It was the story of the nation surviving the ordeal of communism that offered a source of self-identification with the new state for all citizens. The wave of secessions from federation in the aftermath of the Cold War is linked to this renewed salience of national identity rhetoric. Furthermore, and this is significant, despite the instrumentalisation by the communist regimes of varieties of nationalisms at different points in time, national identity did provide a source of oppositional dissent from the notion of 'comradeship' in the totalitarian state. In the immediate context of regime change this oppositional potential gave rise to the discourse of nationalism as hegemonic in the newly democratic states.

The basis of comparability between Bulgarian and Macedonian identity narratives and their transformation within the Europeanisation dynamic is suggested by the many similarities between the two states and the discursive contexts that shaped their post-communist transitions. But at the same time, the two states display specificities that cannot be ignored. They come from different traditions of statehood (unitary state versus federative entity) and this affects the way sovereignty and sovereign territory are interpreted. The type of statehood also has consequences for the perceptions of the integrity of the state. Differences in the domestic accommodation of national minorities (a monolithic-nation constitutional model versus a multi-nationality constitutional model) affect the narratives of nationhood and the interpretations of the meaning of nation in the two states. Unequal positions in the international system of states (recognised statehood versus the issue of acquiring international recognition) and dissimilar positions in regional politics (open disputes with other neighbours in the Macedonian case) lead to different starting positions in joining the dynamics of Europeanisation and consequently divergent paths towards European integration. But irrespective of the precise content of the discursive elements sustaining the identity narratives, they function in a similar way in the entitativity of the identity construction. National identities in the two states had been interpreted exclusively within the logic of nationalism and the limits of political community established by the sovereign nation-state. The high degree of conflictuality of such interpretations interfered with the normative logic of Europeanisation and the formal requirements for joining the process. This was a problem because EU membership had been framed as the strategic goal of the transition and had enabled participants to make sense of the regime change. The discursive clash structured the transition as a 'critical juncture', prompting intensive discursive practice to make the national identity constructions compatible with the dynamic of Europeanisation. Re-narrated within this dynamic, national identity appeared much less antagonistic. This outcome seems to be linked to the modified ethical boundaries of the national political community, which no longer refer to nation-state borders but are capable of including previous national Others into the construction of the national Self. The changed basis of inclusion and exclusion has a direct impact on the legitimacy of political community as a sovereign nation-state participating in a unique

European undertaking. The discursive modifications had become possible through the inclusion of Europe into the national identity constructions. This mechanism of identity change had made European integration an indispensable discursive element of national identity, thus increasing its political relevance and improving the legitimacy of the EU itself. Comparing the different discursive mechanisms of this change in the two states promises to enhance our understanding of it. This chapter establishes the basis of comparison by mapping out the discursive contexts that capture the basic elements of the narration of national identity before Europeanisation.

The context of nationalism in Bulgaria

In the Bulgarian case, just as in all post-communist states, the rise of nationalism in the period after the break-up of communism had its peculiarities. Bulgaria fostered one of the communist regimes that made extensive use of the arsenal of nationalism in tightening its grip on power[1] (Popova and Hajdinjak, 2006). One of its undertakings with most profound consequences for ethno-national peace in the country was the large-scale governmental assimilation campaign initiated in the early 1980s against Bulgaria's Turkish minority, the largest ethno-national minority group in the country (Höpken, 1997). The societal uproar the campaign caused served as a catalyst for mobilising civil and intellectual dissent against the regime and was a factor in eventually negotiating regime change (Poulton and Taji-Farouki, 1997). A strong association was thus created between the communist past and aggressive nationalism. This was taken up by the democratic opposition, which highlighted the link in its attempt to mobilise greater public support for reform. In the rhetoric of the democratic opposition, nationalism is positioned as the exact opposite of democracy, thus reaffirming its incompatibility with the goals of transition. Furthermore, nationalism is repeatedly given as the reason for the continuing inter-ethnic tensions between the Turkish minority and the Bulgarian majority, which characterised the period of regime change negotiations at the Roundtable Talks between December 1989 and March 1990 (Melone, 1994). By radically distinguishing democracy (the possible future) from nationalism (the condemned past) and insisting on their incompatibility, members of the democratic opposition attempted to assert their legitimacy as carriers of the 'future' and thus mobilise as much popular support as possible, including by engaging the votes of the formerly repressed ethnic Turks (Nancheva, 2007). At the same time, however, the centrality of the nationalist motif as a borderline of identification perpetuated the salience of nationalist rhetoric and further politicised the narration of national identity.

---

1. This was not done consistently, however: even though it launched large-scale nationalist campaigns, they were often abandoned half-way through with a change in the Soviet position (such as its policies on Macedonia by 1956) or were initiated randomly with changes in the domestic environment (such as campaigns against ethnic Turks from the 1970s).

The gulf between democracy and nationalism was exacerbated because of the communist successor party's prolonged grip on power (it was known after 3 April 1990 as the Bulgarian Socialist Party): in the first free parliamentary elections in 1990 the socialists won 210 out of 400 seats in the parliament and at the second elections in 1991, 106 out of 240. To regain legitimacy for their presence in the state structures, they tried to dissociate gradually from the negative image of the 'national question' (the term used domestically to designate the inter-ethnic problems inherited from the totalitarian era) without losing credibility in their political stance. Already during the preliminary Roundtable Talks key members of the socialist leadership (Andrey Lukanov, Aleksander Lilov) refused to acknowledge immediate responsibility for the assimilatory campaigns by pointing to the allegedly deep-seated roots of the inter-ethnic problems with the Turkish minority.[2] At the same time, another discursive line taken by the socialist government worked for the reformulation of the discredited notion of 'nationalism' into a political ideology compatible with post-communist politics. In the immediate aftermath of the regime change the contextual usage of the term 'nationalism' referred to the dangers of 'nationalist passions', of 'chauvinist ideas', of dealing with 'nationally-based hatred'.[3] In an attempt to distance the meaning of nationalism from the context of the irrational and destructive, nationalism was subtly being reintroduced to the public in a new light: as the ideology of national unity and the national interest. Evidence of this is the establishment of the Nationwide Committee for the Protection of the National Interests, which legitimately took part in the Roundtable Talks as a nationalist organisation. One of its suggestions was reformulating the controversial Article 1 of the 1971 Constitution to state that 'Bulgaria is a national state' of the Bulgarian nation.[4] Another rhetorical strategy to modify the meaning of nationalism was the constant reference by the socialists to 'the nation' (and not 'the people') as the addressee community of the reforms. Despite the significant overlap of usage between the terms 'nation' and 'people', they are not interchangeable. The move to constitute the community as a 'nation' and not a 'people' appealed subtly to the national sentiment of the majority and suggests the relevance of nationalist policies. Paradoxically, the established formula of 'national unity' (referring to the desired solution of inter-ethnic conflict), turned into one of the consensual catchphrases of the period, also served such a purpose. Its endless repetition during the Roundtable Talks and the numerous documents they produced, as well as during the plenary sessions of the Grand National Assembly, eventually dimmed the paradoxical edges of the idea of 'accommodating' ethnic minorities successfully by consolidating the nation as monolithic. This gave the use of the formula 'national unity' an aura of highest common good, again subtly legitimising

---

2. Verbatim report of Preliminary Roundtable Consultations of the government with leaders of the democratic opposition, 3 January 1990 from 5.30pm.
3. Verbatim report from the Roundtable Talks: 75, 311, 349.
4. Kiril Haramiev, verbatim reports: 360.

nationalist agendas. In the context of an ethnically divided society on the verge of conflict the political use of the adjective 'national' should be cautious because it might not be immediately clear who/what it signifies. Insisting on acting in the interest of 'the nation' (and not the people, society or state) clearly constitutes a political community identified along the lines of nationhood, questioning any minority elements' membership in it, and thus increasing its antagonistic potential.

The strong association of the totalitarian regime with aggressive nationalism on the one hand, and the fact that a vast number of its representatives remained in power after its negotiated change on the other, ensured the relevance of nationalist agendas and rhetoric to everyday politics in the years immediately after the fall of totalitarianism. Despite the democratic opposition's attempts to dissociate the politics of reform from the burden of past nationalism, too much controversy revolved around the 'national question' in the early months and years of the regime change for such a move to succeed (at least in the short term). By refusing to unambiguously accept responsibility for the assimilation campaigns, the socialists also exacerbated the controversy because many of them remained in public office and continued to head numerous state institutions despite their direct participation in the ideological and practical preparation of the 'Revival Process' (the propaganda name of the communist regime's assimilatory campaigns against the Turkish minority). By attempting to redefine the concept of nationalism in line with notions of national uniqueness, national interest and national unity so as to legitimise their stay in power, the socialists impeded the dissociation of politics from the discursive field of nationalism. The increased salience of nationalist rhetoric left its imprint upon the reading of national identity in Bulgaria in the years following the regime change.

Rising nationalism in Macedonia

In line with the rest of the post-communist space, Macedonia also witnessed a rise in nationalist rhetoric in the years immediately following the fall of the Iron Curtain but the subcontexts that facilitated it were distinctly different from what they were in the Bulgarian case. They were determined by the secession from the federation, domestic majority–minority relations and regional inter-state relations.

The context of secession

First recognised as a state within the Yugoslav federation in 1946 (Petroska-Beska and Najcavska, 2004), the Socialist Republic of Macedonia[5] had established the fundament of statehood in the spirit of 'brotherhood and unity' with the other republics of the Yugoslav federation. Even though the republics were instituted along national lines, the national element was formally excluded from the ideology upholding the socialist state. With the disintegration of the federation, nationalism

---

5. Its name from 1963 (when the Yugoslav federation was renamed), replacing the People's Republic of Macedonia.

came to the fore both as a consequence of restated claims for independent statehood along national lines, and as a response to the political uncertainty that these claims created within the federation. Thus, one of the structural factors in the rise of Macedonian nationalism in the beginning of the 1990s was the context of prospective secession from the federation.

Unlike Bulgaria, however, nationalism in Macedonia became associated with change, emancipation and the future, whereas the past remained predominantly linked to the integrationist ideas of commonality within the socialist federation. In the context of renouncing the past and embarking upon the idea of an independent Macedonian state as the grand political project of the present, political rhetoric in the period was distinctly nationalist. The first major theme around which it revolved was, logically, the precise form of statehood that best suited the people of Macedonia. In view of justifying secession from the federation, the discussion interpreted national statehood as ethically superior. The tense inter-ethnic and inter-republican relations in Yugoslavia in the period were pointed to as evidence of the incompatibility of the multinational federative model with the ethical needs of nationhood.[6] The rhetorical renunciation of the federative state as oppressive and the rhetorical vindication of the national community as ethically superior established the context that initially empowered Macedonian nationalism at the beginning of democratic parliamentary life in the republic. At the same time, fully conscious of its negative connotations, the new Macedonian political elite systematically avoided direct references to nationalism in pursuing the project of independent statehood. Instead, its legitimacy was constructed around the discursive element of the Macedonian *people* as the source of state sovereignty, the Macedonian *national interest*, and the Macedonian *national question*. In the context of disengagement from the federation these discursive elements legitimised the claim for independent statehood. Explicit references to nationalism were made only with regard to external and internal Others (Yugoslavia symbolising the federative past, or the sizeable Albanian minority within the Macedonian Republic) and always positioned next to some of its extreme or illegitimate forms, indicating an attempt at rhetorical dissociation from it.

The context of minority accommodation

The second important context that shaped the rise of Macedonian nationalism in the post-socialist years is linked to the internal dynamic of Othering. The underlying feature of the rhetoric preparing the ground for an independent Macedonian state revolved around the idea of a national state for the Macedonian nation. As demonstrated above, the political project of independent statehood was legitimised by pursuing Macedonian national and historical interest, referring to the historical standing of the Macedonian question (Kolishevski, 1981) and confirming

---

6. For example, Tupurkovski and Petrov, 1st plenary session, Parliament of the Socialist Republic of Macedonia, 8 January 1991, 86.

the inviolable sovereignty of the Macedonian people. This legitimisation, however, did not take account of the sizeable non-Macedonian component of the republic – the Albanian minority. Attempting to exclude the Albanians from the political community constituted at state level conditioned a long-term inter-ethnic confrontation and determined to a large extent the type of statehood the newly independent republic achieved in the decade following independence. At the same time this confrontation perpetuated the discourse of Macedonian nationalism, empowered initially with the political project of independence.

Articulating the unambiguous correlation between nation ('the Macedonian people') and state, on the one hand, and denying the same status to any other community[7] on the other, established a clear hierarchy in which the Macedonian national community dominated the project of statehood. This dominant position was further justified by appeals for historical justice, pointing to the Macedonians' long struggles for independent statehood.[8] Categorically stating that the only way to ensure a harmonious relationship with the Albanian community was for them to accept the formula of Macedonian domination prescribed a position of subordination for the ethnic Albanians, whose right to be included in the project of statehood was recognised only as that of one of the 'nationalities'.[9] United with the titular majority along the lines of citizenship, the members of the Albanian ethnic majority could enjoy the same civil rights as other Macedonian citizens. Moreover, they could do so irrespective of their national identity – they were recognised as a nationality. This is in contrast to Bulgaria at that time, where ethnic minorities could participate in the state community only as long as they subscribed to Bulgarian national identity, renouncing their background nationality. In Bulgaria they had been designated as 'ethnic' (not 'national') communities, having Bulgarian national self-identification, despite their different ethnic origins. Macedonia did recognise divergent national identities. However, this recognition served the dual purpose of offering a formula of inclusion into the project of statehood *and* maintaining the status of Otherness. Without a formula of inclusion, however, no meaningful political consensus over statehood could be reached. As the newly elected head of state Kiro Gligorov noted during his inaugural speech in parliament, his election would not have been legitimate had the Albanian minority not participated in it. This recognition speaks to the political bargaining power of the Albanian majority and its role in shaping the identity of the newly independent state. Unlike Bulgaria, where the largest ethnic minority was not included in the Roundtable Talks for negotiating the new power deal, and was offered access to state power only after the negotiations, the Macedonian Albanians participated in the negotiations right from the start.

---

7. Other communities were consistently referred to as 'nationalities', not 'peoples', e.g. Mihail Panovski, plenary session, 8 January 1991, 100.
8. For example, Kiril Kovachevski, 4th parliamentary session, 25 January 1991: 146; Gligorov, 5th parliamentary session, 27 January 1991: 17.
9. Gligorov, 5th plenary session, 27 January 1991: 16.

Fully aware that their inclusion depended on the reformulation of the political project for a Macedonian national state for the Macedonian people, the Albanians attempted to marginalise the 'national' narrative in the project,[10] emphasising instead more universal narratives such as protecting human rights and fostering democracy.

The Albanian context added an important tenet to Macedonian identity at the time. Even though the political project of independent Macedonian statehood demanded a national state for the Macedonian people, it could not acquire the legitimacy it needed unless it articulated a broader criterion for self-identification than nationality. Hence, the consensual formula acknowledging the 'equal and sustainable' participation of other 'nationalities'.[11] This rhetorical move made narratives of Macedonian post-socialist national identity much more inclusive, as compared to what happened in Bulgaria. At the same time, however, it institutionalised Otherness, upholding a state identity destabilised by mutually nourished domestic nationalisms. The internal instability of this identity construction made it more vulnerable to external threats.

The Balkan context

Macedonia staked its claim for independent statehood in a geopolitical environment that was not entirely benevolent. Surrounded by Bulgaria and Greece, which both had certain ideas of 'Macedonian-ness', Macedonia had always had to defend its identity against external encroachment. To Bulgaria, Macedonia was an integral element of the Bulgarian narrative of national pride, sacrifice and loss. Laying claims on the entire region of geographical Macedonia (including Pirin, Vardar and Aegean) as old Bulgarian lands, Bulgaria had not come to terms with Macedonian statehood. To Greece, Macedonia was a central locus of Greek narratives of political and cultural superiority dating back to antiquity. Symbolically, it was an inseparable part of Greek national identity and, as such, independent Macedonian statehood could not be treated as anything but an aberration. Bulgaria and Greece interpreted the fact that they had considerable parts of geographical Macedonia under their sovereignty as evidence supporting their claims and justification for their 'special' positions towards the Macedonian Republic. Appealing to past commonality, Bulgaria fluctuated between the paternalistic tone of an older brother protecting an inexperienced youth and the absolute negation of Macedonia's distinctive identity. Both ends of the spectre denied Macedonia a position of equality in the world of sovereign states and thus contradicted the very nature of the most crucial political project for Macedonia – independent statehood. Greece, in turn, insisted on an essential right over anything Macedonian and categorically refused to acknowledge the

---

10. The 'national key', as Faik Abdi calls it at the 4th plenary session, 25 January 1991, 162.
11. See Macedonian Constitution, 1991, Preamble.

unauthorised use of the name of the republic and of key elements of the insignia of the state. From a position of recognised international authority, this refusal denied Macedonia the freedom to access the most stable of all signifiers of 'Macedonian-ness': the name.

These 'special' positions differed significantly from each other, but in their encroachment over the discursive space of Macedonian identity they both constituted serious threats to its stability. Indeed, the domestic perception of the two neighbours was that of hostility. The experiences of surroundedness and non-acceptance structured the perception of hostility emanating from Macedonia's neighbours and constituted these neighbours as a threat. This was evident in the widely vocalised concern within Macedonia for Macedonian minorities in the territory of the neighbouring states. This excessive preoccupation with the well-being of Macedonian minorities in the surrounding states, however, further exacerbated the reservations of neighbouring states to a sovereign Macedonia, serving as a catalyst to their anti-Macedonian sentiments. The Bulgarian and Greek governments did not hesitate to make these sentiments known in either the domestic or the international context, provoking as a response the mobilisation of Macedonian identity politics and the securitisation of Macedonian national identity. Complemented by complex Macedonian relations with Serbia as the former sovereign, and with Albania, this regional context stimulated the rise of defensive Macedonian nationalism and to a large extent affected the type of national identity it upheld.

Thus, as in Bulgaria, the first years of post-communism in Macedonia were structured by the discursive context of hegemonic nationalism. Understanding this context and its specificities in the two cases under study is the starting point for analysing the meanings upheld by national identity narratives and their modifications within the dynamic of Europeanisation.

The hegemony of nationalism as discursive context

As discussed in greater detail in the first part of the book, nationalism provided the implicit discursive background of modern statehood, thus remaining perpetually relevant to the political background. Both major developments in post-war Europe – the institutionalisation of communism in the East and the project of European integration in the West – attempted to transcend their discursive boundaries, although in very different ways. This temporarily marginalised some of nationalism's interpretations of national identity. In Eastern Europe, the break-up of communism restored their political relevance, particularly in view of the East's initial isolation from the integration processes in the West. The renewed search for collective identity as the unifying centre of political community in post-communist Bulgaria and Macedonia was thus structured by the discursive hegemony of nationalism. National identity narratives of early transition in the two states are exclusionary and highly conflictual, upholding a closed community that was strongly dependent upon past antagonisms. The following section traces some of their most salient interpretations.

Patterns of identity before Europeanisation

Having laid out the discursive context of hegemonic nationalism as structuring the narration of identity in both Bulgaria and Macedonia, the book proceeds to explore the pattern of national identity in the two states before they joined the dynamic of Europeanisation. This section examines three central narrative groups determining the discursive position of Self. These narratives are sustained by traditional discursive elements of political community identifiable in both states: territory, nationhood, national purpose. Tracing dominant interpretations before Europeanisation, the analysis aims to establish the political consequences of identity narration for imagining the community of the state. It also aims to reveal the political consequences of identity narration for perpetuating particular state behaviour. Describing a closed, exclusive community that is highly dependent on historical narrative and thus anchored in the past, national identity narrated within the hegemonic discourse of nationalism perpetuates inter-group, inter-ethnic and international conflictuality. This significantly compromises its credibility as the legitimate source of sovereign power in Europe. With gradual progress towards joining the Europeanisation dynamic, the political relevance of 'European' interpretations narrating the national story increases. Having outlined the discursive pattern of national identity before Europeanisation in this chapter, the analysis will then follow the discursive modifications introduced to it by the dynamic of Europeanisation in Chapters Five and Six.

Bulgarian national identity narratives of Self before Europeanisation

Despite its sedimented quality and increased popular appeal, national identity upheld in an antagonistic manner did not enjoy high credibility as a legitimate state identity in the context of post-communism. Against the imperatives of coming to terms with the past and starting anew, the political community of the state had to be imagined in a different way. The search for a new identity in Bulgaria began in the process of dismantling the totalitarian regime, as discussed in the preceding section. The democratisation process and the project of integration in Europe provided a general direction to this search, but the high salience of nationalist rhetoric and politics prevented immediate progress towards it. This section aims to map out the discursive pattern of Bulgarian national identity in this context of increased instability that was still dominated by the rhetoric of nationalism. By tracing the dominant interpretations of three central elements of national identity and the narratives articulating their meanings, the following paragraphs attempt to identify the discursive logic of the conflictuality they perpetuated. Focusing on one dimension of the identity maintenance dynamic – Bulgarian–Macedonian relations – the analysis explores the political consequences of conflictual interpretations. Assuming that their legitimacy fails in the non-constructive state behaviour they condition, this section ultimately aims to highlight the

Identity narratives of nationhood

omissions of political community imagined within the logic of nationalism. It is against these omissions that the Europeanisation of national identities could enhance the legitimacy of the key source of collective belonging within the nation-state.

High significance in the discursive pattern of national identity is universally attached to the element of nationhood. In post-communist Bulgaria the idea of 'national unity' as the highest priority in safeguarding nationhood sustained the most salient interpretations of its meaning. Rooted in a historical myth from early medieval times and affirmed by the historical narrative of the liberation movement that led to the establishment of the modern independent Bulgarian state (e.g. Roudometof, 2002), at a most basic level the idea of 'national unity' is understood as the natural bond of 'brotherhood'. As with the five proto-Bulgarian brother–princes from a popular national myth,[12] unity is based on a blood relationship, i.e. it suggests a sort of pre-given commonality into which not everybody can share. Although newcomers have traditionally been welcome in accordance with the proverbial call for hospitality, they always remain guests because they do not share this origin (see Stoyanov, 1998 for this problem in view of the Bulgarian Turkish minority). In the context of a threat against the community, the idea of 'national unity' becomes a source of strength against numerous adversaries from both within and without. This is why it acquires a quality of highest value. The period around the negotiated regime change in Bulgaria was a time of utmost uncertainty in an ideological, social, political and economic sense. Moreover, it was a time of serious inter-ethnic tension as a legacy of the totalitarian violence against different ethnicities. In this context of instability the appeal for 'national unity' became increasingly salient.

'Unity of the nation' was the central message of the parliamentary declaration on the national question (televised on 15 January 1990), which officially recognised the responsibility of the totalitarian regime for the nationalist violence of the past in an attempt to appease the protesting crowds throughout the country. Its Article 7 is specifically dedicated to the 'unity of the nation'. Following the declaration, 'unity of the nation' was appealed to endlessly at the Roundtable Talks in brokering the post-communist power agreement, as a formula for consensus and the highest good (Melone, 1994; Elster, 1996). Listing it as one of the basic principles underlying the political system that post-totalitarian Bulgaria needs to establish with the reforms, the then vice chairman of the State Council explained:

> We are introducing new principles [...] such as democratism, humanism, unity of the nation, separation between executive, legislative and judicial powers.[13]

---

12. The fable of Khan Kubrat and his sons: see Lalkov, 1995.
13. Vasil Mrichkov, Roundtable Talks verbatim reports, 19 March 1990, 3.10pm.

From the opposition, a representative of the Club of the Repressed (one of the first activist organisations formed swiftly in the course of the regime change) also listed national unity among the priority goals of the reforms, when appealing for a particular type of electoral system: 'This is particularly important [...] in the name of the consensus, in the name of national unity, in the name of peaceful transition, etcetera'.[14] The lack of theoretical precision in the use and the rhetorical inertia of such statements illustrates the formulaic quality that the phrase had acquired by this time.

The interpretation of the idea of 'national unity' as a highest value upholds a particular vision of national identity that is not necessarily reconciliatory. By emphasising the unity of the national community at any cost, the political actors in effect deny the members of the community the right to differences that transcend the boundary of the nation. At that time, this meant that Bulgarian citizens were not expected to have any different national affiliation if they were to be members of the community of the Bulgarian nation. In the case of national minorities the implication was slightly paradoxical. Their right of belonging was recognised in so far as their 'national consciousness' ('национално самосъзнание') remained Bulgarian, despite ethnic or religious differences. This was the only reasoning that could preserve a cohesive, unified, monolithic nation, while accepting Otherness. But because minorities could not share the bond of blood from the glorious and tragic past, as the Bulgarian narrative of nationhood had it, they inevitably remained something of an aberration. The emphasis on the need for 'tolerance', i.e. acceptance of something one does not necessarily agree with, illustrates this incongruence. The concept of a monolithic nation could simply not accommodate fully and comfortably the idea of national minorities. It would always maintain a fine distinction between 'ethnic minorities and our people'.[15]

This is evident in the discussions on many of the political reforms undertaken with the break-up of communism that the Roundtable Talks showcase, as well as in the legislative decisions taken by the Grand National Assembly following the Roundtable. Political parties, for example, were considered to be 'first and foremost, national organisation[s]',[16] i.e. a clear hierarchy was being established between national and political affiliations in favour of the former. The constitutional provision on political parties, in turn, prohibits 'the incorporation of political parties along ethnic lines'.[17] This precluded the collective right of political representation of (ethno-) national minorities (Jovanović, 2005), which later became particularly controversial in terms of registering parties representing the Macedonian minority in Bulgaria. The registration of the

---

14. Ivan Nevrokopski, Roundtable Talks verbatim reports, 19 March 1990, 3.10pm.
15. Milan Drenchev, Bulgarian Agricultural Popular Union, Roundtable Talks verbatim reports, 12 March 1990, 3.50pm.
16. Mrichkov, Roundtable Talks verbatim reports, 26 March 1990, 9.36am.
17. Constitution, 1991, Art.11, Para.4.

organisation representing the Turkish ethnic minority (the Movement for Rights and Freedoms), on the other hand, was only allowed after a statute modification inviting membership from the Bulgarian majority (i.e. formally, it no longer aimed to represent only the ethnic Turks: see Ganev, 2004). The explicit prohibition of political representation of ethno-national minorities at the level of primary law continued the established hierarchy between national and political, placing ethnicity lower down the hierarchy. This characterised Bulgarian national identity at the time as highly exclusive, constituting a closed community in which belonging is defined by *jus sanguinis* (Roudometof, 2002: 19). Such an exclusive identity fostered antagonism, because it dramatically narrowed the discursive space of the national Self and constituted everybody else in terms of threatening Otherness. In view of Bulgarian–Macedonian relations, such an identity could be disorienting because it conditioned a challenge from within. Historically sedimented narratives of belonging constituted the people of Macedonia as 'brothers': they were included in the same narratives that upheld the community of blood (Roudometof, 2002: Chapter 2). Macedonia's refusal to participate in these narratives threatened their credibility. This was furthermore challenged by the rewriting of the national identity narrative in Macedonia, constituting Bulgaria as the threatening Other. Thus, the dominant interpretation of one of the central discursive elements in Bulgarian national identity – unity of the nation – predetermined conflictuality in bilateral relations with Macedonia.

Identity narratives of territory

Another key element in Bulgarian national identity is articulated on the basis of the meaning of territory. The most salient interpretations of the meaning of national territory in post-communist Bulgaria tell the story of 'territorial integrity'. While preserving the territorial integrity of the state generally leads the security and defence agendas of any state, constituting territorial integrity as a key national identity element serves a different purpose. Originating in the idea of the 'unity' of the Bulgarian nation, in many ways the story of territorial integrity defined the type of state modern Bulgaria became from its independence until the final decade of the twentieth century. Many states contain territorial entities with various degrees of autonomy within their borders, or are part of a federation while still retaining their territorial integrity. In Bulgaria the inherently integral nature of state territory characterised by an equal degree of sovereignty over all its territorial regions has been upheld as sacrosanct. Even the remote probability that the (at the time) loosely organised Turkish minority might demand autonomy for the southern region, which it predominantly populated, was sufficient to generate tension in inter-ethnic relations within the state (Stoyanov, 1998). In their attempts to address the problem in a reconciliatory manner, the government and the democratic opposition discussed an official declaration in which the primary focus was on denying that 'autonomy' had ever come up as a political option. Thus, the leader of the National Union of Students (an active civil society organisation during the anti-regime protests) insisted that: 'Their other demand, for autonomy, which has been flared by the chauvinists, needs to be addressed and denied [in the text of the Declaration]'.[18] The speaker of the democratic opposition continued:

> the Declaration [...] needs to confirm that we have discussed the situation and that the issue of autonomy has not been brought up [...] because they say, rumour has it, that their main demand has been for autonomy.[19]

The attempts to publicly deny even the mention of the idea of autonomy illustrate the explosive potential that this idea might have had on the internal stability of the state. In a telling allegory ('to invite the wolf [into the sheep pen]') the prime minister-to-be insisted that only the word 'separatism' (and not 'autonomy') be referred to when denying any 'anti-state' demands from the minority.[20] The allegory suggests that even though it might have been among the claims of the repressed, the demand for autonomy was categorically dismissed as a possible political solution to the inter-ethnic problem. Territorial integrity as an element in the national identity of the Bulgarian state was non-negotiable.

This is also evident in the text of the new constitution adopted by the Grand National Assembly the following year. Its preamble refers to the 'irrevocable duty [of the legislators] to guard the national and state integrity of Bulgaria'.[21] Article 2 explicitly prohibits any 'autonomous territorial formations' (Para.1) and designates the territorial integrity of the state as 'inviolable' (Para.2). Relevant in this context is also an interesting constitutional provision regulating property rights over land. Foreigners are denied the right to acquire ownership over Bulgarian land and if they inherit it, they need to transfer it immediately.[22] Rare in its juridical formulation, this provision is indicative of the degree of salience of the territorial integrity interpretation in constructing the national identity of the state. In the discursive dynamic determining the positions of national Self and Other such salience clearly designates the 'foreign' as a threat.

Along similar lines, the discursive emphasis on protecting state borders during the negotiation of the reforms reinforces the perception of threat, and is another illustration of the closed character of identity upheld through the national unity and territorial integrity narratives. In the discussion on dismantling the barbed wire fences along state borders the minister of the interior warned of the dangers that such a move would induce and the increased number of guards that it would implicate.[23] Contrasting the idea with the phenomenon of open borders

---

18. Emil Koshlukov, Roundtable Talks verbatim reports, plenary session, 3 January 1990 from 5.30pm.
19. Spasov, Roundtable Talks verbatim reports, plenary session, 3 January 1990 from 5.30pm.
20. Andrey Lukanov, Roundtable Talks verbatim reports, plenary session, 3 January 1990 from 5.30pm.
21. Constitution of Bulgaria 1991, Preamble.
22. Art.22, Para.1 before the amendment of 2005.
23. Atanas Semerdzhiev, Roundtable Talks verbatim reports from 26 March 1990, 9.36am.

in Europe, the minister underlined Bulgaria's unpreparedness for open borders ('[lacking the prerequisites of a] political, economic and social character'), thus increasing the sense of threat. Emphasising the role of state borders had the effect of discursively solidifying them as a source of protection against foreign threats. Such rhetoric increased the antagonistic character of national identity by reinforcing its closed entativity. In view of Bulgarian–Macedonian relations, the salience of the territorial integrity narrative produced a field of political tension focused on the border region of Pirin Macedonia (within the territory of Bulgaria). The independence of the Macedonian state and its claims to protect the Macedonian minority inhabiting this region increased the perception of threat against Bulgarian territorial integrity and considerably strained bilateral relations. This is illustrated by the recurrence of the issue of minorities in relation to territorial integrity in inter-state dialogue between the two states (Chapter Seven).

Identity narratives of national purpose

Another key discursive element in Bulgarian national identity is identified in the meaning of national purpose. Interpreted through the narratives of 'centrality on the Balkans', the dominant meaning of this discursive element at the time was determined by Bulgaria's specific geopolitical position. Encrypted in an almost sacrosanct manner in the national anthem (which demanded dutiful respect, as suggested by the custom of standing up while the anthem is played), it was defined by the centrality of the 'proud' Stara Planina (the transliteration of the name of the Balkan mountain range 'The Old Mountain' into Bulgarian) and delimited by the 'blue' Danube river to the north, the valley of Thrace 'shining in the sun' to the south, and the 'fiery' Pirin mountain to the west (Bulgarian National Anthem, 1964). The mythologisation of national geography as one of the instruments of nation-building constructed a primordial attachment to the land, which became the basis for the claim of sovereignty. Therefore it served the dual purpose of constituting the community as national and legitimising its territorial claims. By revolving its geographical space around the physical backbone of the Balkans – the Balkan mountain range – Bulgaria laid a particular claim to the geopolitics of the entire peninsula: centrality.

Among other things, the Bulgarian president declared in the course of an interview for the democratic opposition's leading newspaper, 'We are the very centre of the Balkans'.[24] 'History has dealt us a key position on the Balkans,' said the vice president a little earlier.[25] The matter-of-fact quality of these statements and the consensual agreement with which they were met across the political landscape are an indication of the high degree of discursive sedimentation of the story of 'centrality'. This is important because it has been rhetorically instrumentalised in justifications of failures in foreign and domestic policy on key political issues.

24. President Zhelyu Zhelev, *Demokratsia* newspaper, 4 January 1992.
25. Atanas Semerdzhiev, Roundtable Talks verbatim reports, 6 February 1990 from 2.35pm.

The story of the nation as the victim of conflicting interests of the 'Great Powers', whose intersection on the Balkans Bulgaria 'tragically' occupies, has been repeated over and over again, with each unsuccessful political move and each loss of position after the series of wars in the first half of the twentieth century, participation in which was motivated by aspirations for territorial unification. The 'unjust' Berlin Treaty of 1878, replacing the 'just' San Stefano Treaty (which incidentally met all territorial claims of the new Bulgarian state), pushed Bulgaria into decades of dramatic effort to complete its national aspirations: 'our righteous aspirations have met nothing but misunderstanding and animosity,' asserted one of the leading historiographers of the communist-era Academy of Sciences.[26] This historically documented conclusion (in the monumental *History of Bulgaria in 14 Volumes* published by the Bulgarian Academy of Sciences in 1979) is also reproduced in the political sphere at the highest level: 'our central geopolitical position] has been a curse for Bulgaria. [...] Bulgaria at the crossroads has always been a victim'.[27] The discursive victimisation of Bulgaria because of its geographical and geopolitical position, projected as something that lies outside the scope of control of the subject (implying its innocence), served the political purpose of transferring the blame for the 'national catastrophes',[28] into which unwise or unfortunate (but otherwise 'righteous') policies had led the state. Reopening the 'Macedonian question' with Macedonia's claim for independence and the ambiguities in Bulgaria's position towards it establishes direct discursive links with this historical discussion on dealing with national loss. The fact that the context that determined Bulgaria's reaction to Macedonia's independence was discursively rooted in the traumas of the past visibly troubled bilateral relations and impeded a solution to bilateral issues in line with the political present.

The political relevance of the narrative on victimisation in the early 1990s can also be linked to the uncertainty caused by the reforms. Rejecting totalitarianism, Bulgaria struggled to redefine its state identity in an entirely novel international environment. Established stereotypes of hostility (of Otherness) naturally resurfaced as points of orientation. However, the context of change, uncertain as it was, brought with it hopes for a new beginning. The fall of totalitarianism promised 'freedom' and opened up the discursive space for new interpretations of what signified national purpose. This is what enabled the transformation of the victimisation narrative into a story of opportunity:

> Today, in the world of modern communications, [our geopolitical] position is a great advantage; we should be the biggest of fools if we do not use our natural advantages.[29]

---

26. Ilcho Dimitrov, interview in *Duma* newspaper, 1 February 1992, Issue 27.
27. Interview with President Zhelyu Zhelev, *Demokratsia* newspaper, 4 January 1992.
28. The term 'national catastrophe' is used in Bulgarian historiography to describe the period after the Balkan wars and the period after the First World War: Bulgarian Academy of Sciences (1999).
29. Interview with President Zhelyu Zhelev, *Demokratsia* newspaper, 4 January 1992.

This interpretation links the idea of centrality to an antithetical discursive line implying uniqueness, significance, responsibility. To begin with, centrality is seen as conditioning Bulgaria's special mission as a factor of stability in the Balkans. This idea was repeated on numerous occasions as the reason and purpose of Bulgarian policies, and was reinforced by external authoritative recognition, which was widely publicised. The American then-Secretary of the Air Force was quoted in a headline to a news article assuring the Bulgarian prime minister that '[your] country is the centre of stability in the Balkans'.[30] Positive pieces on Bulgaria from the European press were another way of suggesting Bulgaria's exceptionalism: 'The little miracle in the Balkans.'[31] Reversing the political sign of centrality to signify stability was an expression of Bulgaria's search for a new state direction and purpose at the beginning of the transition period. Positive self-identification at state level is a good basis for political mobilisation domestically and for successful negotiation internationally. For Bulgaria's smaller neighbour Macedonia, however, the paternalistic tone of Bulgarian foreign policy did not promise good neighbourly relations, particularly in view of Bulgarian ambiguities towards Macedonia as a sovereign nation.

Another aspect of the new interpretation of centrality is directly relevant to Bulgaria's (re-)turn to Europe. Being located near the geopolitical crossroads between Europe and Asia, Bulgaria presented itself as the gatekeeper. In an international context the chair of the parliamentary committee on foreign policy declared:

> The Black Sea has two coastal lines, one European, one Asian. Bulgarians are on the European line and we do not intend to leave it.[32]

Such self-positioning is gratifying because of the claimed mediatory role between two worlds, which are placed in a decidedly hierarchical order, as suggested by the determination with which the claimed position is being defended ('we do not intend to leave' the European line). This formulation was not new to Bulgarian historiography. It implied 'a special duty and a special responsibility before Europe to help solve the problems in the Balkan region', as the Ministry of Foreign Affairs explained.[33] Thus not only was the Bulgarian claim for Europe being staked, but at the same time this claim was being argumentatively backed. Insisting on a special 'duty and responsibility before Europe' arising for Bulgaria from its alleged gatekeeping position also suggested a special relationship between Bulgaria and Europe. Such self-identification aims to discursively enhance the image of the

---

30. Donald Rice, US Secretary of the Airforce, *Demokratsia* newspaper, 28 January 1992.
31. *Züddeutsche Zeitung*, quoted in *Demokratsia* newspaper, 22 April 1992.
32. Aleksander Yordanov, Chair of the Parliamentary Committee on Foreign Policy, *Demokratsia* newspaper, 29 April 1992.
33. Declaration, 18 January 1992.

state. In the longer term it was indicative of the future direction of foreign policy strategy. In view of Bulgaria's international position on the Balkans, however, this self-identification imposed a certain paternalism that Macedonia found particularly irritating, as the second section of this chapter demonstrates. During the early transition, the credibility of 'European' stories of Self was still questionable.

Legitimacy and Bulgarian national identity narratives of Self before Europeanisation

Contextually identifying the dominant interpretations of three of its central elements helps us to imagine the discursive pattern of Bulgarian national identity from the early post-communist period. The notions of national unity, territorial integrity and geopolitical centrality reveal a closed community that was predominantly oriented towards past antagonisms. Self-identification was possible for the community only along the strict lines of nationhood, excluding those who could not partake in the nationhood narrative. Most significantly this category referred to minority communities sharing different national, ethnic, linguistic, or religious backgrounds. Formally accepted in the wider political community, they were discursively marginalised and subtly constituted as internal Other(s). Their Otherness was often transferred to external homelands (i.e. Turkey), constituting various external Others (immediate neighbours) as a threat. The closed character of Bulgarian national identity determined its high degree of conflictuality.

Bulgaria's orientation towards the past, in turn, linked past antagonisms to the present, making them part of the agenda of everyday politics. This orientation impeded processing and coming to terms with the past[34] because it included the past in the discursive field in which the identity of the national Self was being articulated. In the context of post-communist transition, such interpretation of identity became increasingly problematic. In view of Bulgarian–Macedonian relations, in particular, it brought to the fore the narrative of the Bulgarian loss of Macedonia as soon as the issue of establishing bilateral relations at state level was reopened. This inability to dissociate from this narrative determined the conflictual character of bilateral relations and threatened to compromise Bulgaria's regional standing.

An exclusive national identity oriented towards the past is also particularly vulnerable to the destabilising effect of closeness in identity. A national identity oriented towards the past is much more difficult to reformulate because its carrying discursive elements are part of historical narratives with higher degree of sedimentation, i.e. they are more difficult to retell. This is what conditioned Bulgaria's increased perception of threat as a result of Macedonia's claims over some of the discursive elements upholding Bulgarian national identity. The uncertainty caused by the regime change in Bulgaria and the struggle to redefine a post-communist national identity for the Bulgarian state had already challenged

---

34. *Die Vergangenheitsbewältigung*, from the German reconciliation tradition.

the stability of these elements. This opened up the discursive space to alternative interpretations of identity, which promised to reduce insecurity. Joining the dynamic of Europeanisation helped produce the key competing vision of Self, as analysing the narratives in Chapter Six will demonstrate.

Macedonian national identity narratives of Self before Europeanisation

In the context of disintegrating from the Yugoslav federation, accommodating the vocal Albanian minority and struggling for recognition among presumably encroaching neighbours, the Macedonian state sought to project an identity that was capable of making sense of these changes and of reducing the discursive insecurity for its subjects. In the early transition, marked by nationalist rhetoric and politics, however, the most salient interpretations of national identity upheld a highly contentious discursive construction, destabilised from within by unresolved tensions and threatened from without as a consequence of its antagonistic projections. The discursive tension generated by such a contentious identity construction compromised the legitimacy of the national political community and asserted the need for alternative interpretations.

Identity narratives of nationhood

The most salient interpretations of Macedonian nationhood within the hegemony of nationalism struggled with the idea of 'national tolerance'. Their inability to produce a credible narrative of nationhood within the identity construct of the state determined internal instability. On the one hand, the central justification of the project of independence revolved around the vindication of national suffering and the recognition of Macedonians' right of national emancipation. In this sense it upheld statehood as an entirely national project. On the other hand, the historical opportunity for a national state along these lines seemed to have passed because the active political participation of non-Macedonian ethnic minority communities, leading among which the Albanian, prevented the absolute closure of the nationhood narrative in the implementation of the statehood project. Rhetorically entrapped between the dominant story of nationhood and the need for legitimacy, Macedonian statehood had to reach a compromise. This is embodied in its claim to have achieved a just balance between national unity and tolerant inter-ethnic relations. As a discursive element in the national identity construction this claim envisioned a more inclusive national community that, at least declaratively, was not constrained by the limits of monolithic nationhood. This is in contrast to the Bulgarian insistence on an ethnic accommodation model, which could be successful only as long as it excluded divergent narratives of nationhood. Macedonia, unlike Bulgaria, allowed the notion of 'nationalities' in its national identity construct, which justified its claim for national tolerance as the dominant meaning of nationhood in the Macedonian state.

That this compromise was reached as a matter of urgency is suggested in the conflict between narratives of nationhood and the imperatives for legitimacy throughout 1991. In the period leading up to the referendum for the future of Macedonia as an independent state on 8 September 1991 a powerful rhetorical line upheld the statehood project as a national state *per se*. As a national state, the new entity would naturally represent the collective identity of the majority community, the Macedonian nation:

> This is why in the national state we can only speak of equality among the citizens in the protection of their rights and freedoms, and we cannot speak of equality between the nation and the national minorities as collectivities.[35]

Even though absent from the rhetoric of most leading state actors, this line did appear as a narrative at official state level. It is detectable in the parliamentary debates of the entire period. It is the active political participation of the Albanian minority that first began to question this rhetoric:

> I will stand for strengthening national unity but also stabilising inter-ethnic relations, promoting these relations and creating a climate of togetherness on the basis of mutual respect, equality, political rights and freedoms, and mutual trust.[36]

The repeated formula of 'stabilising', 'promoting', 'improving' the inter-ethnic relations suggests that they are under threat and establishes an aim to raise their profile in the first months of the democratic transition, thus leading to their gradual securitisation. Categorically placing inter-ethnic relations on the 'urgent' political agenda of the new Macedonian state, the Albanian political representation called for fair and equal treatment of the national minority communities, putting them on a par with the national majority community. This call attempted to radically reformulate the entire Macedonian statehood project, and, unsurprisingly, was met with fervent opposition from the majority, who insisted on preserving the national referents of the state:

> Nationality [in the constitution] should be specified, Macedonian-ness should be specified, because for the first time in its history the Macedonian people have this chance [to adopt a national constitution].[37]

This argument was taken further in its most radical interpretation, suggesting that treating the Albanian minority on a par with the Macedonian national majority might lead to the paradox of reversing the hierarchical positions: 'it seems, if we continue working like this […], one day we [the Macedonians] will become

---

35. 1st plenary session of the Macedonian parliament, 8 January 1991, 93.
36. Dzheladin Murati, 4th plenary session, 25 January 1991, 75.
37. Branko Crvenkovski, 25th plenary session, 11 November 1991, 25.

the minority and will have to defend our minority rights'.[38] These rhetorical formulations catalysed Albanian discontent with the suggested course of statehood and created an opposing rhetorical current of resentment:

> The Macedonian nation refers to itself as the sole successor of Macedonia. [...] The Albanians seem to be an unwanted constitutive element in this historical context, only because they insist on being an equal subject in the [project of] statehood.[39]

Intensifying the minority protest against alleged unjust treatment clashed with the extreme calls for nationalising the statehood project, thus threatening to escalate the political atmosphere to unmanageable degrees. This is what predicated the need for an inter-ethnic compromise.

Pointing to the inter-ethnic conflicts that tore Yugoslavia apart, the prime minister-to-be emphasised Macedonia's 'vital interests', which could not be realised unless 'we tried to establish tolerant relations between all of us'.[40] Cevenkovski saw these 'vital interests' as 'completing statehood and acquiring independence and sovereignty', 'protecting territorial integrity' and 'entering the European processes of integration'. This was the context within which the notion of constituting the state identity as a community of citizenship, rather than of nationhood, gained prominence: 'at this moment in Europe there is no single state that is constitutionally defined as a national state'.[41] The speaker of parliament reinforced the argument in favour of civic, rather than national, statehood:

> our Macedonian state [...] contains its own national aspect [...] but now we need to move forward to a civic state, because Macedonians are not simply a members of the nation, but are members of the nation as citizens, as enlightened individuals[.][42]

Rhetorically positioning the national and civic statehood in a hierarchy in which citizenship is placed higher, as a more 'enlightened' stage of statehood, was an attempt to justify the necessary modification of the Macedonian independence project. Emphasising that the national character of the state would not be removed, the speaker demonstrated how a state community organised along civic lines would be a community better suited to the political present ('we need to move forward'). What prevailed on the side of a civic community is the European perspective ('no other state in Europe'), as will be demonstrated in more detail below.

The obvious hesitations in taking the independence project from national to civic statehood tell of an internal undecideability in Macedonian identity.

---

38. Todor Petrov, 25th plenary session, 11 November 1991, 54.
39. Ismet Ramadani, 25th plenary session, 9 November 1991, 45.
40. Branko Crvenkovski, 25th plenary session, 11 November 1991, 25.
41. Ibid.
42. Stojan Andov, 25th plenary session, 9 November 1991, 192.

Even though the particular issue that caused such heated debates (removing the 'national' denominator from Article 1 of the 1991 Constitution) was resolved in favour of civic identity, the national marker continued to designate the community of the state (as evident from the Preamble of the Constitution). In the ambiguous story of national tolerance, this internal tension destabilised Macedonian identity when it needed affirmation and recognition from both within and without. In this sense it actually increased conflictuality. Unlike Bulgaria, which fixed its post-communist identity by openly refusing to accommodate divergent narratives of nationhood, Macedonia formally acknowledged domestic Otherness. Unable to completely detach from the narrative of nationhood, however, it created a context of domestic antagonism that affected its national and international standing for the following decade.

Identity narratives of territory

In contrast to Bulgaria, national territory was interpreted in Macedonia not as integral and indivisive, but as perpetuating the national story of belonging. The uncertainties surrounding the status of the territory of Macedonia throughout most of the nineteenth and twentieth centuries and the territorial aspirations of neighbouring sovereign states towards it left its population no other stable source of collective self-identification but the name of the land they inhabited. 'Macedonia' as the locus of their struggles for political emancipation from empire began to define the identity of a people that was contested on all other grounds. Caught between conflicting narratives of nationhood (Bulgarian, Serbian, Greek) but unable to subscribe to any one of them, the people of Macedonia could effectively declare their own identity only by the name of their land. Because of this specific historical role, to an extent replicated in the federation, the story of territorial belonging took a central position in the narration of Macedonian identity.

> Macedonia is all we have![43]

> Our negotiating position starts from the inviolability and entirety of the [political and national subjectivity and] the territorial, the total integrity of Macedonia. We have no right to even discuss these categories with anybody. We will reject a priori any pressure or usurpation integrity of Macedonia whatsoever.[44]

The fact that the geographical land of Macedonia was a primary source of self-identification had an important implication for imagining the community at state level. Macedonian state borders included about one-third of the entire

---

43. 5th plenary session, 27 January 1991, 25.
44. Vladimir Mitkov, Chairman of the Republican State Council, 1st plenary session, 8 January 1991, 85.

geographical region that was historically referred to as 'Macedonia'; the rest of it was part of neighbouring states. The implication, therefore, is that of incompleteness, of a severed whole. This was indicated in the numerous references in Macedonian political rhetoric of the time to 'unification' and to the 'Macedonian national question'[45] as well as in the extraordinary concern for the 'parts of the Macedonian people' in neighbouring states.

> Macedonia never has had and never will have territorial aspirations towards its neighbours because one can only have territorial aspirations towards something that is not one's own.[46]

Even though such explicit formulations were, indeed, rare, they were indicative of the implicit understanding that 'Macedonia' as a self-identification category referred to a larger community. This understanding was one of the key reasons for the high degree of antagonism in the Macedonian state's bilateral relations with its neighbours. In Bulgarian–Macedonian relations in particular, it contained an implicit claim over Pirin Macedonia and its people. These relations were further strained by the conflicting claim on the Bulgarian side over the exclusively Bulgarian character not only of the Pirin region, but also of the rest of Macedonia.

Another implication of the story of territorial belonging for the pattern of Macedonian national identity was the increased symbolic significance of the name. Being a primary signifier of identity, the name 'Macedonia' was non-negotiable. This became evident in the context of the name dispute with Greece and the grave consequences that Greek disaffection had had on Macedonia's economic and political stability in the Balkans caused by the Greek embargo (Panagiotou, 2008), as well as on its progress in Euro–Atlantic integration. Even beyond the logical line of argumentation on Macedonian side that choosing a name for their state was an exclusive prerogative of state sovereignty, the firm Macedonian position in the dispute displayed, besides everything else, Macedonia's inability to discuss anything less than the constitutional name ('Republic of Macedonia'). Conforming with the formulations acceptable to Greece, such as 'Vardar Macedonia', for example, would have involved a dramatic reduction of the discursive space delimiting the community, even though it precisely corresponded to the territorial space of the state.

Thus the salience of nationalist interpretations of territory in Macedonia perpetuated a collective identity that was incongruent with political realities. On the one hand, this reinforced a domestic perception of being besieged by malevolent neighbours. On the other hand, it projected an external impression of threat towards the political *status quo* in the region. Both dynamics worked against the discursive stability and security of collective identity in the various contexts

---

45. e.g. Vasil Tupurkovski, 1st plenary session, 8 January 1991, 92.
46. 1st plenary session, 8 January 1991, 97.

within which it operated. This is evident in the insistence in repeating the adjective 'Macedonian' as a nominal modifier of everything:

> We, the Macedonians [...] have this constant urge to prove ourselves. We would be happy if we could mention in every article [of the new Constitution] that it was 'Macedonian': the Macedonian legal system, Macedonian television, Macedonian this, Macedonian that. We are constantly proving ourselves with the subconscious feeling that maybe all this is threatened, it is not recognised, and we need to repeat it and convince ourselves that it is so.[47]

Referring to the reliance on the name 'Macedonian' as reassurance of one's own identity, the Macedonian president exposed this insecurity and denounced it as unnecessary. In the Balkan context, and particularly in view of Greek non-recognition of the name, he called for greater self-esteem because '[the name] is [...] beyond any real and comprehensible enquiry, meaning: [our state] is called Macedonia'.[48] This was a discursive attempt to confirm the stability of Macedonian identity and neutralise the perceptions of external threat against it.

In the domestic context, and particularly in view of accommodating the Albanian minority, the excessive preoccupation with the 'Macedonian' denomination of the signifiers of the state strained inter-ethnic relations. It added unnecessary emphasis to the discussion of Macedonian priorities and rights over non-Macedonian ethno-national communities by virtue of the 'Macedonian' character of the state.[49] This also became evident in the spirited debates in parliament over the exact text of the constitutional preamble referring to the character of the state. The various formulations revolved around the necessity of insisting on the 'fatherland' implication of the national denominator. A powerful discursive line advised against such a formulation:

> It is normal that [we] crave recognition, and above all, collective recognition. And our insistence to make this constitution a national landmark and give it a national character is understandable. But does this really fulfil our intention? [...] To whom do we need to prove that this is the state in which the Macedonian people accomplishes its statehood: to ourselves or to others? [...] There's no state in Europe [...] defined in its constitution as national.[50]

It was noted that such insistence on nationality would reveal the instability of Macedonian identity ('to whom do we need to prove') and, furthermore, would distance Macedonia from its prospective European aspirations. However, insistence

---

47. Kiro Gligorov, 25th plenary session, 15 November 1991, 46.
48. Gligorov, ibid.
49. For instance in the debates over the official languages in the state, 25th plenary session, 78–83.
50. 25th plenary session, 11 November 1991, 27–8.

on the formulation of 'national state of the Macedonian people' indicated that the imperative of collective recognition along the lines of 'Macedonian-ness' could not be easily ignored.

Thus, the story of belonging to Macedonia as a geographical land implied a discrepancy between the politically established limits of Macedonian discursive space and its imagined boundaries. Externally, it projected the image of a national community that was significantly larger than the one demarcated by the territorial borders of the state. This suggested a possible future course of aligning the two contours, left a perception of threat among Macedonia's neighbours, and reinforced their already cautious policies towards the new state. National identity upheld through these narratives prepositioned its own Others in a conflictual manner, intensifying the conflictual potential of external relations. Internally, this interpretation increased the significance of the name 'Macedonia' as denominator of the nation, marginalising community members who could not share in the Macedonian nationhood narrative. In this sense it damaged inter-ethnic relations by establishing a contested hierarchy between the majority and the minorities and by intensifying antagonistic discourses of domestic nationalisms. Overall, nationalist interpretations of territory had a destabilising effect on Macedonian identity by increasing its external and internal insecurity.

Identity narratives of national purpose

The perception of insecurity in Macedonian identity had its roots in its interpretation of Macedonian history. The narratives of victimisation, suffering and injustice are integral elements of it. Their taken-for-granted quality is evident in the multiple purposes these narratives served in the discursive space of Macedonian politics. Referring to the insecurity in Macedonian identity, the president mentioned in passing the probable explanation: 'perhaps because of our very difficult history, that has been our fate'.[51] The suggestion does not question the adjectives ('very difficult'), it only modifies their explanatory value in this precise case ('perhaps'). The resignation with which the difficulties are accepted ('[it] has been our fate') is indicative of a deeply sedimented narrative of victimisation that stands out as an important signifier of Macedonian national identity in the early years of transition to democracy: '[Ours] has been, after all, the most contested people today and throughout history'.[52]

The narrative of victimisation can be identified in numerous and varied interpretations. It might refer to the Macedonian land, to the Macedonian people, to its dignity, to the wrongdoings the Macedonian people have suffered, or to the territory's isolation and helplessness. Many major political undertakings in the course of preparing and declaring independence were justified by the narrative of victimisation. Electing a president was important for 'finding a place under the

---

51. Kiro Gligorov, 25th plenary session, 15 November 1991, 46.
52. 25th plenary session, 11 November 1991, 27–8.

sun for this long-suffering patch of land [that is Macedonia], to call our own'.[53] The president, in turn, saw his elected post as a mission to 'bring Macedonia back its dignity'.[54] Exactly the same appeal was taken up by the newly elected vice president a week later: 'Let's bring Macedonia back its dignity!'[55] This was not accidental. The suggestion that Macedonia had been dishonoured apparently had very wide political resonance. It was used for mobilisation purposes because it was discursively linked to the notion of vindication and the need for recognition. These ideas underlay the central lines of justification of the grand political project of the time: independent statehood.

The notion of vindication was visible in the appeal to the Macedonian people to renounce the role of victim and finally take hold of their own destiny. The only way to do this was through independent sovereign statehood because, it was argued, Macedonia had never actively participated in the organisation of matters within the Yugoslav federation. Pointing to the very beginning of Macedonian statehood – the sittings of the popular front,[56] which negotiated the foundations of socialist Yugoslavia – a couple of speakers at the first session of the democratic parliament expressed their fears of 'being caught in the snow': a historical reference to the inability of the Macedonian representatives to get to the sitting because of the deep snow.[57] Even stronger satire is evident in the allegory of Macedonian hesitation in breaking from the past and choosing a new president:

> [as before], Santa Claus will come and will open our little gift box and will hand us down our president of the republic [...] on whom the entire political life of this republic will depend.[58]

The political call for Macedonia's active participation in the crafting of its own fate was therefore based on its dissociation from the passivity of the federal past and finding its own place 'under the sun'.[59] The formula 'own people on own land' was repeated as an invocation throughout the year preparing for independence. In Macedonian, the saying 'свои на своето', which cannot be translated literally, implies the feeling of being among close people in one's own home. Independent statehood comes to discursively represent staking out one's rights over one's own land. Thus denouncing the discourse of victimisation becomes rhetorically linked to embracing the project of independent statehood. This reveals its constitutive role in the new Macedonian identity.

---

53. Tito Petkovski, 5th plenary session, 27 January 1991, 6.
54. Kiro Gligorov, 5th plenary session, 27 January 1991, 24.
55. Ljubco Georgievski, 6th plenary session, 1 February 1991, 44.
56. AVNOJ, abbreviation for the Anti-Fascist Popular Council for the Liberation of Yugoslavia (1942, 1943, 1945).
57. 1st plenary session, 8 January 1991, Bogdan Nedelkoski, 65, Todor Petrov, 91.
58. Todor Petrov, 1st plenary session, 8 January 1991, 91.
59. 5th plenary session, 27 January 1991, 6.

An identical link exists between the victimisation narrative and the call for recognition. The political project of independence was being interpreted as a substantially new stage in Macedonian statehood. This is illustrated in the formulaic references to creating 'a completely autonomous, independent and sovereign state called the Republic of Macedonia',[60] 'longing for an autonomous and sovereign state',[61] defending the integral 'legal, political, cultural, national subjectivity' of Macedonia (the first plenary session), the need to acquire 'international legal subjectivity',[62] etc. These widely used formulae suggest that despite the claims of continuity in Macedonian statehood, Macedonia's statesmen were conscious of the categorically new political opportunity for the Macedonian state. Hence, their depiction of the political time as a historical turning point enabling the desired emancipation of the Macedonian nation from the assumed compromise of federative statehood to 'autonomy', 'sovereignty' and 'subjectivity'. It was viewed as the logical culmination of the long struggle of the Macedonian people for 'national liberation',[63] thus juxtaposing the independence project with the narrative of victimisation as its just end point.

Irrespective of its justness, however, entering this new stage of emancipated statehood could not be finalised by a unilateral decision. Hence the awareness of the need for and the call for external recognition:

> the legally schooled should know best that Macedonia [...] does not have internationally recognised continuous legal subjectivity, regrettably. [...] The Basque country also has its own history [...] but it is not a state. And so do the Kurds.[64]

The rhetorical parallel with the Basques and the Kurds is not legally (or historically) accurate but it emphasised the argument for the difference between the historical continuity of the Macedonian state, which was not questioned, and its legal continuity, which was. The parallel with stateless peoples was also meant to add urgency to the call for recognition, and was articulated at every significant political juncture. The need to rewrite the constitution for instance, the first crucial task after the referendum in favour of independence, was framed in this call for recognition of the republic's international legitimacy.[65] Its link to the renounced victimisation narrative, however, perpetuated the discourse of Macedonian nationalism and increased the conflictuality of the collective identity of the new state.

---

60. 25th plenary session, 9 November 1991, 18.
61. Ismet Ramadani speaking at the 25th plenary session, 9 November 1991, 45.
62. Stoile Stojkov speaking at the 25th plenary session, 9 November 1991, 86.
63. See, for instance, 25th plenary session, 9 November 1991, 45.
64. Stoile Stojkov speaking at the 25th plenary session, 9 November 1991, 86.
65. See the five sittings of the 25th plenary session from 9 to 17 November 1991.

In the domestic context an expression of this increased conflictuality was the rearticulated call for recognition of the Macedonian state as a state of the Macedonian nation, already referred to above. In the regional context too, this narrow interpretation generated more conflictuality because of its unrealistic call for the alignment of the notions of nation and state.

> In view of international recognition [...] the Serbs recognise the Macedonian nation, but do not recognise a state. The Bulgarians say they recognise the territory but do not recognise the nation, the Greeks practically deny both, whereas the Albanians [...] remain lukewarm [...] [But] how do we seek international recognition when we ourselves say that we are nobody's state? [...] we ourselves say we do not have a state but ask the neighbours to say 'it's yours'.[66]

Equating the omission of a direct constitutional reference to the Macedonian nation with relinquishing ownership of the state aimed to demonstrate the unacceptability of such a political option and to justify imagining the state as a national state. A political community organised along strictly national lines, however, inevitably excluded major parts of the population and its legitimacy was thus challenged. It was not a stable political option and its perpetuation created a deep divide in the political independence project, threatening to destabilise the identity of the Macedonian state. In the context of regional hostility such identity was even more vulnerable to encroaching Otherness, which presupposed its higher conflictual potential. Thus the salience of the victimisation narrative incorporated the notion of nationhood in the independent statehood project in a manner that challenged its internal credibility and increased its external instability. At the same time, dissociating from the victimisation narrative implied a major reformulation of the notion of vindication that was central in the justification of independent statehood. It therefore conditioned a discursive contradiction within the political statehood project that needed to be solved before the new state could uphold a stable and politically legitimate national identity.

Legitimacy of Macedonian national identity narratives of Self before Europeanisation

Macedonian national identity in the early years of democratic transition was revealed as highly divided and controversial. Identifying the dominant interpretations of its central discursive elements highlighted a declarative national tolerance of Otherness that was not entirely supported by political practice, the notion of belonging to a divided territory, and dissociation from the victimisation narrative through the call for vindication and recognition. Within the discursive context of hegemonic nationalism and its interpretations, Macedonian national identity was torn between projected ambitions and political constraints. It constituted a political

---

66. 25th plenary session, 9 November 1991, 162.

Identity without Europe | 75

community shaken by instability and insecurity, generated by an inability to decide between the narrative of nationhood and the narrative of citizenship as the story of the state. The decades-long ambition of the Macedonian people for a sovereign national state finally arrived at a political opportunity with the disintegration of the Yugoslav federation. However, its political environment prevented the realisation of the statehood project within the national frame. The struggle to accommodate the civic imperatives of a non-monolithic nation into the national narrative of statehood propelling the independence project produced a series of political compromises whose internalisation required time. The collective identity that they attempted to construct and uphold at state level was torn between the nationhood narrative's traditional orientation towards the past and the citizenship narrative's typical detachment from the past. The internal tension generated by narratives of 'Macedonian-ness' destabilised Macedonia's national identity construct at a time when its legitimacy was being put in doubt.

Instability was also generated in the external projections of Macedonian identity. The articulations of more inclusive and open identity narratives were instrumentalised by Macedonia in its bilateral relations in the region. Faced with suspicion from neighbouring Bulgaria and Greece, Macedonia attempted to affirm its position by demanding from its neighbours similar formally inclusive and open treatment for Macedonian minorities on their territories. These demands were met with distrust and lack of understanding, first because Bulgarian and Greek national identity constructs were much more closed and exclusive and their treatment of minorities was organised on completely different terms. But second, and more significant here, Macedonian calls for recognition of minorities were met with a lack of understanding because its neighbours also refused to acknowledge Macedonia's legitimacy as a sovereign legal subject. In this way the projected image of Macedonian national identity provoked external animosity and had a negative impact on Macedonia's regional standing. This seriously compromised nationalist interpretations of identity. In the discursive vacuum of halted international recognition and Macedonia's inability to access the legitimacy resources of the Europeanisation dynamic, which was made available to Bulgaria much sooner, it dramatically increased the instability of the Macedonian national identity construction and largely determined the course of its transformation.

Comparability between Bulgarian and Macedonian national identity narratives of Self

Identifying the carrying discursive elements of the key narratives of Bulgarian and Macedonian national identity constructions and the discursive patterns in which they appear highlights the roots of conflictuality in Bulgarian–Macedonian relations, which will be further analysed in the next chapter. Table 4.1 helps us to visualise the way interpretations of national identity related to each other in the two states. It is notable that while discursive elements of identity occupied similar discursive positions, the meanings they contained were very dissimilar. The discursive position of the nation, for instance, was interpreted in two diametrically different ways in the different contexts in which the element of nationhood operated. The attempt to discursively imagine the nation against the backdrop of ethnic differences was driven by identical ethno-national configurations in Bulgaria and in Macedonia: a dominant national majority, one dominant national minority and a range of smaller minority groups. The political context in the two states, however, varied, prompting divergent models of accommodation in the political community. In Bulgaria the dominant national minority was not given access to active participation in the deal on political power transition. This prevented its inclusion in the official narratives of national identity and permitted the narrative constitution of nationhood in monolithic terms. Hence, the salience of the story of national unity. In Macedonia, in contrast, the dominant national minority was already actively participating in renegotiating the political contract and this did not allow the majority to codify a monolithic national construct. Instead, the notion of intra-national balance retold a more inclusive national story permissive of national difference. Hence developed the notion of national tolerance.

The different interpretations of the discursive position of the nation had important implications for the conflictual interaction between the two states. Bulgaria, whose notion of a unitary nation included 'Macedonia' as a key historical narrative, had difficulties in coming to terms with the distinctiveness of a separate, non-Bulgarian Macedonian nation precisely because of the salience of the national unity story in its national identity construct. Macedonia, whose formulations of a diverse national community included the people born in the non-Macedonian parts of the Macedonian region, insisted on recognition of national minority status and granting made on the immediate external Other from the particular discursive interpretations of the nation turned out to be mutually exclusive. Meeting them required a major reformulation of the meanings attached to the nation and its discursive position. This compromised the political hegemony of nationalism in interpreting national identity and preconditioned the need for alternative visions.

A very similar dynamic is notable in the discursive position of territory. The salience of the territorial element in Bulgarian national identity emphasised integrity, determining the high security context in which (even the suggestion of) any of its territorial regions having a special status was framed. This included the taboo of recognising any degree of political or territorial autonomy for minority-populated regions (Pirin Macedonia is discussed in these terms). The historical sedimentation of the territorial integrity element also explains the continued political relevance of territories previously included in the Bulgarian national narrative (Vardar Macedonia is one of them). The discursive position of territory was interpreted differently in Macedonia. Its centrality increased the salience of the story of belonging since the name of the geographical territory provided an unambiguous source of collective self-identification for a state and nation struggling for recognition. The discrepancy between geographical and legal 'Macedonia' is what was perceived as a threat to both the territorial and discursive spaces of neighbouring states. The most salient interpretations of territory in the

Table 4.1: Discursive patterns of national identity before Europeanisation: Bulgaria and Macedonia

State community	National identity narratives of Self		
	Nationhood	Territory	Purpose
Bulgaria	Increased salience of the idea of 'national unity': • belonging by jus sanguinis • monolithic nation, no 'national' minorities acceptable • exclusive membership	Territorial integrity: • equal sovereignty over the entirety of national territory • non-negotiable in terms of minority demands • prohibition of land ownership for foreigners • state borders encapsulating the community	Centrality on the Balkans: • increased attachment to national geography as an indicator of belonging • key element is the 'Balkan' mountains, suggesting territorial uniqueness on the peninsula • victimisation narrative based on the idea of centrality on the Balkans • basis for the claim to 'Europe'
Macedonia	National tolerance formally upheld as a compromise between the project of national statehood and the need for legitimacy: • increased inter-ethnic tension in stabilising the compromise • unsuccessful attempt to articulate national statehood in civic terms	Territorial belonging: • the narrative of severed national integrity • the centrality of the narrative of 'unification' • increases symbolic significance of the name 'Macedonia'	Victimisation narrative: • sovereignty as 'vindication' • active vs passive national role • centrality of the imperative for recognition • salience of the narrative of national statehood in its narrow interpretation

two national identity constructs increased the significance of borders, border regions and border populations as gatekeepers. But in emphasising Otherness, they also intensified bilateral antagonisms.

The interpretations of the discursive element of national purpose are conflictual, too. National purpose in both states was related to stories of victimisation. Narratively, however, these stories were put to different purposes. In Bulgaria they were inextricably attached to the discursive position of 'Macedonia' as part of the Bulgarian national story, and in this sense they referred to dealing with national loss. The stories of victimisation attempted to find justification for this loss in a self-esteem-boosting manner, articulating meanings of centrality, uniqueness and special responsibility. These meanings were not necessarily conflictual. But within the discursive hegemony of nationalism, the paternalism in policies towards Macedonia that they implied naturally subverted the notion of equality and antagonised an already fragile relationship. In Macedonia the stories of victimisation referred to the historical impossibility of national statehood. They were linked to the call for vindication of 'Macedonian-ness' and the call for recognition of Macedonian sovereignty justifying the legitimacy of the strategic political project of the time: independence. Again, this interpretation was not necessarily divisive, but in the specific context of rising nationalism it reinforced the boundaries between national Self and Other and increased the political indispensability of such boundaries. Demanding a position of equality for their state, which its external Others refused to acknowledge, the victimisation narratives preconditioned the antagonistic potential of interpretation of national purpose.

Interpreted within the discursive logic of nationalism, the narratives of Bulgarian and Macedonian post-totalitarian national identities span a field of conflicting meanings. Investigating the key features of these interpretations suggests that without a major reworking of the discursive patterns of both national identity constructions, the conflictuality they perpetuated could not be overcome. The analysis of the three central narratives of Self before joining the dynamic of Europeanisation also reveals the incompatibility of such national identities with the changing discursive contexts of decommunisation and democratisation. The high conflictual potential and the imperatives of the transition highlighted the need for re-imagining the community of the state. The goal of joining the common European processes of cooperation and integration gave the process of re-imagining a clear direction: a return to Europe. The following two chapters will explore how embracing the long-term goal of Europeanisation by the two states affected imagining the national community and began to transform national identity narratives. By upholding new inclusive interpretations of national identity, Europeanisation facilitated reconciliation along the lines of bilateral relations, and emphasised the political relevance of integration. This enabled the imagining of national Other(s) in terms of cooperation and commonality, and gradually included Europe into the narration of the national Self. As a result, the boundaries of the national political community dramatically transformed.

Chapter Five

From Conflict to Reconciliation: The European Ways

Exploring and contrasting national identity narratives in Bulgaria and Macedonia prior to Europeanisation reveals their incompatibility with the changing discursive contexts of democratisation and the requirements for participation in the common European processes. Interpreted within the logic of nationalism, narratives of identity determined a high degree of conflictuality in state behaviour caused by exclusionary, divisive visions of political community. This was confirmed in both the domestic inter-ethnic relations and the external inter-state relations of the two states. While the previous chapter traced interpretations of three key elements determining the discursive position of Self and conditioning conflictuality domestically, this chapter will follow narratives of identity determining the discursive position of Other and governing external relations. The chapter is divided into three sections, each focusing on one aspect of conflictuality maintained by antagonistic interpretations of national identity. These have been selected on the basis of their political salience in both states: recognising statehood, solving the language dispute, and granting minority status. The analysis follows the dominant interpretations of the discursive elements upholding the stories of conflict. Tracing the evolution of bilateral relations, the three sections uncover transformations in the narratives of identity enabling (or disabling) reconciliation. The findings of the investigation suggest that with the progress of Europeanisation, reconciliation was made possible around most of the conflictual points. This in turn facilitated preparations for joining the integration process. Overcoming bilateral conflictuality and making progress towards EU membership helped 'imagine' the national political community in an inclusive, positive, self-enhancing and optimistic manner. In this way the discursive dynamic of change enhanced the key functions of national identity. This improved the legitimacy of the political community that the state represented and linked it to the logic of integration. The following three sections describe the discursive mechanisms that enabled this change.

Narratives of recognising statehood

As in Chapter Four, this section starts by mapping out the specific discursive context that structured bilateral relations prior to Europeanisation. The section goes on to trace the identity narratives that governed bilateral behaviour around the issue of recognising the international subjectivity of the Macedonian state.

Exploring the links between these narratives and the specificities of the process of Europeanisation in the two states, the analysis then follows post-recognition narratives of identity to see how the discursive position of the Other has changed.

The context of inequality and distance

Around the beginning of the post-communist transition the relationship between Bulgaria and Macedonia was not one of equality. Beside domestic interpretations of national identity, which attempted to establish hierarchical positions, inequality was also determined by the specific international legal and political context of the time. Even though Bulgaria emerged from one of the rigid totalitarian systems as a loyal Soviet satellite, its international legal subjectivity had not been questioned since it formally declared independence from the Ottoman Empire in 1908. So when it began to dismantle its totalitarian structures in 1989 in line with the processes in the rest of Eastern and Central Europe, Bulgaria launched its transition to democracy as an independent sovereign state. Macedonia started its democratic transition on completely different terms. The Macedonian state had only enjoyed international legal subjectivity as a constituent republic of the Yugoslav socialist federation (Hristov, 1971). Modern Macedonian statehood had not been possible before 1944. Therefore, when the socialist federation began to disintegrate and the Macedonian Republic decided to seek independence as a sovereign state in 1991, it had yet to deal with the issue of international recognition. As it turned out, its international legal subjectivity was challenged on several grounds (leading among which were Greek objections to the state's name), which seriously impeded international recognition. In this context, the post-totalitarian relationship between Bulgaria and Macedonia began as that of an international sovereign and one bidding to be recognised as such. This naturally distorted the discursive power balance of the interaction. In Bulgaria it initiated the paternalistic rhetoric on the subject of Macedonia that discursively reaffirmed inequality and visibly obstructed bilateral relations. In Macedonia it gave rise to the rhetoric of defiance, which further damaged relations and antagonised narratives of Otherness in the two states.

The distance between national Self and Other along the axes of bilateral relations was increased by the rhetorical strategies of differentiation determining the meaning of identity. Bulgaria had always held a special position on Macedonia because 'Macedonia' had been a central element in the narration of Bulgarian nationhood. In the post-communist period the renewed relevance of the Macedonian question was deliberated on the basis of this special position. 'Macedonia' as a significant point of reference in the Self–Other dialectic had no equivalent in Bulgarian national identity narratives. Macedonia, on the other hand, attempted to belittle Bulgaria's significance rhetorically in Macedonian narratives of nationhood by discursively positioning it in a chain of equivalence with the rest of Macedonia's neighbours. The consistency in this discursive strategy did not allow Bulgaria any special status in Bulgarian–Macedonian relations. This act of distancing along the Self–Other nexus was an effort on behalf of Macedonia to play down the inequality of the relationship. Thus, the discursive constitution of Other in the two states disabled reconciliation with Otherness. This in turn reinforced the perceptions of threat that initiated the dynamics of distancing in the first place.

It is clear from this that the context framing Bulgarian–Macedonian relations in the early post-totalitarian period was not conductive of amity. Quite to the contrary, it positioned the major outstanding issues between the two states along the lines of conflictuality. As a matter of foreign policy order, the first issue that needed to be addressed in the bilateral relations was international recognition of Macedonia. In view of the regional ambiguities about the name of the newly independent republic, the need to recognise Macedonia's constitutional name officially appeared simultaneously with the recognition of statehood on the political agenda. Narratives of recognition structured the first post-communist interaction between the two states but, affected by the context of inequality and distance, their interpretations differed significantly.

Bulgaria's and Macedonia's strategic orientation towards participation in the processes of European integration, however, gradually began to establish a field of commonality. Europeanisation positioned the national Self into a markedly different Self–Other dialectic in which all participants shared. Pushing the boundary of Otherness from national borders to the discursive borders of the Europeanisation space, the process radically changed the basis of belonging. Upon joining the process of Europeanisation, Bulgarian and Macedonian leadership and their publics began to speak of national identity in different ways. The changed stories of national identity engaged European signifiers within the discursive patterns of national identity and facilitated partial or complete reconciliation along the Self–Other nexus in the narratives of recognition. Their 'European' re-narration added legitimacy to the post-totalitarian reading of national identity by disabling conflictuality. This in turn stabilised the discourse on Europeanisation in both states. The following section sets out to explore how this happened.

International recognition of Macedonia's name and statehood

The Macedonian referendum on the future of the state of September 1991 confirmed popular support for the independent statehood project and initiated the Macedonian quest for international recognition. Formally marking a new stage in Macedonian statehood, this was obviously a significant moment in the Macedonian national story. However, it also represented a turning point in Bulgarian nationhood narratives. 'Macedonia' as an integral element of the story of national Self in Bulgaria had managed to accommodate Macedonian statehood within the Yugoslav federation with the help of the 'Greater Serbia' plot (Tröbst, 1983). Macedonia's dissociation from the Serbian-dominated federation without demonstrating any signs of wanting to return to its 'Bulgarian origins' presented Bulgaria with the laborious task of having to retell the 'Macedonian story' in order to take account of Macedonia's self-reliance. This required modifying the narrative of national catastrophe and loss, justification for which had comfortably been found in Bulgaria's 'righteous' struggles for Macedonia.[1] The complexity of the undertaking determined Bulgaria's initial unpreparedness to deal with the prospect of Macedonia's independence. This is visible in the reluctance that accompanied the discussion about raising the 'Macedonian question' during the first year of Bulgaria's transition.[2]

With the declaration of Macedonian independence from the disintegrating Yugoslav federation, the issue of redefining Bulgaria's position on Macedonia acquired renewed political urgency. It is important to highlight that from the very beginning non-recognition was not a viable political option (there was no mention of it in official positions). The controversies rather revolved around the modalities of recognition: the exact timing and manner. The idea that recognition should be postponed was central in the socialists' position, which was unsurprising given their greater attachment to nationalist rhetoric and the key position that Macedonia played in the national stories.[3] The actors mainly responsible for the decision, however (the prime minister, the president and the foreign minister), represented the democratic forces and their ambition to demonstrate detachment from nationalist politics became central in the decision-making process. This was evident from their reliance on the European Arbitration Commission's report on the status of the former Yugoslav republics (the Arbitration Commission of the Peace Conference on the former Yugoslavia headed by Robert Badinter), which the government awaited before deciding on the form and the timing of recognition. Linking Bulgaria's reaction to the European stance might have been a sign of insecurity in the face of a potentially conflictual outcome, but it helped frame the entire rhetoric of Bulgaria's position in the rhetoric of 'European-ness':

> Bulgaria appreciates the European Community member states' unity of action on the crisis in Yugoslavia […], [Bulgaria] accepts and supports […] Brussels' approach of equality […], we also entirely share the recognition criteria [listed in the EC's declaration], [which is why] we will soon recognise Macedonia's independence[.][4]

---

1. Ilcho Dimitrov, interview in *Duma* newspaper, 1 February 1991, Issue 27.
2. See verbatim reports from the Roundtable Talks and from the Grand National Assembly, in the context of the ethnic minority tensions and the status of the claimed Macedonian minority in Pirin Macedonia.
3. See verbatim report of the reactions in parliament, 15 January 1992; also report in *Demokratsia* newspaper headlined 'The socialists did not welcome the recognition', 16 January 1992.
4. Message from President Zhelyu Zhelev to President Kiro Gligorov, 11 January 1992, BTA Courier Service.

This was declared several days before recognition. On the day the prime minister announced in parliament that the government had reached the decision to recognise Macedonia, he insisted that 'this act expressed our willingness to preserve peace and security on the Balkans and in Europe'.[5] The chair of the parliamentary committee on foreign policy also confirmed that the government's decision was congruent with the European Arbitration Commission's report on the legal basis for independence and 'secures [Eastern European states' place] in the common European processes'.[6] In his televised address to the nation on the evening of the decision, the president declared:

> The decision [to recognise Macedonia] is another confirmation of Bulgaria's unswerving pursuit [...] of facilitating the actual unification of Europe [in line with] the aims of the common European policies of today.[7]

A couple of days later the Ministry of Foreign Affairs publicised a declaration, again referring to Bulgaria's 'special duty and responsibility before Europe':

> Democratic Bulgaria seeks to implement European policies on the Balkans sustainably and will coordinate its decisions with the common positive processes on the continent, headed by the European Community.[8]

The decision to recognise Macedonia's independence was Bulgaria's first significant foreign policy act in the post-communist period. Following a year of relative international self-isolation as a result of the intense domestic negotiations on the regime change and the new constitutional order, Bulgaria sought to reclaim its international presence and, more significantly, position itself in the realm of 'Europe'. Thus the rhetoric of 'European-ness' surrounding the recognition of Macedonia is in effect a call for European recognition of Bulgaria and the first Bulgarian identity claim for 'European-ness' voiced in the international space after the break-up of communism. In this sense non-recognition would have represented international silence and it would have deprived the new democracy of a 'European' voice. In terms of identity politics, this is what explains the fact that non-recognition had not been considered as a political option.

Another key reason for Bulgaria's affirmative position on Macedonian independence had to do with the central place of the 'Macedonian' element in the Bulgarian nationhood narrative. In it 'Macedonian' represented to a large extent part of what was thought of as 'Bulgarian'. Discursive illustration of this is the systematic reference to the Macedonian people as 'brothers' or 'Macedonian brothers' (whereas the rest of the former Yugoslav republics are referred to, in

---

5. Filip Dimitrov, 28th plenary session, 15 January 1992, 45.
6. Aleksander Yordanov, 28th plenary session, 15 January 1992, 76.
7. President's address to the nation, 15 January 1992, BTA Courier Service.
8. Declaration of the MFA, 18 January 1992, BTA Courier Service. Reprinted in *Demokratsia* newspaper, 18 January 1992.

contrast, as 'our friends in Slovenia, Croatia and Bosnia and Herzegovina').[9] This suggests that the relationship was seen as one of 'blood', i.e. Macedonians were made part of the Bulgarian national community constituted along these lines. Moments of rhetorical emotion took this suggestion even further:

> We are witnessing a moment that takes us back down the lane of history and simultaneously opens for us a door to the future. [...] Today Bulgaria is making a fateful step. It is making a step [...] *towards our Bulgarian brothers in the Republic of Macedonia*. [Applause on behalf of the majority, acclamations 'Bravo!' – stenographer's note.][10]

The emotional approbation with which referral to the Macedonian people as 'Bulgarian brothers' was met in parliament (at that coming from a position of responsibility in foreign policy) is indicative of the implied meaning of the 'brotherhood' narrative. It is not surprising then that in its relationship with Macedonia Bulgaria sought a special position. Postponing recognition until the international reaction had crystallised would not have given it such a position. The only chance of obtaining a special position was deemed to be recognising first. Indeed, the Bulgarian government took the decision in favour of recognition on the day following the EC declaration on the juridical validity of Macedonia's claim for independence (15 and 14 January 1992 respectively) before any other state had reacted. This swift action should not only be interpreted in the light of good neighbourly relations,[11] even though this might have been the case in recognising Slovenia, Croatia, and Bosnia and Herzegovina. More than anything, it was meant to articulate Bulgaria's position as that of Macedonia's special protector and defender:

> It is well known that Bulgaria is in favour of a free and independent Macedonia, which will finally be defended against the territorial aspirations of its neighbours. [...] Bulgaria does not have and has not had any other wishes for Macedonia but to see its population free and capable of deciding its own fate.[12]

Obviously, the Bulgarian president did not include Bulgaria in the list of neighbours threatening Macedonian territory. Quite to the contrary, he presented Bulgaria as the benevolent patron ('wishes to see') of the vulnerable Macedonia ('be defended against'). The implicit notion of 'patronage' was confirmed by the suggestion that Macedonia was not 'free and capable of deciding its own fate' yet because this was Bulgaria's wish for Macedonia's past and present. This notion in effect reinforced

---

9. See Aleksander Yordanov at the plenary session of the Bulgarian parliament, 15 January 1992, 77.
10. Ibid., 80 (emphasis in the original).
11. It was described as an 'important step towards even closer cooperation with all of our neighbours' in the President's address to the nation, 15 January 1992, BTA Courier Service.
12. Message from President Zhelyu Zhelev to President Kiro Gligorov, 11 January 1992.

the idea of an asymmetric relationship. Another significant discursive element in the president's message for the Macedonian president was his avoidance of the term 'Macedonian people': the formulation 'Macedonia's population' was used instead. The omission of the national denominator 'Macedonian' against the background of the president's declarations from the summer of the previous year (that even though Bulgaria recognised the Macedonian state, it would never recognise the Macedonian nation) is indicative of the reasons for Bulgaria's claimed patronage over Macedonia: it was thought of as 'Bulgarian'.[13] This position was an adaptation to the new political situation of the Bulgarian 'Macedonia' narrative . It offered the opportunity of re-affirming the hierarchy of the relationship in a legitimate manner, while seeking to preserve Bulgaria's special status in it. It was also in concordance with Bulgaria's ambition to represent itself as a key stability factor in the Balkans.[14] This was another way in which the swift recognition of Macedonia upheld a particular vision of Bulgarian national identity that was not necessarily 'Europeanised'.

This vision of Bulgarian identity was also not particularly compatible with Macedonia's vision of Bulgarian identity, nor was it with Macedonia's vision of Macedonian identity. Its articulation allowed taken-for-granted references in Bulgarian public space to the 'so-called Macedonian nation' and the 'Bulgarian roots' of Macedonia.[15] It permitted Bulgaria's foreign minister to publicly announce that he would postpone establishing diplomatic relations with Macedonia 'until Macedonia's attitudes towards the issues of giving up territorial aspirations and the non-existence of minorities in neighbouring countries crystallise'.[16] Such rhetoric helped Macedonia to constitute Bulgaria in terms of malevolent Otherness. This is reflected in the regular use in Macedonia of the pejorative denominator 'bugarashi' (a derogative word for Bulgarians in the Macedonian language) as the ultimate label of national betrayal in Macedonian political discourse. Systemically used against the opposition party VMRO–DPMNE[17] because of its pro-Bulgarian leadership (Ljubco Georgievski was its leader at the time) for example, the label 'bugarashi' was meant to discredit the party's political standing, calling it on numerous occasions to redeclare its Macedonian loyalty (Georgievski, 2007). Another way in which Macedonian visions of Bulgaria were

---

13. Ilcho Dimitrov calls the people of Macedonia 'Macedonian Bulgarians' in an interview for *Duma* newspaper, 1 February 1992.
14. 'Expresses Bulgaria's aspiration to be a stabilising factor on the Balkans': from Zhelev's address to the nation, 15 January 1992, 'The Bulgarian Government believes that its position will contribute to the stability of the Balkans as part of the new Europe': declaration of the MFA, 18 January 1992, etc.
15. See, for instance, Velizar Enchev in *Otechestven vestnik* newspaper reporting on Skopje's reactions to Bulgarian recognition, 16 January 1992.
16. Stoyan Ganev in an interview for *Demokratsia* newspaper, 8 February 1992.
17. The abbreviation from the transliteration in Macedonian and Bulgarian of the party's name, the Internal Macedonian Revolutionary Organisation – Democratic Party for Macedonian National Unity, standing for democratic rights.

incompatible with Bulgaria's claimed patronage had to do with the portrayal of Bulgaria as Macedonian occupier. Rooted in the notion of belonging to the land of Macedonia, which was a key element in Macedonian identity as noted earlier, it assumed that important parts of Macedonia were 'occupied' by Bulgaria and the fate of the Macedonian people living in those parts was uncertain. Suggesting inherent malevolence and Otherness, this interpretation of Bulgaria did not allow any approximation between the two national identity images.

In the context of this general negative attitude towards Bulgaria, which had already been built up during the period of preparation of independence, Macedonia's reaction to Bulgarian recognition was unsurprisingly reserved. Cautious of the hierarchy that Bulgaria's patronage attempted to reinforce, Macedonian public discourse even aired the idea that Bulgarian recognition was undesirable since it would improve Bulgaria's public standing in Macedonia.[18] This accompanied the realisation that international recognition was the inevitable result of Macedonian independent and autonomous policies pursued so far,[19] and was not subject to the fortuitous positions of its neighbours. In this context, the emphasis was put not on Bulgaria's public declarations of support but on the inherent flaws in Bulgaria's official position. The Macedonian president confirms:

> we are experiencing particularly painfully the attitudes of those of our neighbours who, instead of helping us because we are the last nation on the Balkans to achieve our independence and international recognition, are contesting either the name of our state or the name of our nation.[20]

Drawing on the popular repertoire of victimisation rhetoric to construct justification for support ('instead of helping us'), the Macedonian president unambiguously identifies enemies without naming them: Macedonia's name was contested by Greece and its nationhood by Bulgaria. Their malevolence is implied ('we are painfully experiencing [their] attitudes') but at the same time belittled:

> We have an understanding of these neighbours and their problems, or if you wish, delusions, we think of them [...] without rancour [...], [we wanted to show them] our goodwill[.][21]

The dignified acquiescence that the neighbour's 'delusional' animosity is met with attempts to reverse the hierarchy in the relationship by changing its organising criterion from power to morality: on the moral scale it is suggested

---

18. *Nova Makedonija* newspaper, 16 January 1992.
19. Kiro Gligorov, 31st plenary session, 10 January 1992, 7–8 ('sooner or later we shall be independent').
20. Kiro Gligorov, 31st plenary session, 10 January 1992, 9.
21. Kiro Gligorov, 31st plenary session, 10 January 1992, 9.

that Macedonia should be the stronger side. This discursive move was repeated in front of different audiences. Immediately after Bulgaria's official recognition of Macedonian independence, the Macedonian president gave an international press conference in Skopje, in which he declared, among other things, that:

> Macedonia welcomes Bulgaria's recognition but is not interested in its historical prejudices, which are its domestic problem and not a topic of inter-state dialogue.[22]

The same recognition of Bulgaria's domestic 'problems' aimed to confirm Macedonia's moral superiority and reverse the hierarchy of power. The formulation of equality used to characterise the relationship ('inter-state dialogue') reinforced this effect.

Another discursive strategy that aimed to diminish the possible significance of Bulgaria's swift recognition of Macedonia attempted to establish a chain of equivalence between Macedonia's allegedly malevolent neighbours. This was already visible in the texts cited above: they did not single out the responsible malevolent subjects but put them under a common denominator, 'our neighbours'. An even more explicit illustration of this strategy can be found in the leading media:

> As we can see, Bulgaria [...] intends to put conditions [on establishing diplomatic relations], following the example of Greece. Seeking to push Macedonia into relinquishing its national minorities in the neighbouring states, if it gets to that, will uncover the whole game around the supposedly principled, historical, non-strings-attached recognition of Macedonia's independence by Bulgaria. [...] This all demonstrates that Bulgaria's position approximates Greece's position on Macedonia, which Bulgaria had initially denounced as absurd.[23]

Equating Bulgaria with Greece and suggesting that its foreign policy act contained conditions unacceptable to Macedonia ('to relinquish its national minorities') discursively minimised the significance of the fact that Bulgaria was the first state to recognise Macedonian statehood. Furthermore, equating Bulgaria with Greece implied an equal degree of negativity, even though Greece's refusal to recognise Macedonia under its constitutional name had far more negative consequences than Bulgaria's difficulties in assimilating the idea of a Macedonian nation could have had, because of Greece's Euro–Atlantic standing at the time.

Overall, it is obvious that the special status sought by Bulgaria was not accepted by Macedonia, despite the declarative support extended in the

---

22. Kiro Gligorov, Press conference, Skopje, 16 January 1992, reported by BTA.
23. Commentary on an interview by the Bulgarian foreign minister Stoyan Ganev, *Nova Makedonija* newspaper, 12 February 1992.

swift Bulgarian recognition. Furthermore, in the discursive space upholding Macedonian national identity, the Bulgarian recognition was seen as a latent threat and resisted – despite awareness that it could protract Macedonia's international isolation. Viewed in light of the identity construction dynamic producing conflictual narratives of Self and Other, this outcome was not unusual. Bulgaria was struggling to accommodate the new Macedonian status in its own historical narrative of nationhood, one of whose central plots revolved around Macedonia. Attempting to preserve the special status of the relationship, Bulgaria reinforced a hierarchy of inequality in its attitude towards the new state that was unacceptable to Macedonia. This hierarchy was the only discursive space within which the key elements in Bulgarian narratives of Self continued to contain unmodified meanings. From protecting the territorial integrity of the state against possible threat, through preserving the unity of the nation against division, to promoting Bulgaria's role as a central factor of stability in the Balkans and Europe, Bulgaria's position towards Macedonia around the time of the declaration of independence was determined by a particular (nationalist) vision of Bulgarian national identity. Macedonia also behaved in accordance with salient nationalist interpretations of its identity, articulated domestically. Its call for recognition and for vindication of the long-suffering Macedonian people could not accommodate patronising attitudes because for Macedonia they represented the renounced past. The salience of the narrative of territorial belonging did not permit abandoning the aspiration for a close relationship with Macedonian territories under foreign sovereignty. Its notion of national tolerance demanded the same for Macedonia's claimed minorities abroad. Within the logic of nationalism, the community of the state was imagined through mutually exclusive or highly conflictual meanings. Against their hegemony, even the 'European' references that had already begun to appear in national discursive spaces were interpreted in an antagonistic manner. This disabled any rapprochement in the relationship between Self and Other, as visible from the underlying animosities feeding back into the domestic discursive spaces.

Reinforcing domestic antagonisms in the context of nationalism

The visible political presence of former communists in Bulgaria was what mostly affected the way recognition was interpreted domestically. Recognition was constructed as a threat to Bulgaria's national security and international standing. Picking up on the indecisiveness in the government's foreign policy between declarative support and national interest considerations, the socialists pointed to the most intractable issues in bilateral relations to interpret them as threatening central elements in the national identity. Recognition of the Macedonian state was thus rhetorically linked to the imperative of recognising the Macedonian nation and national minority, a prospect that Bulgarian national identity narratives were unable to accommodate at that stage because of the salience of the national unity narrative. The possibility of demanding autonomy for the Pirin Macedonia region, which the socialists associated with recognising Macedonian nationhood, threatened, on the other hand, the interpretation of integrity and inviolability of the territory of the state:

> [O]ur recognition of Macedonia could bring Bulgaria to the verge of territorial and national separatism. Embracing European standards on human rights and minorities [...] could be utilised to inspire (cultural, political and territorial) autonomy in Pirin Macedonia [and its] consequent annexation [...] by the Republic of Macedonia. Under the principle of the domino effect such aspirations might rise among the Turkish minority and lead to reciprocal actions on behalf of Turkey.[24]

The reference to embracing European standards and their potential negative consequences is of significance here. Bulgaria's presumed 'European' behaviour was articulated as consequential because of its incorrect interpretation by the reciprocant, also implying inferiority. Such rhetoric was potentially subversive because it suggested the irrelevance of European standards to bilateral relations and offered absolution from them. By sounding the familiar 'Turkish alarm' the urgency of the situation was significantly increased because of the still too recent inter-ethnic tensions in Bulgarian society.

Another discursive line adopted by the socialists emphasised that recognition, even though necessary, had been too hasty and untimely, and promised international isolation as a consequence of unwise foreign policy. It placed the issue in the realm of 'high politics' (foreign policy, security policy, defence), which politicised recognition in an urgent manner. This was also significant because it suggested a threat to another key element in Bulgarian narratives of Self: the aspiration to be a factor for stability in the Balkans:

> The length of the period in which Bulgaria remains the first and the only state to have recognised Macedonia (not counting the 'recognition' by the illegitimate North Cyprus Republic [...]) enormously increases the risk potential for our national security [...]. [Our] looming isolation on the Balkans threatens [...] to largely restrict our foreign policy manouverability. [...] A hostile constellation is being created which leaves Bulgaria [and Macedonia] with a single open door – towards the Bosphorus.[25]

Raising again the prospect of dependence upon Turkey, Bulgaria's most significant historical antagonist, placed Bulgaria's support for Macedonia in the context of short-sightedness and treated it as a foreign policy lapsus. This line of analysis was maintained in other key articles as well. The established historian and academic Professor Ilcho Dimitrov judged the recognition as a hasty blunder.[26]

---

24. Professor Anton Parvanov, 'Bulgaria, the Balkan Syndrome 1913, and the Macedonian Rubicon', *Duma* newspaper, 5 February 1992.

25. Ibid.

26. See Ilcho Dimitrov, 'From recognition – onwards', *Duma* newspaper, 1 February 1992.

The threat of international isolation, when all Bulgaria's behaviour began to focus on a search for assertion and visibility on the international scene and a 'return to Europe', implied a negative evaluation of the act of recognition and warned against further support. In this sense Greek disaffection was particularly concerning because of Greece's position as an immediate neighbour situated within the European political space. The socialists did not miss the opportunity to emphasise this, quoting the Greek foreign minister as saying:

> Even in the future [the hasty recognition of Macedonia] will be an obstacle for Sofia's European orientation. […] [This] misguided [foreign policy move] annihilated the trust [between Greece and Bulgaria].[27]

Even though it is voiced by political representatives from Bulgaria's past, this interpretative line became increasingly salient because it linked popular rhetorical imperatives of the past to Bulgaria's ambition for the future. It demonstrated that the attempt to preserve its special status in its relationship with Macedonia had jeopardised its position in the Balkans and its future in Europe. The socialists instrumentalised this tension between past and present in the act of recognition for the purposes of gaining political leverage. This suggests that while operating within the hegemonic logic of nationalism, 'European' signifiers could be harnessed to serve nationalist purposes.

Similar entanglement in politics dictated by attachments to the past could be observed in Macedonia. Upheld by nationalist interpretations, Macedonian identity narratives of Self were unable to accommodate rapprochement with Bulgaria, despite the presumably amicable act of recognition. If taken up, Bulgaria's declarative support could mean breaking Macedonia's international isolation by establishing its first diplomatic relations. But, at the same time, too much political proximity with Bulgaria threatened the credibility of narratives upholding Macedonia's national identity discourse. Having just shed the patronage of Serbian-dominated Yugoslavia, Macedonia could not oblige another big patron because much of the identity narration of post-federation Macedonia was upheld by the claim for emancipation and vindicated independence. Operating within the hegemonic logic of nationalism, the Macedonian leadership could not make use of Bulgaria's support, even though it might have facilitated the declared goal of asserting Macedonia's place in the Balkans and in Europe. The salience of the interpretations of severed territory and divided nation also prevented repositioning Bulgaria from the position of a malevolent Other. These interpretations used Bulgaria's recognition to perpetuate domestic identity conflictuality.

Bulgaria was repeatedly portrayed as an aggressor in references to 'Bulgarian aspirations' for Macedonia.[28] On the political front accusations that they favoured

---

27. Tsocho Shatrov reporting for *Duma* newspaper, 17 January 1992.
28. Vladimir Goluboski, 52nd plenary session, 10 December 1992, 134.

an alleged Bulgarian–Macedonian confederation began to appear much more frequently as an instrument for summoning political support. Areas of geographical Macedonia within Bulgaria's borders were referred to as the 'oppressed parts of Macedonia'.[29] Macedonia's active interest in the fate of people living there was debated as an official position of the state:

> We do not want anything else from Bulgaria. The only thing we ask of them is to recognise the rights of our minorities, in line with the demands of Europe [and the UN].[30]

The assumption of violated rights highlighted the distance between 'us' and 'them', while the reference to Europe added value to the justness of the demand ('to recognise the rights of our minorities'). Bulgaria's refusal to even discuss this issue was interpreted in the most extreme terms:

> the genocide over the members of the Macedonian nation [...] in Bulgaria [...] (43rd plenary session, 2 July 1992, 35), [...the] open fascism, which labelled all of Bulgaria's citizens as 'bulgarians', among them the Macedonians, the Turks, and everybody else, and which even tried to change their names[.][31]

References to 'genocide' and 'fascism' articulated Bulgaria's position as universally unacceptable in moral and political terms. They tried to justify Macedonia's concern with the fate of the people of Pirin Macedonia under Bulgaria's sovereignty, even in matters of the exclusive authority of the state, such as the organisation and result of the population census:

> [...] when we speak of the vital interests of the Macedonian national unity abroad, as in the particular case of the Bulgarian national census, which performs legal denationalisation of the Macedonians [we should not be silent].[32]

Such rhetoric fed into Bulgarian nationalist interpretations of threat and reinforced them. Thus, realising the project of independent Macedonian statehood, articulated within the context of nationalism, prevented dissociation from conflictual narratives. It disabled the narration of recognition as anything but a threat to the new state that perpetuated already conflictual interpretations of identity.

By interpreting Bulgaria's support for Macedonia as destructive of Bulgaria's and unacceptable for Macedonia's international goals, nationalist rhetoric

---

29. 41st plenary session, 27 October 1992, 80.
30. 43rd plenary session, 1 July 1992, 101.
31. 41st plenary session, 27 October 1992, 120.
32. 52nd plenary session, 10 December 1992, 143.

framed it as ultimately incongruent with the identities representing the two states and in effect proscribed further rapprochement along the Bulgarian–Macedonian relationship. By bringing back the dominant political rhetoric to the notions of 'national interest', 'national self-consciousness', 'national responsibility', it attempted to reinforce the hegemony of nationalism, which had been challenged by the signifiers of the 'European' ('European norms', 'European standards', 'European common processes') that structured early narratives of the recognition of independence. The intense domestic struggles for political hegemony, characterising the transfer of power between the old and the new ruling elites, took much political energy out of the bid for Europeanisation and redirected it into the search for solutions to domestic problems caused by uncertain political rules and identities.[33] Ultimately, the overall political, economic, social and cultural reforms undertaken in the complex processes of transition challenged established norms and institutions and eventually created a general context of uncertainty that destabilised traditional discursive hegemonies. It visibly compromised the credibility of national identity narratives upheld within this uncertain context.

In Bulgaria this was reflected in the instability of the governments, the persistent grip on power by representatives of the former totalitarian regime, the political and economic insecurity caused by the unsteady transition to democracy and market economy, the questionable legitimacy of the privatisation processes and the widespread perceptions of corruption and lawlessness (Krastev, 2004). At the state level this context of uncertainty opened the political space for the discursive realm of Europeanisation, which offered alternative interpretations better suited to articulating meanings of purpose and role in the new context of demanding change. They were able to threaten and dislocate key interpretations of nationalism, particularly in view of its failure to provide in any convincing way a positive source of

---

33. This discursive dynamic prevented subsequent attempts to bring the two states closer on various issues of mutual concern. In the Macedonian parliamentarian elections, for example, the affair of the so-called 'Bulgarian leaflets' acquired unimaginable dimensions. Sparked by the pre-election distribution of old leaflets in the Bulgarian language from the time before the formal codification of Macedonian language, the scandal eventually aimed to discredit the oppositional party VMRO–DPMNE by exposing its 'pro-Bulgarian' character. Insignificant in anything but its dimensions, the affair is illustrative of the enormous negative potential of political association with 'Bulgarian-ness'. A similar affair in Bulgaria, popularised by the media as 'Mishev-gate' (after the name of a notorious informer from the communist security services in Bulgaria whose name first appeared in the arms scandal that brought down Filip Dimitrov's government, see http://www.trud.bg/Article.asp?ArticleId=808098, accessed 10 February 2012), which accused Dimitrov's government of an arms deal with Macedonia, had an even stronger discrediting impact. It eventually led to a no-confidence vote for the government. Even with the president's repeated mandate, Dimitrov could not gain the necessary support in parliament to form a new government. This is illustrative of the political unacceptability of any relationship with Macedonia other than the one prescribed by the discourse of Bulgarian nationalism.

collective self-identification against the background of looming poverty. In this sense the difficult transition challenged the discursive hegemony of nationalism, but it also impeded immediate achievements in the process of Europeanisation. This is illustrated by the perpetuated conflictuality in relations with Macedonia, which was still governed by key interpretations of nationalism.

In Macedonia the process of discrediting the hegemony of nationalist interpretations was even slower because of the peculiarities of transition there. Besides the complex processes of democratisation and market liberalisation, post-communist Macedonia also had to address a series of issues arising from the imperative of consolidating statehood and deep inter-ethnic division, as well as to overcome the impediments before international recognition. The Albanian blockade of the Macedonian referendum for independence[34] warned of the need to redefine the basis of Albanian participation in the statehood project. The Albanian minority's perception that it experienced exclusion and injustice deepened domestic division and created a discourse of domestic Albanian nationalism that challenged notions of 'Macedonian-ness' and antagonised politics in the new republic. This enormously troubled Macedonia's transition and in important ways threatened the internal stability of Macedonian national identity. Interestingly enough, Albanian nationalism soon took recourse to European rhetoric in its bid for just political accommodation, thus challenging Macedonian nationalism from within. This determined the initial discursive tension between Macedonian nationalism and Europeanisation. Europe's reservations to Macedonian independence, the postponed recognition from the European Community, and the conditions imposed on the international use of the republic's name as a consequence of Greek objections, did not help the normative power of Europeanisation in the newly independent republic. The few tentative steps in the direction of Macedonia's European orientation did not provide sufficient basis for substantially rethinking the dominant narratives of 'Macedonian-ness' until well into the 1990s. This is reflected in the intransigence in the relationship with Bulgaria, which was still predominantly governed by the meanings of Macedonian nationalism. Although tentative, however, the first steps towards Europe were taken in both states as a consequence of the search for better versions of political community.

Empowering Europe in Bulgaria

In Bulgaria references to Europeanisation were taken up by the democratic opposition primarily as an anti-communist alternative to the power establishment associated with the communist past. The opposition interpreted communism as an aberration from Bulgaria's European trajectory. This interpretation, perpetuated

---

34. 23rd plenary session, 17 September 1991.

by the first democratic coalition government, attempted, largely successfully, to construct Europe as a counter discourse to the communist past in terms of 'European legal standards and the ethical and material values of Europe'.[35] In this sense the appeal of making references to Europe was initially provided by the notion of 'return'. It interpreted the communist experiment as a passing moment, a lapsus, in Bulgaria's European trajectory:

> The Road to Europe is not new for Bulgaria. [It] will just be a difficult return after 45 years of forcible exile in the misanthropic communist camp. *Bulgaria has been and will be an inseparable part of Europe!*[36]

This is repeated on numerous occasions. On an official visit to Turkey, a leading Bulgarian parliamentarian asserted, among other things, that 'there is no democracy where the former communists are in power, under any form whatsoever'.[37] This radical break from the communist past also implies dissociation from communist nationalism in domestic and foreign policy. In the European context, Bulgaria's Balkan policies were framed by entirely different principles:

> Bulgaria sees as its mission to implement European policies in the Balkans, free of historical prejudice [...], good neighbourly relations with all neighbouring states, [...] independent foreign policy which can turn Bulgaria into a factor of stability on the Balkans and in Europe.[38]

Focusing on a familiar interpretation of the meaning of its national purpose ('factor of stability'), the democrats link the discourse of Europe to a new, non-nationalist foreign policy ('free of historical prejudice') that was detached from the imperatives of the past ('good [...] relations with all neighbours'). This was a major modification of the established narrative of a 'special status' in its attitudes towards Macedonia. It signifies detachment from a dependence upon stories of national loss and national tragedy over Macedonia. The rhetorical effect of this interpretation comes from establishing a causal relation between 'returning' to Europe and overcoming bilateral conflictuality:

> Before the Balkans can become an inseparable part of a truly united Europe, the states from the Balkan region need to walk the avenue of understanding and sincere cooperation. Bulgaria is aware of this responsibility.[39]

---

35. National Conference of the United Democratic Forces (UDF), 14 April 1992, BTA Courier Service.
36. Report on the National Conference of the UDF in the *Demokratsia* newspaper 15 April 1992, emphasis in the original.
37. Aleksander Yordanov quoted in *Demokratsia* newspaper, 29 April 1992.
38. Report on the National Conference of the UDF, *Demokratsia* newspaper, 15 April 1992.
39. National Conference of the UDF, 14 April 1992, BTA Courier Service.

And since the Democratic Party tapped into the resources of the 'Europe' rhetoric in order to gain leverage in the political game, references to it began to appear increasingly in everyday politics:

> This is Bulgaria's chance: it has managed to push the representatives of the [former communists[40]] out of all electable posts. Precisely because of that in a few days we will be able to regain our self-esteem as Europeans [by being admitted to the Council of Europe].[41]

The first tangible success in Bulgaria's general strategy of 'return to Europe' – the successful bid for membership in the Council of Europe – even though significant in many ways, was rhetorically magnified by the democratic media in order to emphasise the vision of the democratic government and assert the political and symbolic meaning of the accomplishment. Headlines such as 'Democratic Bulgaria appears on the big European stage',[42] 'Bulgaria returned to the bosom of the European family',[43] 'It is the European hour of stardom for new democratic Bulgaria',[44] and 'Hello Europeans!'[45] illustrated this rhetoric. At the same time, the fact of membership was interpreted as Europe's recognition of the new Bulgarian state's democratic character and as such an authoritative external confirmation of the aspired new identity. Highlighting the specific achievements of democratisation, the Bulgarian president emphasised the importance of this:

> Membership in the Council of Europe is not a benefaction or a privilege [...]. It is recognition of the democratic changes which the people have made happen in their own state; it is recognition of the people's maturity and wisdom; it is recognition of political culture and civilisation. [...] For two and a half years the Bulgarian people created a multi-party political system, independent syndicates, free press, independent radio and television, autonomous universities, democratic multi-party elections, a parliament with an opposition, a president elected by the direct vote of the people.[46]

The president's address represents an act of 'European' identity articulation. Equating the state with its people, Zhelev completely marginalised the nation as the nationalist source of self-identification and legitimacy. Even though he used the national denominator ('Bulgarian'), the president was consistent in his

---

40. The official name of the party at this point was the Bulgarian Socialist Party (Communists).
41. *Demokratsia* newspaper, 4 May 1992.
42. *Demokratsia* newspaper, 5 May 1992.
43. *Demokratsia* newspaper, 6 May 1992.
44. *Demokratsia* newspaper, 8 May 1992.
45. Ibid.
46. President's address to the nation, Dr Zhelyu Zhelev, Republic of Bulgaria, Sofia, 7 May 1992, BTA Courier Service.

reference to 'the people'. Considered against the taken-for-granted references to the state community as the 'Bulgarian nation' in the political rhetoric of the time, this nuance was significant. The omission of the 'nation' signifier allowed the constitution of the community along the lines of moral categories ('people's maturity and wisdom') and universal values (democracy, 'political culture', 'civilisation'). Listing particular steps of the democratisation process, as declarative as they might be (the independence of Bulgarian media had been questioned many years after 1992, for instance), aimed to materialise the achievement, improve its credibility and highlight its significance. In his address to the nation the president continued to point to the 'deprivations and difficulties' that accompanied the reforms.[47] The reference aimed to address popular discontent with the economic crisis and the overall uncertainty created by the transition. By emphasising that it was these deprivations and difficulties that eventually enabled such great success for Bulgaria, he addressed the omission of nationalist discourse that mostly destabilised its hegemony: its failure to address looming poverty in the country. Invoking the familiar interpretation of its purpose ('[the Bulgarian people] turned [their country] into a stability factor in the Balkans'), the president immediately linked his rhetoric to the principal new strategic goal of Bulgaria's politics: membership of the European Community:

> This is why I will not be too surprised if by the end of the year Bulgaria becomes an associated member of the European Community. [...] Our people deserves this. It demonstrated it with its deeds.[48]

By presenting association status as a credible political prospect for the near future and as a prospect dependent upon the merit of 'the people', the president rhetorically increased its attractiveness and called for popular support. At the same time he summoned again the civic community of the state – and not the nation – as the referent of an optimistic future.

The prime minister performed an identical rhetorical move: linking the tangible international success of Council of Europe membership to the imperative of the key international strategic goal, associated membership of the European Community:

> Our inclusion in the Council of Europe is enormously significant but it needs to be followed by other initiatives and decisions by the end of the year, which should lead to associated status with the European Community.[49]

---

47. Address to the nation, Dr Zhelyu Zhelev, Sofia, 7 May 1992, BTA Courier Service. He talked of both political and economic reforms even though the criterion for Council of Europe membership refers only to democracy.
48. Ibid.
49. Filip Dimitrov at a celebration event of the National Club of the Friends of the European Community, National Palace of Culture, Sofia, 9 May 1992, BTA Courier Service.

The logical link established between the two goals and the already magnified significance of the first aim to construct association with the EC as an even greater success, summoned political support and justified prospective policies. The prime minister, in line with the general line of his party, also fell back on the discursive opposition between Europeanisation and the renounced political experiment of the communist past: 'We repeat the word "Europe" over and over again, so that it sounds almost like a spell that will stop communism from ever happening again'.[50] The 'enchanting power' of repeating the word 'Europe' suggests that Europe had by then become a positive point of reference, all the more attractive because it was associated with renouncing the communist past.

Against the background of this positive prospect, the strategic goal of European Community membership, declared from the very beginning, seemed more desirable and more achievable. This was confirmed by the insistence that joining the Council of Europe was meant as 'simply the first step on our integration into the community of democratic states and, in the future, the European Community';[51] this was repeated on numerous occasions and from various positions of authority. The credibility of these claims is reinforced by Europe's declarative rhetoric, which was popularised by the Bulgarian media on the occasion of every contact with representatives of EC member states. At the Bulgarian–Portuguese meeting of foreign ministers, for example, the Portuguese foreign minister is quoted as saying, 'I can express my hope that in May [1992] Bulgaria will be given a green light to initiate [association] negotiations with the European Community.[52] This was published in a report under the headline 'Support on our way to Europe' and, with the repeated comments of the Portuguese foreign minister concerning the 'green light' for negotiations with the EC, it sent a clear message: all effort should be put in direction of achieving the desired status in Europe, which was already so close. The same function was performed by the publicised address of the European Commission vice president on the occasion of a celebratory event at the Bulgarian National Palace of Culture: the vice president expressed 'the European Community's wish to start negotiations for associated status'.[53] Even though the beginning of negotiations for associated status was the preliminary step to the loosest form of institutionalised contact with the EC and could hardly be interpreted as a particular achievement,[54] this extensive rhetorical preparation of the event,

---

50. Ibid.
51. Speaker of Parliament Stefan Savov in an interview for *Demokratsia* newspaper, 30 May 1992.
52. Portugal's foreign minister João di Deus Pinheiro, Lisbon, 29 April 1992, BTA Courier Service.
53. Frans Andriessen, Vice President of the European Commission, 9 May 1992, BTA Courier Service.
54. Especially given the fact that several Central European states are already registering progress as associated members at the time (Poland, Czechoslovakia, Hungary).

officially confirmed several days later (12 May 1992), rendered it politically more significant and increased its popularity:

> Let no one be fooled that [these achievements] are not connected with the two events of the most recent elections – the coming to power of the Union of Democratic Forces [...] and the moving to opposition of the Bulgarian Socialist Party.[55]

The discursive line of associating 'return to Europe' with the policies of the democratic coalition government demonstrated the manner in which the rhetoric of 'Europe' was utilised in the political power game: it was meant to increase popular support despite the economic crisis. It also illustrated the process of gradually increasing the normative power of Europe in Bulgarian politics.

Even though associated membership status was not confirmed until 1993 (March 1993, signing of the Association Agreement) or enforced until 1995 (1 February 1995), the beginning of negotiations marked Bulgaria's step-by-step progress in its aspirations towards Europe. The utilisation of the 'European' rhetoric in the democratic party's power struggle ensured the invariable presence of 'Europe' on the political agenda of the state. The systematic approach of negotiations applied the 'Europe' *problématique* to all aspects of policy. The asymmetric format of the negotiations (a state applying for associated status in a community of states), on the other hand, enabled their portrayal as a learning process,[56] and as a strategy of self-improvement,[57] thus highlighting the general need for change in every relevant aspect of statehood. In this sense it prompted the credibility of the interpretation of 'return to Europe' as a process of thorough collective identity transformation.

The aspiration for full membership in the European Community, declared as soon as negotiations for associated status began, indicated the desired direction of this transformation. By the end of the year when associated membership status was enacted, the government and parliament had agreed upon and sent to the European Council Bulgaria's formal application for full membership of the EU.[58] Even though the first decision on the application was negative (1997), which is unsurprising given the total breakdown of Bulgaria's financial credibility by 1997 and the acute governmental crisis of the winter of 1996–7, the political consensus on Bulgaria's aspirations for full integration into the EU had not changed.

---

55. Ilko Eshkenazy, chief negotiator in the associated membership negotiations of 14–15 May 1992, *Demokratsia* newspaper, 12 May 1992.

56. 'Brussels teaches Sofia a lesson in economics', *Demokratsia* newspaper, 15 May 1992.

57. 'The European Community Association agreement: Bulgarian's European bible', *Demokratsia* newspaper, 14 May 1992.

58. European Council, Madrid, 15–16 December 1995.

Against the background of an unsteady transition and increasing popular discontent with its course, giving up the European aspiration would have meant depriving the state of any meaningful sense of direction. This was significant. By the late 1990s Bulgarian nationalism discourse, constituting a closed, self-reliant national community of people united by a common narrative of past tragedy and grandeur, had already become discredited because it no longer provided a positive image of collective Self. Mired in poverty and deprived of any immediate prospects of prosperity, Bulgarians could no longer identify with the vision upheld by the rhetoric of nationalism, which had structured their ideas of purpose at the beginning of transition. The attraction of the 'European' rhetoric was conditioned by its radical dissociation from the past, by its promise of economic stability, and, to no lesser a degree, by its elusive attainability. So while Bulgaria's identity of the immediate post-communist period had already been destabilised by pessimistic political realities, Europeanisation proposed an alternative model for self-identification that seemed both positive and optimistic. This was what conditioned the normative power of 'Europe' and determined its impact on the transformation of Bulgaria's national identity. The reciprocal incentives provided by Europe throughout the process, marked by the formal start of accession negotiations in 1999, confirmed the credibility of this identity choice (the decision was taken on 10 December 1999 at the Helsinki European Council).

Empowering Europe in Macedonia

Macedonia took a different path to empowering European rhetoric. European references were present in the Macedonian public sphere from the very beginning of transition. They revolved around notions of democracy, peace, economic prosperity, inter-ethnic tolerance, human rights protection, regional and international cooperation and integration.[59] These were typical European points of reference in the majority of Central and Eastern European transitioning states. But while in Bulgaria the rhetoric of Europe was taken up as an oppositional discourse against the establishment representing the past, ensuring its political salience, in Macedonia the past was renounced with the rhetoric of national emancipation and independence, which ultimately operated within the logic of nationalism. The European references were meant to uphold the national narrative in a positive, optimistic manner, but their role at the beginning of transition was only supportive: they were to provide long-term direction and guidance. The immediate strategic goal of independent statehood was defined by the logic of Macedonian nationalism.

This discursive configuration might have been just as successful in empowering Europe in Macedonia as in Bulgaria, if the particular domestic and international contexts framing Macedonia's independent statehood project had not significantly

---

59. See 5th plenary session, 27 January 1991 for the more solemn occasion that this session provides: the inauguration speech of the newly elected president Gligorov.

diverted politics from the direction of Europeanisation. In the first place, the political leadership of the Albanian minority saw in the European rhetoric a legitimate discursive strategy for advancing the needs and demands of their electorate. It systematically resorted to European references in order to counteract the nationalist rhetoric of the majority and to ensure fair inclusion of the Albanian element in the statehood project:

> the democratic forces in Macedonia will not allow the state to become captive of the calculations for national exclusivity because as such we will never be part of Europe or close to it[.][60]

The overall perception among the minority representatives was that this goal was not accomplished, which is evidenced by the general Albanian voting abstention.[61] Their rhetoric of discontent, which called for justice on the basis of European norms, was logically opposed to the majority's position, thus juxtaposing the European references with the logic of Macedonian nationalism:

> The event of Europeanisation raises a series of issues of principle [...]. It exercises pressure over state sovereignty and state stability. Whether willingly or not, [Europe] interferes in the domestic affairs of the state, particularly a 'newly-composed' state [such as ours].[62]

Calling upon the grounding principle of the modern state system – the inviolability of state sovereignty – the commentary presented Europeanisation as an intervention and intrusion, rather than a learning process of socialisation into the European normative space. The quoted European categorisation of Macedonia as a 'newly-composed state' aimed to highlight the unacceptability of Europe's position: it contradicted the central Macedonian narrative of the continuity of its national identity. The moral standing of Macedonia's reluctance to allow interference was supported by Europe's recognition of its civic liberalism. An expert representative of the Council of Europe was quoted as saying that she did 'not know any country in Western Europe which gives national minorities such freedom'.[63]

It is important to note, however, that even though the discursive attempts at decoupling European references from the Macedonian narrative of nationhood were already evident in 1991, they did not immediately succeed. Quite to the contrary, there is evidence that Macedonian elites attempted to modify their

---

60. Seyfedin Haruni at the 25th plenary session, 9 November 1991, 69.
61. 22nd plenary session, 2 September 1991 in the run-up to the referendum; for the post-voting discussions, see 23rd and 24th sessions, 17 and 23 September 1991.
62. 'Europeanisation "happening": unfortunately, the European models for democratic society cannot be copied in Macedonia', *Puls* newspaper, 4 March 1994.
63. Lenz-Cornette, quoted in ibid.

nationalist rhetoric in order to accommodate Albanian demands. This is visible in the majority's strong line of argumentation in favour of a civic organisation of the state, despite popular visions of a national state:

> we need to respect the opinion of those who said that at this moment no state in Europe has a national constitution and no state in Europe is defined as a national state in its constitution. [they are all] civic states. [...] It's up to us to decide whether we will follow [...] the conditions prescribed by Europe or not.[64]

The normative power of the European reference was suggested by the speaker's rhetorical strategy of leaving the options open ('it's up to us to decide'), even though it was implied which was the correct option. This boldness of argumentation, however, gradually began to sound unconvincing. First, it was voiced from the political left, which was associated with the non-national statehood model of the past. It therefore lacked sufficient credibility as a viable narrative of independent statehood. Second, lack of majoritarian support for it failed to satisfy Albanian discontent, which further discredited its salience. Third, Europe largely failed to provide any substantial incentives in order to reinforce its credibility and increase the political relevance of Europeanisation processes that could have upheld it. The consequences of this triple dynamic prevented the European reading of the organising principles of statehood from stabilising. The call for fairness upheld by the Albanian political elite increasingly captured the European references and decoupled them from the central narrative in the majority's justification of independent statehood: a Macedonian state for the Macedonian people.

The discursive current working against the normative power of Europe in Macedonia was significantly reinforced by Europe's reservations in recognising Macedonia's international subjectivity in view of Greece's objections to the republic's name. Without explicitly endorsing Greek intransigence in the name dispute, the European Community's hesitation undermined Macedonia's international standing and had an extremely negative effect on popular consensus about Europe. This was recognised publicly by Macedonia's president in the months following Macedonian independence:

> Our recognition by the European Community is already a matter of morality and if it does not happen soon, there will be a defeat of European policies [in Macedonia].[65]

The delayed recognition not only challenged the normative power of Europe in Macedonia, it had a destabilising effect on the entire construction of Macedonian national identity because it questioned the validity of its central

---

64. Branko Crvenkovski, 25th plenary session, 11 November 1991, 27–8.
65. President Kiro Gligorov quoted 14 April 1992 by BTA from Belgrade.

political form: the independent Macedonian state. Europe's inability to address Greek demands on Macedonia in any meaningful way was interpreted as particularly damaging:

> today Europe, again, is trading with the national feeling of this people and the dignity of all citizens of Macedonia, when without any legitimacy it has taken the [...] decision to recognise the state without the name; there is no citizen in this unrecognized Macedonia who does not feel violated, belittled, injured.[66]

Calling upon arguments from the spheres of morality and legality, such rhetoric exemplifies the damages that non-recognition and partial recognition inflicted upon Europe's standing in the discursive space of Macedonian nationhood. This perception of unfairness began to decouple the Macedonian nationhood narrative from European references in a more categorical manner than the Albanian claim for abidance by Europe. In order to recreate a credible narrative of national direction and purpose, Macedonian political elites resorted to more exclusively nationalist rhetoric at the expense of European interpretations, particularly in their defence against Albanian demands for parity in the state.

> [We are] concerned about whether we meet some European standards. If we do not meet them, the European Community will sanction us, so we must. But why don't these standards apply to Bulgaria, why don't they apply to Serbia, why don't they apply to Greece, why don't they apply to England? Isn't England a democracy but in the name of nationality [and nationalism] bombs explode in London every day because [Northern] Ireland wants independence and [England] won't give it.[67]

The fact that the framework for minority rights in Europe was still rudimentary (Toggenburg, 2000) and that Europe itself was highly undecided about the type of protection it wanted to provide, increased the perception of double standards valid for Macedonia but not for Macedonia's protagonists, nor for Europe itself. The vague reference to these standards ('some standards') confirms the diminished credibility that European norms of minority–majority accommodation had come to enjoy in Macedonian political discourse on this issue. The suggestion that democracy did not preclude nationalism ('isn't England a democracy?') reinforced this notion.

The period between Macedonia's declaration of independence and the first major act of international recognition (membership of the United Nations in 1993) had a general destabilising effect on Macedonian national identity construction and on its domestic and regional security. Evidence for this is the fall of the

---

66. Blagoy Handjiski, 43rd plenary session, 1 July 1992, 78–9.
67. Trajan Mitsevski MP representing the Macedonian majority, 41st plenary session, 28 October 1992, 74.

non-partisan government of Kljusev by mid-1992 and the return to power of the former communists under the leadership of Branko Crvenkovski, which put the process of democratisation in the country in serious doubt. It was also interpreted domestically as a distancing from Europe:

> [I]f [there were] people in power who had had nothing to do with communism but were concerned with true democracy, [we] would have taken a different road, which would have taken us faster to Europe.[68]

The discreditation of the democracy narrative and the divisions maintained by Albanian discontent challenged the discursive construction of Macedonian national identity from within, threatening the strategic political project of statehood.

Macedonian identity was further destabilised from without. The fact that UN recognition had been conditional – membership was agreed under the name acceptable to Greece, namely the Former Yugoslavian Republic of Macedonia (FYRoM), and not under Macedonia's constitutional name – did not remedy Macedonia's international and regional standing in any radical way. A compromise agreement with Greece brokered by the UN did not result in lifting the Greek economic blockade over Macedonia until 1995, which, together with the UN embargo over Yugoslavia and the reluctance to establish any meaningful bilateral ties with Bulgaria, sealed Macedonia from its main trading partners and pushed the country into economic isolation that was just as pernicious as the international political vacuum that surrounded it. This had a destabilising effect on the legitimacy of Macedonia's national identity as it caused a deep economic and societal crisis. Accompanied by the general loss of national direction as a result of the intractability of the dispute with Greece and the halt in Macedonia's international positioning, by the mid-1990s its deep international isolation threatened to destabilise the very project of Macedonian statehood.

To avoid this, the Macedonian leadership declared its readiness to discuss Greek demands and make progress in overcoming the dispute with Greece. Other than the name objection, Greece laid claims on key identity formulations in Macedonia's constitution[69] and key Macedonian national symbols (the so-called Virginia sun that appeared on Macedonia's first national flag, which had to be changed for the sake of appeasing Greece). The fact that Macedonia was willing to give these up in order to break its international isolation testifies both to the destabilisation that had shaken the construct of Macedonian national identity and to the search for new direction that was illustrated by the desire to relaunch the Europeanisation project.

In view of Macedonia's new placatory policy towards Greece and the progress made in the bilateral dispute, Europe was finally ready to establish diplomatic relations with Macedonia (1995) and begin granting assistance under the Poland

---

68. 49th plenary session, 3 September 1992, 117.
69. The formulation of duty of care for Macedonians in neighbouring countries was interpreted as irredentist: Constitution, 1991, Art.49, which Macedonia had to amend.

and Hungary Assistance for the Restructuring of the Economy programme (PHARE) (1996). This enabled, for the first time in years, an improvement in the credibility of Macedonia's European option making European references to Macedonian politics more relevant. It was the breakthrough in economic and political isolation and the first European funds that upheld optimistic narratives about trade and development and gradually reintroduced European norms as guidelines into Macedonian politics. Whether debating tax and tariffs, wheat production, education or elections, policies were gradually beginning to be measured against the 'European standards'.[70] This conditioned the possibility of re-narrating Macedonian national stories with reference to Europe despite the operationalisation of European meanings by Albania's political leadership and its initially divisive effects.

As in Bulgaria, membership of the Council of Europe was considered a stepping stone in the Europeanisation process. Even though it, too, was postponed until 1995, when the problems with Greece began to be resolved, it marked the start of the Europeanisation process being institutionalised in Macedonia. Even though the strategic goal of European integration was not an immediate political option, dialogue with European institutions, established by the mid-1990s, initiated the steady process of empowering Europe. Not unlike Bulgaria, Macedonia embarked on its way to Europe because it lacked any other sensible political alternative. On the one hand, the imperatives of the transition to democracy and market economy indicated this clearly. On the other hand, the process of consolidating statehood, halted by the country's embroilment in a severe inter-ethnic crisis (culminating in the civil conflict of 2001) and strained regional relations, also suggested European integration as an adequate solution. In this sense, albeit later than in Bulgaria, the political will for Europeanisation produced a similar dynamic of engaging European references in the re-narration of national identity. But it was not until 2001 that an association agreement was signed between Macedonia and the EU. Immediately after its entering into force in 2004, Macedonia applied for EU membership and was granted official candidate status the following year. This (delayed but) incremental progress towards Europe ensured the legitimacy of the European narration of Macedonian identity, which reached out to include national Others and to make Europe an indispensable element in the identity construction.

Europeanisation effects on Bulgarian–Macedonian post-recognition narratives of Otherness

Investigating the narratives of recognition and post-recognition in Bulgarian–Macedonian inter-state relations of the early transition reveals interesting, albeit still subtle, modifications in both states' national identity constructions (Table 5.1). Initially, narratives of recognition were interpreted predominantly within the

---

70. Plenary sessions from 29 November 1995 to 2 April 1996 provide examples of the debates on these topics and the European indicator.

Table 5.1: Identity narratives of recognition and post-recognition in Bulgaria and Macedonia

State	Bulgaria	Macedonia
Meanings upheld by nationalism	International voice	Vindication
	Special status towards Macedonia	Renouncing protectionism
	Protecting territory against threat	Links with adjacent Macedonian territories
	Preserving the unity of the nation	Close relationship with Macedonian minorities on the other side of the border
Meanings upheld by Europeanisation	Overcoming nationalist conflict and upholding civic nationhood as indicative of break from the past	Non-national statehood as remnant from the past
	Good relations with neighbours as a sign of progress	Civic statehood as accommodating Albanian minority on a par with the majority
	European incentives increasing political relevance	Compromise not encouraged through international recognition

logic of nationalism. They upheld mutually exclusive identity constructions, which were inevitably conflictual. The presumably amicable act of recognition performed in reference to Europe was interpreted within this logic as consequential and hostile. This suggests that within the realm of nationalism, identity-based conflictuality could be reproduced even by formally non-antagonistic state behaviour. In a context of democratisation and Europeanisation, this worked against the legitimacy of identities narrated through nationalist interpretations. With the gradual empowerment of Europe, however, alternative interpretations of recognition and post-recognition began to structure bilateral relations. Where they managed to provide credible alternative readings of central discursive elements in the identity construction, these interpretations reduced conflictuality, thus boosting the legitimacy of national political communities as stable and peaceful. In Bulgaria, the credibility of the European reading of identity was improved by immediate incentives received from Europe. The optimistic, positive identity of deserved progress, which it upheld, prompted fewer antagonistic interpretations of the Macedonian Other, while at the same time boosting the legitimacy of the national political community. It also increased the appeal of Europe as a rhetorical self-enhancement strategy and stabilised the Europeanisation process. In Macedonia Europeanisation did not provide sufficient incentives for a credible reading of Macedonian national identity at the time. It increased the salience of interpretations that conflicted with sedimented meanings of national identity elements, without providing a credible alternative. Within the discursive field of Europe, therefore, narratives of recognition and post-recognition upheld a discouraging vision of

Macedonian identity that was seen domestically as largely pessimistic, unfair and undeserved. This compromised the appeal of Europeanisation and perpetuated nationalist antagonisms until a more tangible notion of Europe was able to provide a more credible reading of Macedonian national identity.

Narratives structuring the language dispute

Exploring modifications along another group of identity narratives determining the meaning of Otherness – the language dispute, which increased in salience during a later phase of the transition – reveals further aspects of the discursive mechanisms through which Europeanisation upheld stories of national identity and increased the legitimacy of the national political communities they referred to. Chronologically, the language dispute governed Bulgarian–Macedonian relations from the mid to the late 1990s. The period was characterised by very different political contexts and outcomes in the two states. Progress made towards Europeanisation and the increased relevance of Europe had already begun to transform discursive realities even though nationalist hegemonies had proven difficult to shift. The different progress towards Europeanisation in the two states under study helps highlight the discursive logic of capturing the same discursive elements of identity in different contexts, and discursively repositioning them in a new vision of Self. Inevitably, this dynamic also impacted bilateral conflictuality and ultimately facilitated reconciliation. Interpreting the solution of the language dispute as a key achievement on the path to Europe significantly improved the legitimacy of national political communities by providing evidence for constructive political behaviour, bilateral cooperation, good neighbourly relations, stable regional policies and a common vision for the future.

Changed contexts

By the mid-1990s the exhilaration of the first post-communist years had waned to give way to the pragmatic politics of transition and international repositioning. Both Bulgaria and Macedonia had initiated the transition to a functioning democracy, and both states had also seen representatives of the former communist elites return to power in the course of the democratic electoral competition. But while in Bulgaria the partial retreat of the democratic opposition meant a temporary reinforcement of nationalist rhetoric, in Macedonia it was associated with a further destabilisation of national identity within the logic of nationalism. This is displayed in the dynamic of domestic inter-ethnic accommodation. In Bulgaria it followed the model designed during the negotiated regime change under the patronage of the former communists and, in view of their return to power, it was neither challenged nor changed. In Macedonia, in contrast, the return to power of the former communists ensured increased political participation for minority elites whom the Macedonian national statehood project had not been fully prepared to accommodate. This perpetuated the inter-ethnic divide in the country (Stoyanov, 1998; Daskalovski, 2004).

The transition to a market economy had also been initiated in both states and as this led to major restructuring of their whole economies, it was accompanied by serious economic hardship and increasing poverty among their populations. In Bulgaria the economic crisis stimulated significant rethinking of the meanings of national direction and purpose and facilitated Bulgaria's orientation towards Europe as a symbol of economic prosperity and stability. Together with their first successful steps in the process of European integration, this consolidated the normative power of Europe and permitted its gradual attachment to the national stories. In Macedonia, however, this process was hampered by Europe's reservations about recognising Macedonian statehood and establishing a dialogue with the independent republic. Against the background of the Greek economic blockade of Macedonia, the UN embargo on Serbia and only limited trade ties with Bulgaria, Macedonia quickly lapsed into deep isolation, which affected the functioning of its economy and deepened the economic crisis. This challenged the meaning of key national identity elements. In the lack of immediate optimistic prospects and European incentives, meanings of identity were seriously destabilised, leading to a widespread perception of national insecurity.

So, while in Bulgaria the process of consolidating the post-totalitarian statehood and rethinking nationhood in the context of transition actually facilitated Bulgaria's (re-)turn to Europe, in Macedonia it deepened international isolation and initiated a process of introspective reformulation of Macedonian identity, challenged from within by the political struggle for ethnic accommodation. Eventually the process did produce an interpretation of national identity that was compatible with the meanings of Europe but it took longer and was more cumbersome. Macedonia's first successful steps towards European integration, even though delayed, greatly facilitated the empowerment of this re-narration of identity in view of the strategic goal of Europeanisation, and helped to stabilise it.

Bulgarian–Macedonian relations evolved in congruence with these domestic and international contexts. The high degree of instability initially perpetuated bilateral antagonisms and raised further issues of disagreement between the two states. With the gradual progress of Europeanisation, however, and the reinterpretation of national identity narratives associated with it, a notable relaxation in bilateral tension was made possible. This is testified by the significant progress in resolving the inter-state language dispute that had frozen Bulgarian–Macedonian relations for more than half a decade.

The language dispute and its conflictual (non-)narratives

The Bulgarian–Macedonian language dispute, like other lines of conflictuality between the two states, was predicated on two mutually exclusive interpretations of Otherness. The first was Bulgaria's claim of patronage over everything Macedonian. The second was Macedonia's denial of commonality with anything Bulgarian. As two extreme interpretations of the historical past of the region, identity narratives retelling the story of Other in these terms logically positioned Bulgaria and Macedonia in a relationship of irreconcilable antagonism. Elaborating on historical narratives of commonality, popular Bulgarian attitudes claimed that, because of the great degree of similarity of the language spoken in Macedonia with South-Western dialects of the Bulgarian language, Macedonian was, in fact, Bulgarian. Pointing to the late codification of Macedonia's official state language (1944, compared to the first Bulgarian codification in 1878), Bulgarian narratives aimed to demonstrate the 'artificial' character of Macedonian and reveal its 'true' nature as a dialect of Bulgarian.

Macedonian narratives, on the other hand, attempted to deny any substantial commonality with the Bulgarian language, pointing to the scientifically proven autochthonous character of Macedonian, and referring to its historical standing through the centuries. The Macedonian national language, which was capable of articulating national uniqueness despite the internal and external contestations against the state's identity, had a central position as a discursive element of the identity construction: 'Language is our only fatherland'.[71] This awareness of the significance of Macedonian language as the ultimate locus of Macedonian-ness impervious to foreign intrusion is not new. But at a time when Macedonian identity was being redefined, with the internal and external insecurity that this process generated, national language began to fix identity in a categorical way like no other identity signifier. The formal codification of Macedonian language concurred chronologically with the first recognised Macedonian state (within the Yugoslav socialist federation). In this sense it established tangible links with Macedonian statehood. The project of renegotiating the terms of statehood of the early 1990s went back to the state's political agenda as evidence of its viability. Narratives upholding the centrality of national language in the imagining of the national community dominated the discursive space of Macedonian politics around the time of the declaration of independence.[72]

At an official level these narratives first clashed with the Bulgarian national stories in an inter-state dispute in 1994, around the time of the first state visit of the Macedonian president Kiro Gligorov to Bulgaria at Bulgaria's invitation. There had been language-related incidents earlier in the year, but they had not acquired such salience because of the lower (ministerial or ambassadorial) level at which they had occurred. One had involved the refusal of the Bulgarian minister of education to sign bilateral agreements in the Macedonian language discussed with his counterpart in Skopje.[73] A similar issue had arisen around the Bulgarian ambassador to Skopje earlier in the year.[74] With the expected publicity surrounding the visit of President

---

71. Blazhe Koneski quoted in *Puls* newspaper, 13 May 1994.
72. Kiro Gligorov, speaking at the 5th plenary session, 27 January 1991, 19: 'against all our discontent, we dare not forget that today our language is a European language, that for 45 years only it developed and made our literature, poetry and art flourish, which is what determines the cultural face of a nation.'
73. Minister of Science and Education Professor Marko Todorov during a visit to Skopje, 14 April 1994, BTA Courier Service.
74. Anguel Dimitrov, commenting in parliament, 20 April 1994, 43.

Gligorov to Bulgaria, however, these incidents culminated in a full-blown diplomatic scandal. The particular reason for it was disagreement on the wording describing the official languages of the two states. This issue quickly became central during the official part of the visit because of the series of bilateral documents that had been prepared for signing by the presidents. In line with the governmental guidelines, Bulgaria insisted that the documents be signed in 'the official *language* of the two states as per their constitutions', without further specifications (Guiannakos, 2001). The assumption was that the two states shared a language. Macedonia, on the other hand, insisted on mentioning the Macedonian national denominator when specifying what the official language of the state was. The two demands eventually prevented the signing of any of the prepared documents during the visit. The political impossibility of superseding these formulations in any constructive way during the following years in effect completely froze Bulgarian–Macedonian relations and blocked all inter-state dialogue at a time when both states could have benefited enormously from bilateral cooperation.

To fully understand the meaning of this diplomatic and political deadlock and how language became such a crucial inter-state problem, it is necessary to understand the identity narratives that conditioned it. Language represented a central element of national identity constructions in both states. Different nationalist visions, however, produced divergent interpretations of it.

For Bulgaria, linguistic similarity with the dialects spoken in Macedonia had provided justification for Bulgaria's historical claim for patronage over the people living there. Despite the different political path that Macedonia had taken over the course of the twentieth century, Bulgaria had continued to commemorate and cultivate historical commonality with it. On the basis of their shared history, 'Macedonia' had come to represent an important aspect of Bulgaria's cultural heritage: many classical works of Bulgarian literature treat Macedonia and its tragic loss as a key element of the Bulgarian national story (one prominent example is Dimitar Talev's (2001) four-volume epic novel on Macedonia). This story, supported by Bulgarian national historiography, translated 'Macedonia' into the Bulgarian political space as originally Bulgarian in ethnicity and culture. The linguistic similarity of the Macedonian language with Bulgarian was interpreted as further evidence of this. Against the background of the general salience of language as a key element of Bulgarian nationhood, treating Macedonian as a language of a foreign state posed a serious threat to Bulgaria's national identity construction. In a time of general insecurity caused by the deepening economic crisis, this was politically dangerous. Already destabilised by the reforms and still without tangible European incentives, Bulgarian narratives of national identity could not accommodate the threat. Instead, they resorted to familiar interpretations of nationalism. This rhetorical (re-)turn was facilitated by the democratic government's collapse in 1992 (followed by two technocratic) and the looming electoral victory of the former communists, who formally returned to power in 1995.

'Recognizing the state but not recognizing the nation' (Zhelev, 2005), the ambiguous formula, declared as early as 1991 at the prospect of Macedonian independence, came to structure Bulgaria's position in the language dispute despite the inherent contradiction in it. Sovereign statehood carries with it the legitimacy to decide on domestic state affairs, one of which is choosing an official state language. The way nationhood is constructed usually predetermines the choice of language. Bulgaria's ambiguity attempted to present recognition as an act of condescension, assuming a role in the process that it did not have. The assumption was highly contested in Macedonia because of the notion of patronage it imposed. Introducing historical narratives into the political discourse as valid political argumentation, Bulgaria's position firmly linked policy on Macedonia to the narratives of the past. Their high degree of sedimentation prevented the establishment of constructive inter-state dialogue, which might take account of differences in the interpretations of nationhood. Language, as a key element in the constitution of the Macedonian national community, was one of the national identity elements most bitterly contested by Bulgaria, not least because of its central role in the construction of Bulgaria's own national identity. Pointing to the 'artificial' and 'invented' character of the Macedonian language ('demonstrated' by Bulgarian linguistics and historiography, see Stankov, 2003; Tyulekov, 2007), Bulgarian nationalist discourse began to treat its use, as an official language of another state, as an encroachment upon Bulgaria's cultural heritage. Macedonia's official declarations of the autochthonous character of its national language were taken as an affront to the memory of the dead in the Bulgarian struggles over Macedonia (Dragnev, 1998). These interpretations made impossible any official acknowledgement of Macedonian as another state language within the discursive space of Bulgarian nationalism. Thus the concrete steps the government of Filip Dimitrov made in order to activate bilateral relations with Macedonia were hamstrung by formulations that were unacceptable to Macedonia. Against the background of more pressing international imperatives for both states, this regional stand-off was not widely problematised but by the mid-1990s it had already become an intractable inter-state dispute that discredited the two states' claims for democratisation and Europeanisation.

It is significant that Bulgarian public space was predominantly silent on the subject. Recognising the priority of historical narratives of nationhood over economic interest considerations would have caused a serious erosion of legitimacy even within the logic of nationalism. History was called upon, instead, to serve a different, more legitimate, purpose:

> In their [Balkan and European] aspirations Bulgaria and Macedonia will walk together, because this is what history obliges us to do, because this is what our present and our future summon us for.[75]

If cooperation is dictated by history, then failure to achieve it defies the credibility of historical narratives. The identity of the Bulgarian national political

---

75. Concluding speech by Aleksander Yordanov, speaker of the Bulgarian Parliament, 364th plenary session, 26 April 1994.

community, still oriented towards the past and embedded in stories of national Self referring to past glory and grandeur, was not ready to accommodate such a challenge. This is why Bulgaria's insistence on the controversial formulation went widely unacknowledged in Bulgaria. When responsibility for the bilateral deadlock had to be taken, it was sought in Macedonia, not in Bulgaria. Pointing to the straightforward way in which cooperation agreements were signed with the Albanian president at the time, President Zhelev is quoted as saying, 'It is so easy, you see, when politicians do not meddle in the work of linguists'.[76]

Implying that politics and linguistics should be kept separate (a task Bulgarian identity narratives failed to achieve, not least in the rhetoric of the president), Zhelev attempted to rhetorically transfer the responsibility for this failure, because of its incompatibility with the state's official position:

> Establishing friendly and ever closer relations of cooperation with the Republic of Macedonia [...] requires mutual trust and denouncing some prejudices from the recent past.[77]

It is unsurprising then that Bulgaria's inability to align its behaviour with its political rhetoric was not widely discussed in the public sphere. It remained a missed opportunity for advancing relations with Macedonia, which for the next half-decade remained at a complete standstill. The lack of any political will to find a solution that was acceptable to both sides was not problematised in the context of domestic instability.

As pointed out above, in Macedonia, too, language had been one of the central elements of national identity. Against the background of contested nationhood and conditional statehood, language had come to represent Macedonia's categorical distinctness within the federation of which it had been a part and amidst encroaching neighbours. Precisely because of past commonality with Bulgaria, the Macedonian nation-building process had taken particular care to limit similarities with Bulgarian when codifying the national language. This had been accomplished by adopting a cultural vocabulary of non-Slav origin, by introducing non-Cyrillic alphabet signs, by changing the orthography of common words in order to avoid signs used in Bulgarian (Koneski's *Grammar of the Macedonian Literary Language*, 1982). Beside the differences fostered with the codification of the Macedonian language, the half-century of modern Macedonian statehood had cultivated a national linguistic community that had grown apart from Bulgaria. In this sense commonality with the Bulgarian language had notably diminished by the early 1990s. So when Macedonian publics and elites were faced with the renewed Bulgarian claims of patronage, their indignation stirred a wave of anti-Bulgarian rhetoric.

---

76. At the meeting with the Albanian President Berisha upon signing the bilateral agreements in both Bulgarian and Albanian language, *Puls* newspaper, 13 May 1994.
77. Introductory speech by Aleksander Yordanov, speaker of the Bulgarian Parliament, 364th plenary session, 26 April 1994.

This happened at a time when Macedonian statehood was struggling against external non-recognition and almost complete international isolation. In the absence of any tangible European incentives, Macedonia turned to the rhetoric of nationalism to address the challenge to its national identity. The return to power of the former communists (their party, the Social Democratic Union of Macedonia, was re-elected in 1992 and governed until 1998) and the demands of the Albanian political leadership, however, posed another domestic challenge to the Macedonian nationalist discourse and the identity construction it upheld. Destabilised from within and threatened from without, Macedonian nationhood could preserve its discursive stability only if it did not react to Bulgarian claims. This conditioned Macedonia's retreat from inter-state dialogue with Bulgaria and contributed to the prolonged freeze of bilateral relations.

The retreat was noted in Macedonian public space. The leading media reported Macedonian reactions to the language dispute as 'either silence, or no comment'.[78] At the same time, these reactions were assessed as 'paradoxical' against the background of the excessive preoccupation of Macedonian politics with the issue of organising and carrying out a national census in six languages:

> The paradox here results from the greater [need] to protect the Macedonian language in our own state than against Bulgaria's official refusal to acknowledge it.[79]

The commentary points to the domestic threat against national language as an element of identity that diverted political attention from addressing the bilateral problem. At the same time Macedonian public rhetoric did not omit the significance of this problem and the implications it might have had. They pointed to its discrepancy with the 'time of democracy and attempts for Europeanisation of the Balkans', as well as to the threat it posed to national freedom, national memory and national culture. This reveals the central position of language in the construction of nationhood: 'without language, without identity, without nation, there is only naked territory and geographical space.[80] The intricate link established between language, identity and nation points to their significance for the state's national identity and aims to justify the categorical position of the Macedonian leadership. It continues the long-standing tradition of defence against similar attacks, arguing that these issues are subject to domestic political consensus and cannot be an object of international debates and contestation: 'The Macedonian language is part of Macedonia's national identity and this is a topic that cannot be discussed [by anybody else but Macedonia]'.[81]

---

78. *Puls* newspaper, 13 May 1994.
79. Ibid.
80. Ibid.
81. *Puls* newspaper, 29 April 1994.

Discarding Bulgaria's historical claims as irrelevant and inappropriate, Macedonian rhetoric refers to the 'reality' of Macedonia and its 'happening' and 'occurring upon' Bulgarian politics.[82] The verbs of action discursively reinforce the notion of 'reality'. From the viewpoint of 'reality', this rhetorical line goes, there could have been no other Macedonian reaction despite Macedonia's complicated international and domestic situation. Furthermore, because of the complications, this reaction is interpreted in heroic terms:

> In extremely heavy and difficult political, economic and military realities and various combinations against Macedonia by its neighbours and the wider world, Macedonia managed to promote, again, in the face of the Bulgarian state, its position of autonomous subject of statehood and nationhood.[83]

The implicit heroisation of the stance taken by Macedonia in the bilateral relations performed the function of justifying the negative consequences ensuing from it. In the context of complete international isolation and deteriorating internal stability, closing what was possibly the only door open to Macedonia in the region required serious discursive argumentation. Explicit analytical formulations appeared to address this need:

> It seems that not signing the agreements was, in fact, the best that could have happened: Bulgaria found itself, once again, facing straight into the reality called Macedonia. And this was the first step in the long march of renouncing the illusions of history.[84]

Discursively presenting the two states' failure to reach any form of agreement and sign any particular document of cooperation as 'the best' possible outcome was a strategy to reduce the political impact on Macedonia. Placing the event in a chain of supposedly systematic efforts on the part of Macedonia ('once again', 'the first step') to stand its ground before its historically 'deluded' opponent, was also an attempt to depict it as the desired political outcome rather than as a serendipitous course of events. The same purpose was served by analysing the economic and political situation in Bulgaria as 'full of contradictions': 'People's lives get worse every day, inflation grows and the value of the Bulgarian Lev against the dollar is declining'.[85] References to the high level of corruption and the criminalisation involved in Bulgaria's transition[86] attempted to play down the potential value of

---

82. Described as 'independent sovereign state, equal political subject in the international relations and stable partner in the dialogue with everybody, including Bulgaria', *Puls* newspaper, 29 April 1994.
83. Ibid.
84. *Puls* newspaper, analysis, 29 April 1994.
85. Ibid.
86. Ibid.; including detailed material on the Bulgarian corporation Multigroup, which was notorious for its links with organised crime cartels.

any inter-state dialogue with Bulgaria and to understate the potential losses of failing to sign the planned bilateral trade and business agreements. At a time of isolation and crisis in Macedonia, the political responsibility for unconstructive foreign policy behaviour could be too risky. Presenting dialogue with Bulgaria as non-productive, besides being offensive to Macedonian nationhood, served the purpose of neutralising these political implications.

Narratives of reconciliation – resolving the language dispute

With the gradual progress in Bulgaria's preparation for joining the European integration dynamic, however, the language dispute began to attract political attention, mainly because of the questions it raised about the conflictual nature of Bulgaria's relations with its neighbours. In view of Bulgaria's formal application for full EU membership from the end of 1995 and the prospects for its success, its official position on Macedonia began to receive criticism. In an editorial piece, the democratic party mouthpiece (*Demokratsia* newspaper) analysed modern Balkan nationalism as an idiosyncratic element of the of the twentieth century's worst inventions that paralleled Barbarianism under the Roman Empire. The language dispute with Macedonia was interpreted as a remnant of this 'Barbarianism' of modern nationalism:

> [We risk] star[ing] in awe outside New Europe [like the ancient barbarians in front of the Empire], while it tries to understand exactly what language dispute there is to solve […] and how it threatens our national identity.[87]

Similar rhetoric began to come even from socialist ranks. This is remarkable because it was precisely the policies of the socialist government that reinforced the freeze in Bulgarian–Macedonian relations by politicising controversial nationhood narratives in the first place. Speaking as a representative of the socialist leadership, the future Bulgarian president confirmed:

> We need to admit that our two states have better relations with their other neighbours than with each other, which is incongruent with the good historical, economic and cultural ties traditional between us in the past.[88]

The statement still operated within the familiar Bulgarian narrative of shared past but represented an important modification. It avoided the conflictual interpretation of 'brotherhood' by emphasising the amity in the relationship ('good […] ties between us'). This made it potentially acceptable to the

---

87. Ivo Berov, 'United Europe, the barbarians and civilisation', *Demokratsia* newspaper, 2 February 1999.
88. Georgi Parvanov, Vice Chairman of the Supreme Council of the Bulgarian Socialist Party, in an interview for *Puls* newspaper, 26 April 1996.

Macedonian side, which was not comfortable with the insistence on 'excessive closeness'[89] with Bulgaria. It also enabled problematising the freeze in bilateral relations:

> We have been unable to establish the optimal environment for development of our relations [...] and we have lost from this. The peoples on both sides of the border have lost, families have lost, businessmen have lost, those who needed the intellectual contact with the other side have lost, [geopolitically] which is most important, we have lost from this.[90]

Interpreting the lack of good bilateral relations as a 'loss' and emphasising the many implications of this loss at the personal, economic, cultural, and national level represented a significant change in narratives on Macedonia. Coming from the lines of the socialists who were the ruling party at the time, it signified a detachment from the traditional nationalist narrative of a closed community defined through its losses in the past, and signalled an orientation towards the benefits of the present. Articulated by the leader of the renewed socialist party bidding for a turn in power, this interpretation indicated political legitimacy. Framing the discussion on Macedonia in these terms helped to identify specific reasons for the freeze in bilateral relations, thus opening up the discursive space to the search of possible solutions:

> We need to admit that both in Sofia and in Skopje there are reporters and publics and political figures who, with their statements and actions, malevolently increase reservations on both sides of the border.[91]

Singling out those held responsible for the general deterioration of relations among a group of journalists and opinion-makers is a clear indication of an attempt to acquit the government in its official position. Immediately, this pointed to the most controversial issue – the language dispute – and the possible avenues for its closure:

> The issue of the language in which the documents between Bulgaria and Macedonia should be signed is a matter of secondary importance, and its current escalation is fed by factors and powers disinterested in developing our relations in a positive direction. [...] Our party and parliamentary group are actively working to find a formula around the language issue that would be acceptable to both states.[92]

Interpreting the language dispute as a matter of secondary importance is already an attempt at depoliticising it and taking it off the 'urgent' political agenda. This

---

89. Ibid.
90. Ibid.
91. Ibid.
92. Ibid.

discursive move was performed repeatedly (in the same interview duplicating 'this is not even the most important issue' and on further occasions, see Parvanov speeches), thus emphasising its validity.

With the fall of the socialist government in the following year and the electoral victory of the democrats, this rhetoric was taken up as an official governmental policy on Macedonia. 'Solving' the language dispute with Macedonia became one of the primary foreign policy goals of the Kostov government (1997–2001, elected with the mandate of the democratic party), both as a publicity-generating strategy and as an attempt to take credit for the Europeanisation of Bulgaria's relations with its neighbours. The change in government in Macedonia as a result of the electoral victory of the Macedonian right[93] stimulated a similar dynamic. The new Macedonian prime minister Georgievski, often attacked for his moderate position in Macedonia's Balkan policies and accused of being 'pro-Bulgarian', was also a factor in reaching a compromise. His leadership encouraged an intensified bilateral dialogue with Bulgaria. Starting at ambassadorial[94] and ministerial[95] level, the two governments began gradually to normalise the political rhetoric surrounding bilateral relations by attaching it to the practicalities of mutually beneficial cooperation in particular areas. Subjects for discussion included the establishment of a free trade zone between the two states, agreements avoiding double taxation, agreements on the protection and promotion of mutual investments, cooperation in air and rail transport, etc. The issues of possible bilateral cooperation were organised into a total of twenty-three agreements whose signing had been blocked since the beginning of the language dispute in 1994. Framing the relations between the two states in the rhetoric of mutual interest logically raised the question why this had not been done earlier and enabled declarative certainty of progress in the conflictual areas:[96] 'By the time [these agreements] are enforced, the 'language dispute' will have been solved by the diplomacy of our two states.'[97] Avoiding contentious abstract formulations in the everyday political talks between the two states helped achieve progress in these efforts because it allowed their depoliticisation. By taking the focus off matters of principle, the political dialogue centred around improving the cooperation framework in specific areas. This emphasised the pragmatic benefits of a good relationship and the missed opportunities of the prolonged bilateral freeze.

---

93. Internal Macedonian Revolutionary Organisation – Democratic Party for Macedonian National Unity headed by Ljubco Georgievski, formed the new government in November 1998.

94. Briefing on the Bulgarian ambassador to Skopje's approval of a preliminary text of a prospective bilateral agreement, *Demokratsia* newspaper, 8 February 1999.

95. Macedonia's economic minister Nikola Gruevski visited Bulgaria for a meeting with his Bulgarian counterpart Valentin Vassilev to discuss the particulars of prospective economic cooperation, 9 February 1999, BTA Courier Service.

96. 'Relief in trade contacts with Macedonia from the beginning of 2000', *Demokratsia* newspaper, 10 February 1999.

97. Press conference by the economic ministers Valentin Vassilev and Nikola Gruevski, Sofia, 9 February 1999, BTA Courier Service.

Against the background of Bulgaria's active efforts for Europeanisation and intensified dialogue for cooperation in a series of areas, the Bulgarian leadership was eventually able to produce a formal position on the controversial issues in Bulgarian–Macedonian relations, which could gain political legitimacy and be officially accepted. The special position that Macedonia occupied in Bulgarian national narratives represented a particular challenge in this task. Engaging the Europe rhetoric and including European references to the issue proved capable of providing an interpretation of this position that simultaneously preserved Macedonia's special status and removed the conflictuality surrounding it. At an official celebration of the anniversary of Bulgarian parliamentarism, the Bulgarian prime minister chose to declare:

> Going back in history I would probably not err if I said that, after the word 'Bulgaria', the most frequently repeated word on the premises of the Bulgarian parliament has been the word 'Macedonia'. Looking into the future, however, I am convinced, the most frequently repeated word [here] will be the word 'Europe'.[98]

Highlighting the reorientation dynamic of Bulgarian nationhood narratives from the past to both present and future, the prime minister emphasised the role of European references in overcoming Bulgaria's obsession with the Macedonian narrative. Repositioning the narrative from the distant past (and the stories of national tragedy and loss associated with it) to the beginning of inter-state dialogue between Bulgaria and Macedonia (Bulgaria's recognition of Macedonian independent statehood), made possible as a result of this reorientation, is what enabled the non-conflictual reinterpretation of Bulgarian–Macedonian relations:

> The governments of the Republic of Bulgaria and the Republic of Macedonia reached an agreement [as] a natural consequence of the historical fact that Bulgaria first recognised the independence of the Republic of Macedonia.[99]

Framed within the rhetoric of Europe, this chronological repositioning of the historical dependency of Bulgarian–Macedonian relations increased its legitimacy:

> the two states found a way to begin to speak in the language of a united Europe, the language of friendship, of understanding, of tolerance and of mutual respect [...]. This is Bulgaria's piece of European news.[100]

---

98. Ivan Kostov, Prime Minister, at the celebratory plenary session of Bulgarian parliament, 10 February 1999.
99. Ibid.
100. Ibid.

Establishing an equivalence between behaviour guided by the norms of Europe ('to speak the language of [...] Europe') and the moral categories characterising a relationship of friendship attempted to discursively delegitimise the conflictuality in Bulgarian–Macedonian relations. Emphasising the breakthrough that such amity marks ('piece of [...] news') and labelling it as European rhetorically interpreted the event as a success.

This notion was reinforced by the overblown declarations of approval coming from domestic and international sources of authority. The Bulgarian foreign minister defined the decision as a 'sign of civility and European behaviour'.[101] The chairman of the foreign policy committee in the Bulgarian parliament saluted the 'remarkable consensus on unblocking the relations with Macedonia'.[102] The Bulgarian president also lent his absolute support to the agreement by confirming that he had been part of the efforts that led to it:

> this issue is about to be closed in an extremely satisfactory manner for both sides, keeping the dignity of both Bulgaria and Macedonia. This opens an avenue for pragmatically resolving all problems that stand between us.[103]

Linking the resolution of the dispute to the notion of pragmatic politics was a discursive strategy to emphasise its compatibility with Bulgaria's national interests. The explicit confirmation that Bulgaria's dignity as a sovereign state had not been affected in the bilateral compromise reinforced this idea and demonstrated that a new interpretation of what represented 'Bulgarian-ness' had occurred.

Framed within the positive stories of European-ness, publicised external approval added legitimacy to the policy of rapprochement with Macedonia and served the purpose of neutralising nationalist arguments against it:

> Obviously, the two states managed to [...] overcome history. This is [...] a European approach to solving the problems. [...] The agreement between Bulgaria and Macedonia is truly a European solution.[104]

Associating the lower salience of historical narratives with European-ness ('European approach', 'European solution') indicated the reorientation required of Bulgaria in its interpretation of Bulgarian-ness. Detaching the national identity narratives from their focus on the past and reorienting them instead to the present and future was what enabled the 'overcoming of history'. At the same time, the modified interpretation of Bulgarian-ness retained familiar elements of

---

101. Nadezhda Mihailova at the Committee for International and Integration Policy, quoted in *Demokratsia* newspaper, 12 February 1999.
102. Assen Agov at the Committee for International and Integration Policy, quoted in *Demokratsia* newspaper, 12 February 1999.
103. President Petar Stoyanov quoted in *Demokratsia* newspaper, 11 February 1999.
104. Avis Bowlen, US ambassador to Bulgaria, 11 February 1999, BTA Courier Service.

national identity that preserved the continuity of the nationhood narratives. This was illustrated by the emphasis on the significance of Bulgaria's new policy on Macedonia to the stability of the Balkans:

> Bulgaria did a lot to contribute to stabilising the region. [...] What the Prime Minister just announced will additionally help improve the future stability of the Balkans.[105]

Bulgaria's traditional interpretation of its national purpose – the role of the state as a factor in stability in the Balkans – was being highlighted to help accomplish the discursive move of re-narrating Bulgarian national identity within the discursive space of European integration without losing credibility. The fact that recognition of this Bulgarian role came from Europe (in the shape of the German ambassador) increased its discursive significance.

The same purpose served the immediate rhetorical link established with the notion of national interest:

> Having succeeded in finding again a common language with Macedonia, there will be no barriers in front of us to stop us from speaking it in the name of the national interests and the national ideals, which should be our only guide in our service.[106]

Linking the Europeanisation of bilateral relations with Macedonia with the notion of national interest is meant to confirm the compatibility of the move with the meaning of Bulgarian nationhood: it was emphasised that both the 'national interests' and the 'national ideals' are adhered to in an improved dialogue with Macedonia.

The change in the official rhetoric on Macedonia illustrates the modifications in identity narratives that occurred in the course of transition. In view of Bulgaria's new political priorities and policy goals and its gradual progress towards Europeanisation, the national community needed no longer be constituted around historical narratives of past grandeur and glory. It had a clear perspective for the future that could provide an optimistic, positive source of self-identification: 'returning' to Europe. This is what suggested the decreased political significance of historical narratives about Macedonia and the increased significance of narratives of good neighbourly relations. With important implications for the contents of national identity, the depoliticisation of historical narratives on Macedonia produced, eventually, a rearrangement of the identity pattern. The change is evident in the new interpretation of the meaning of national interest: making specific steps in the direction of Europe, one of which was improving relations with neighbouring countries.

---

105. Peter Metzger, Germany's ambassador to Bulgaria, 11 February 1999, BTA Courier Service.
106. Prime Minister Ivan Kostov at the celebratory plenary session of Bulgarian parliament, 10 February 1999.

The particular formula that enabled the improvement of Bulgarian–Macedonian relations was nothing new: it had been discussed previously by the governments of Zhan Videnov and Branko Crvenkovski and had been discarded as unacceptable. Its wording stipulated that the Joint Declaration between Bulgaria and Macedonia be signed in duplicate copies 'in the official *languages* of both states: Bulgarian under the Constitution of the Republic of Bulgaria, and Macedonian under the Constitution of the Republic of Macedonia'.[107] The fact that almost exactly the same formula had hitherto been seen as unacceptable is an indicator of the changed political environment that enabled the general consensus in Bulgaria around Macedonia.

It is important to note, however, that the deep sedimentation of Bulgarian narratives on Macedonia did not permit their dislocation from the national discursive space. Even though the language dispute was gradually moved down the state's political agenda, the interpretations of 'Macedonia' that caused and perpetuated it did not disappear. Because of their historical intertwinement with the narratives of Bulgarian nationhood, they could not be completely removed from the national discursive space. Bulgaria's difficulties in acknowledging the distinctiveness of the Macedonian national language continued to plague narratives on Macedonia. This was particularly visible in the reactions to the announced Joint Declaration in Bulgaria's right-wing political space:

> In no case should this be interpreted as recognising the Macedonian language. [...] I repeat, it does not follow that we recognise such a language on Bulgarian territory and this is clearly formulated.[108]

The duplicated confirmation that the official position on the nature of the Macedonian language and its use in Bulgaria had not changed attempted to appease the nationalists' concerns. It also aimed to restore the balance in the familiar national identity narrative, which was accomplished by two explanatory interpretations of the Joint Declaration's language formula. One concerned the practicalities of the political process that led to it. It explained that this formula was a step forward from the proposal of the Macedonian government, presumably demanding the unconditional recognition of the Macedonian language.

> The position of the previous governments in Skopje sounded very like an ultimatum. It demanded that we recognise the existence of a Macedonian language and that the documents be signed in Bulgarian and Macedonian without any qualifications. [...] The formula now accepted guarantees both our historical interests and our national security in view of any future demands.[109]

---

107. Text of the Joint Declaration of the Prime Minister of the Republic of Bulgaria and the Prime Minister of the Republic of Macedonia, 1999.
108. Krasimir Karakachanov, leader of the Bulgarian VMRO in an interview for *Demokratsia* newspaper, 11 February 1999.
109. Ibid.

The statement aimed to demonstrate that the national position had been asserted and championed: the reference to 'historical interests' and the consideration of 'national security' issues confirmed this. Transferring political responsibility for past intractability on the issue to Skopje reinforced the idea that concerted effort had been made and progress had been achieved on the part of the Bulgarian government, thus highlighting the outcome as a success.

The second interpretation concerned general principles that underlie the new policy. It upheld the idea that pragmatic national policies should not be driven by considerations of history:

> Historical claims are not the job of politicians. [...] Language and nation, let alone history, are not to be recognised. A nation or a language either exists or it does not. It would be silly to continue arguing about history.[110]

The discursive separation between the historical and the political is the main change in Bulgaria's rhetoric. Denouncing the political relevance of historical arguments as 'silly', the nationalist leader attempted to close the dispute without compromising core nationalist assumptions.

The timing of the move was repeatedly justified with reference to the change of power in Macedonia, aiming to reinforce the idea that Bulgaria's position had always been amicable:

> Bulgaria has long been ready for this day. Our foreign policy towards Macedonia has always been consistent and tolerant, and European values are the criterion that we use to solve contentious issues. This is the language that Europe speaks today. When Skopje began to speak this language, our domestic language dispute became unnecessary.[111]

This rhetorical realignment of Bulgarian foreign policy with European values essentialised Bulgaria's position and problematised Macedonia's: the responsibility for the previous freeze in the relationship should be transferred to Macedonia because Bulgaria 'has always been [...] tolerant' and 'European'. In stark contrast with the intransigence of Bulgaria's previous official position on Macedonia, this claim represented an attempt at domestication of the discursive transformation that enabled the breakthrough in the relationship. The only voices that contradicted it came, predictably, from the ranks of the socialists, now in opposition, who suggested that the solution of the language dispute with Macedonia implied a 'grave compromise' with the Bulgarian national interests.[112] This deviance from the consensual approval for solving

---

110. Ibid.
111. Aneliya Dimitrova, 'Language', commentary, *Demokratsia* newspaper, 11 February 1999.
112. Georgi Daskalov, leader comment in *Demokratsia* newspaper, 16 February 1999.

the dispute, however, was marginalised as 'nationalism' unworthy of the new 'European' character of Bulgarian politics:

> whether the socialists have the courage and resources for a candidly nationalist campaign *against* the normalisation of Bulgarian–Macedonian relations [or not], the damage of such campaign for both Bulgaria and Macedonia is guaranteed.[113]

Contrasting the European-ness of improving bilateral relations with damage from nationalist politics was the discursive dynamic that enabled the overcoming of antagonisms from the past. Associating Bulgaria's prosperous future with Europeanisation, and articulating amity with Macedonia as the only European option for progress in bilateral relations, facilitated the historical narratives on Macedonia to be taken off the political agenda and marginalised as remnants of the nationalist (communist/socialist) past. This helped to initiate a bilateral institutional dialogue that eventually led to negotiating a legitimate solution to the language dispute.

The political narratives around the actual signing of the Joint Declaration between Bulgaria and Macedonia, which put an end to the language dispute, confirmed the increased salience of the signifiers of 'European-ness'. 'Respect for European principles in the interaction with partners', a 'European solution to Balkan problems',[114] 'saluted' and 'appreciated' by the EU,[115] represented common approaches to covering the event in the leading media. Even though sceptics criticised the event as a gesture to impress Europe rather one that would benefit Macedonia, it had important implications both for improving Bulgarian–Macedonian relations and for consolidating the power of Europe. The policies of the new democratic coalition government in Bulgaria were already framed within the context of Europe as a general strategic goal. This facilitated the overall institutional consensus on solving the dispute with Macedonia and enabled the signing of the Joint Declaration, as well as a whole spectrum of subsequent bilateral documents advancing relations in various sectors. Ranging from economic cooperation (free trade, investment plans, transport links) to cooperation at the level of 'high politics' (defence and security[116]), the joint initiatives opened up the bilateral discursive space for normalised political dialogue. Guided by references to European behaviour and European values such as trust, tolerance, amity, pragmatism, the progress in the bilateral relations marginalised the nationalist interpretations of identity as detrimental and irrelevant to the many aspects of possible cooperation. In this sense,

---

113. *Demokratsia* newspaper, 16 February 1999. Emphasis in the original.
114. *Demokratsia* newspaper, 23 February 1999.
115. *Demokratsia* newspaper, 24 February 1999.
116. Including plans for joint military training events, and Bulgaria's big donation of military arms and equipment to Macedonia, 1999.

Europeanisation produced a less antagonistic interpretation of collective state identity. As this interpretation was more in line with the imperatives of joining the EU, it was also considered more legitimate.

But while the process of Europeanisation in Bulgaria had already achieved several tangible results, which enabled the sustainable empowerment of Europe over the entire discursive space of Bulgarian politics and facilitated the general institutional consensus on overcoming the freeze in the bilateral relationship, Macedonia was at a different stage in its efforts towards Europeanisation. As a result of the delay in international recognition and the continuing domestic problems with minority accommodation, Macedonia had not been able to initiate an institutional dialogue with the EU as early as Bulgaria. By the time Bulgaria was already officially an applicant state (December 1999), Macedonia was about to begin its associated membership status negotiations (April 2000). This determined the decreased political relevance of Europe and its only partial appropriation in the discursive space of Macedonian politics. A domestic political factor also contributed to Macedonia's ambivalence on Europe. While the Bulgarian democratic coalition had replaced the former socialist elite in all institutional positions of leadership, Macedonia was experiencing a deep institutional divide between the presidency (still headed by the functionary from Yugoslavian times, Gligorov) and the government (already led by the democratic party leader Georgievski). The clash between the two institutions divided Macedonian politics on key political issues[117] and was displayed in debates over the advancement of Bulgarian–Macedonian relations. Thus, even though the prime minister and his government referred to Europe to justify their policy on improving relations with Bulgaria and gain legitimacy for it, Europeanisation was not empowered consensually, as it was in Bulgaria. The salience of nationalist rhetoric (perpetuated by the socialists around the former Macedonian prime minister Crvenkvoski, whose central theme was anti-Bulgarian rhetoric) demonstrates this.

The leadership of the Macedonian socialists claimed that the compromise reached by the two states had been a fatal error. Insisting that the formula of the compromise (signing the documents 'in Macedonian language under the constitution [of Macedonia]') limited the Macedonian language to the boundaries of the constitutional jurisdiction and did not imply recognition of its existence outside of it, the former Macedonian ambassador to Bulgaria denounced it as 'unacceptable'.[118] He demanded that it be accompanied by an explicit declaration from Bulgaria recognising the Macedonian language. Such a declaration, already demanded officially by the previous Macedonian government, had obviously not been deemed possible by Bulgaria. Inquiry into the aspects of the agreement that remained contentious between the two states had a destructive effect on the prospects of bilateral cooperation. By insisting on these aspects, the Macedonian

---

117. See the debate between the president and the prime minister at the parliamentary session, 23 February 1999; also enquiries at the parliamentary committee on security, etc.

118. Georgi Spasov for *Dnevnik* newspaper, 15 February 1999.

socialists attempted to secure popular support by utilising the salience of nationalist narratives constituting Bulgaria as the threatening Macedonian Other. Even so, the oppositional voices of the socialists were steadily marginalised, particularly with the stepping into office in December 1999 of the new president Boris Trajkovski, who came from the lines of the democratic party VMRO–DPMNE, not least because the Albanian minority's political representation, in line with the government, had also subscribed to the rhetoric of Europeanisation as a tool against Macedonian nationalism. The prime minister defended his policy of normalising relations with Bulgaria by calling upon the realm of commonality that this discourse upheld:

> Is there a person who could be bothered by normalising relations between two Balkan states [...] particularly between Macedonia and Bulgaria? [...] Yesterday the European Union expressed support for normalisation [...], in the morning Great Britain sent us congratulations for the courage and the manner in which we acted. [...] And instead of being proud [...] that once and forever we overcame this dispute [...], we are now starting all over again to search for problems and faults.[119]

Juxtaposing the notion of 'normalisation' and its universality as a value with the 'abnormality' of conflict, Georgievski emphasised that Europe was entirely in favour of normalisation. Therefore, the ones seeking 'problems and fault' would be the 'abnormal', non-European elements in Macedonian politics. This is a discursive attempt to delegitimise the dispute and the narratives associated with it, thus justifying the policy of the government as the only legitimate option:

> We do not intend to be in a situation of frozen relations, martial relations, to be constantly threatened. We want security for the Republic of Macedonia. Is there a better example of security than good relations with this [the Bulgarian] state?[120]

Transferring improved relations with Bulgaria to the realm of 'high politics' (threat and security) highlighted their significance and aimed to justify the government's policy of rapprochement. Reversing the familiar Macedonian narrative of Bulgaria as a threat, the prime minister insisted that 'good relations' with Bulgaria signalled the best way to ensure Macedonian security. Bulgaria's post-declaration donation of military equipment was used as an illustration of this claim:

> We should once and for all forget about the schemes that somebody will attack us from Bulgaria. Apparently, they are the ones arming us[.][121]

---

119. Ljubco Georgievski at the 12th plenary session, 23 February 1999, 13–14.
120. Ibid.
121. Ibid., 14.

From conflict to reconciliation | 125

Table 5.2: Narratives of the language dispute in Bulgaria and Macedonia

State	Bulgaria	Macedonia
Meanings upheld by nationalism	Compromising nationhood	Asserting statehood
	[Silence]	[Silence]
Meanings upheld by Europeanisation	Good relations with neighbours	Normality
	Regional amity, trust and tolerance	National and regional security
	Pragmatic politics, national interest	Pragmatic politics

This was a powerful change in the official interpretation of Bulgaria in the Macedonian public sphere. Traditionally positioned among the many Balkan enemies of the independent Macedonian state (a habitual reference used the allegory of 'sheep among wolves') with a mainly anti-thetical discursive role, Bulgaria now became a partner, and amity with Bulgaria began to signify security and normality. These were key elements in the European rhetoric in Macedonia and as such they realigned good bilateral relations with Europeanisation. This is the dynamic that attempted to marginalise nationalist narratives on Bulgaria, while empowering Europeanisation.

Unlike Bulgaria, Macedonia still needed to see Europe as a tangible political prospect in the near future in order to establish general institutional and political consensus on its European option. The delay on the road to Europe had a detrimental effect on the normative power of Europeanisation in Macedonia. On the issue of resolving the language dispute, the partial empowerment of Europe in the Macedonian discursive space was complemented by Bulgaria's determination to demonstrate reconciliatory regional policies in order to facilitate its own integration efforts. This greatly assisted the resolution of a dispute that had been initiated in the first place by Bulgaria's intransigence on the issue of language, and determined its amicable outcome.

Europeanisation effects on identity narratives of the language dispute

Bulgarian and Macedonian post-communist identities were initially upheld by narratives steadily anchored in the past. This is what determined the stark dependence of Bulgarian–Macedonian relations upon historical antagonisms. Political rhetoric in both states reflected the inadequacy of such identity narration in the general silence on the language dispute (Table 5.2). Despite the visible importance that was given to the issue as central in the identity constructions, it did not head the political agendas in the two states. Another context within which the language dispute seemed incompatible with the political priorities of the period was the prospect of preparing to join the dynamics of integration. The gradual marginalisation of the former communists from the centres of state power and the constitution of democratic governments as a definitive break from the past, well into the transition processes, enabled the adaptation of national identity narratives to the political imperatives of the time. Focusing on the opportunities for cooperation placed bilateral relations on the plane of pragmatic politics and facilitated the marginalisation of conflictual interpretations impeding cooperation. Transcending conflictuality was discursively attached to references to Europe interpreted in terms of security, stability and normality. Against the background of a strategic reorientation of national politics towards European integration, this increased the appeal of the new narration of national identity and significantly improved the legitimacy it lent to political community.

Narratives on recognising national minorities

The investigation of national identity narratives determining the discursive position of Other in Bulgarian–Macedonian relations has focused so far on two narrative groups. In the first years of transition it followed modifications in narratives of recognition and post-recognition. From the mid-1990s to the end of the first transitional decade it explored changing narratives of language and the way they facilitated reconciliation of the language dispute. Conditioned by different factors in the two states (domestic political struggles, minority–majority relations, international status, etc.), both narrative groups tended to display similar discursive modifications. First, the general orientation of national identity constructions shifted from past to present and future. This reorientation helped depoliticise conflictual historical narratives and take them off the 'urgent' political agenda of the state. Second, the narration of national identity began to increasingly include European references to describe the meaning of key discursive elements. This dynamic turned Europe into an element of the national and significantly increased the realm of commonality between the two states, thus transcending the boundary between collective Self and Other set by national borders. Third, political priorities began to be determined more by pragmatic rather than ideational interpretations of interest. This helped to avoid conflictual formulations of principle and concentrated bilateral relations on the possibilities for mutually beneficial cooperation. As a result, the meaning of the national Other could be detached from antagonistic narratives, and be re-narrated as a partner. Overall, these discursive transformations adapted the national identity constructions to the changing political imperatives. By providing a positive and optimistic reading of national identity, they also improved the legitimacy of the political community it represented.

The salience of the two narrative groups discussed in the previous two sections of this chapter increased at two different points in time. Recognition became an issue at the very beginning of transition, while language was problematised towards the middle of the first transitional decade. Modifications in the identity narratives reflect this chronological difference, because it is related to different degrees of progress towards Europeanisation. While in 1991 Europe was merely a distant vision, an idea that had little immediate political relevance in the context of utmost insecurity created by the regime changes, in 1999 it was already a foreseeable political prospect. The normative power of Europe was gradually increasing as a result of the more visible relevance of the integration processes and of Europeanisation. Therefore, narrating national identity through the meanings of Europe seemed to have become easier over time. Tracing modifications of meanings in another narrative group – narratives on national minorities – whose salience was highest late in the transition period, helps us to fully grasp the logic of this discursive dynamic.

Inextricable from the historical narratives of nationhood, the issue of national minorities at home and abroad defined one of the central lines of conflictuality in Bulgarian–Macedonian relations. Shaped by antagonistic interpretations of Other, the stand on minorities in the two states differed in view of the different identity patterns and the different interpretation of the meaning of central elements of the national identity constructions.

Building on its central interpretation of national unity, Bulgaria rejected the notion of 'national minority' altogether. In the legal framework for the protection of minorities, the state operationalised the term 'ethnic minorities' and treated their members as Bulgarians of different ethnic origin. This interpretation upheld the monolithic character of Bulgarian national identity, at the same time as granting necessary protection. Short of collective political rights, which were unconstitutional under Bulgarian legislation,[122] members of these minorities in Bulgaria enjoyed the full spectrum of rights granted to others. The ethnic accommodation model negotiated at the beginning of Bulgaria's transition to democracy provided the rules for sufficient political participation of the largest minority group, the Turks, so there were no further political imperatives for rethinking the framework. Externally, Bulgaria had no consistent policy towards its minority communities in neighbouring states, but had a specific position on Macedonia. Because of the historical interpretation of Macedonia as part of the Bulgarian nationhood narrative, the common story was that of Serbisation and communisation of the originally Bulgarian national identity of the people living in Macedonia (Angelov, 2004). Where these processes had failed, Bulgarian narratives assumed, there were still people professing their 'original' Bulgarian consciousness, despite the threat of repression. Bulgaria's official position was that of encouraging this presumed target group and protesting against Macedonia's repressive policies. But it did not demand special minority status, because recognition of a Bulgarian minority in Macedonia would imply the clear distinction between the Bulgarian nation and the Macedonian nation. Bulgaria was far from adopting this position.

Macedonia took a much more clearly defined stand on national minorities. In view of the complex processes of inter-ethnic negotiations and the active participation of the sizeable Albanian minority in the political processes of transition, the notion of national minorities became a permanent part of Macedonian

---

122. Constitution of the Republic of Bulgaria, Art.11, Para.4.

national identity narratives. Accommodated through the formula of national tolerance, it secured a range of cultural and political rights for all minority groups on the territory of the republic. However, Macedonia never acknowledged either the existence of a Bulgarian minority group or the significance of a Bulgarian element in its national identity construction. Bulgarian presence in Macedonia was retold as foreign occupation and professing Bulgarian national consciousness was interpreted as a form of treason (Georgievski, 2007). In this sense minority protection in Macedonia was never extended to Bulgarian minority groups. But in view of the salience of the narratives of national territory and the notion of territorial belonging, Macedonia sought to secure it for Macedonian minorities abroad. As already noted, concern for Macedonians living in parts of the region under foreign sovereignty was a high priority foreign policy issue and interpreted as one of the state's main external responsibilities. This is confirmed by the constitutional provision explicitly stipulating this role.[123] In the context of Bulgaria's narration of national identity as monolithic and the Bulgarian ambiguity on Macedonian nationhood altogether, this concern of the Macedonian state was perceived as a particular threat. In Bulgaria it was interpreted as a national security problem.[124] Placing the discussion of minorities on the agenda of security politics in Bulgaria further politicised the minority issue in Macedonia and reinforced antagonistic narratives on Bulgaria.

It is evident from this that Bulgarian and Macedonian national identity narratives clashed both internally and externally on the issue of national minorities and created one of the most intractable conflictual fields in their bilateral relations. The conflict was maintained by three key narratives: the perception of threat to the territorial integrity of the state, incompatibility with the historical narratives of nationhood, and unrecognised minority status and minority protection. These narratives placed the issue of national minorities on the agenda of national and state security policies, which significantly impeded their normalisation and depoliticisation. With the first positive steps towards Europeanisation, the insecurity generated by the complex transition processes began to subside. (Re-)turning to Europe posed particular practical demands on the two states, among them good bilateral relations and a framework for minority protection. This streamlined bilateral relations into the rationality of Europeanisation policies and helped take conflictual interpretations off the political agenda. Even though the two states did not agree on a mutually acceptable interpretation of the contentious formulations, they managed to avoid them in their inter-state dialogue, thus reducing their political relevance. Tracing the changed articulations along the three key conflictual narrative lines on national minorities demonstrates the mechanism of this discursive dynamic.

---

123. Constitution of the Republic of Macedonia, Art.49.

124. As was Macedonia's concern about its minorities under Art.49 seen by Greece: it was stated as one of the reasons for the Greek economic blockade. For an overview of what led to this extreme regional position, see for instance Danforth (1993).

Narratives on national minorities and the threat to territorial integrity

Narratives of territorial threat signalled one aspect in which the issue of national minorities affected Bulgarian–Macedonian relations. Linking national minorities to a territorial threat was based on historical references in the identity construction and was determined by conflictual interpretations in the two states. The relations of the Bulgarian communist party with socialist Yugoslavia in the first decades of communism had brought about a series of rather controversial political campaigns directed at the population of the region of Pirin Macedonia in Bulgaria (Angelov, 2004). Initially they had been aimed at fostering a distinct Macedonian identity in line with Bulgaria's warm relations with Josip Broz Tito. After the split between Tito and Stalin, Bulgaria's communist policies had changed course and had redeclared the Bulgarian character of the region and its population. Eventually the issue had been completely closed, particularly in view of communist historiography's nationalist interpretation of Bulgaria's new history and its tragic narratives on Macedonia (Bulgarian Academy of Sciences, 1999). The heated debates at the very beginning of the democratic transition borne by the 'national question' and the repressed Turkish minority's need for redress did not reopen the issue of the Macedonian minority in Pirin because the latter minority was not officially recognised[125] and did not have any political voice.[126] It was not until Bulgaria's recognition of Macedonian independence that the issue was placed on Bulgaria's 'urgent' political agenda in view of Macedonia's official concern for its national minorities abroad.

From the very beginning of the formal inter-state relations between Bulgaria and Macedonia, the issue of national minorities was treated with utmost urgency because of its discursive association with the prospect of territorial separatism. The strong link between nation and territory, a classical tenet of nationalism, formed the justification for Bulgaria's official policy of non-recognition of minority status and minority rights for the contested minority in Pirin Macedonia. The significance of this link is demonstrated in the context of establishing diplomatic relations between Bulgaria and the newly independent Macedonia. Despite Bulgaria's declarative act of international recognition and its pledged support for the former Yugoslav Republic, it was almost two years after recognition that it opened an embassy in Macedonia. Indeed, diplomatic relations had already been established, but with more than eight months' delay and at consular level only. When asked by the press why he was delaying his first formal visit to Macedonia even though he had received an official invitation, the Bulgarian foreign minister pointed precisely to the claim for recognising Macedonian national minority and the related 'territorial claims'.[127] Linking minority status to protecting the official territorial borders of

---

125. An insignificant number of people had declared that they were of 'Macedonian' ethnic origin in the official censuses, see official information available at http://www.nsi.bg/Census/Ethnos.htm (accessed 1 June 2015).
126. Roundtable discussions, verbatim reports, 80–1.
127. Stoyan Ganev quoted in *Duma* newspaper, 12 February 1992.

the state inevitably placed the discussion of minorities on the agenda of 'high politics' (national security and defence) and prevented its normalisation. Taken up by the socialists, this theme became central in narratives on Macedonia for a long time, discursively delegitimising the possibility of recognising minority status and excluding it from the policy options of the state.

Indeed, Bulgaria's official position never acknowledged any national identity for the people in Pirin Macedonia other than Bulgarian, and refused to discuss their status in terms of minority rights and protection, despite the lack of any reasonable concern for Bulgaria's territorial integrity in view of Macedonia's position (Macedonia's virtually non-existent army during the first half of the 1990s). The language dispute reinforced nationalist interpretations of Macedonian calls for minority protection as a hidden agenda for territorial demands. This is illustrated by the high priority that the matter assumed when Bulgaria's political will for overcoming the language dispute changed. It became the subject of one of the two key provisions that enabled the breakthrough. Together with the formulation on language, Bulgaria's efforts in the negotiations that led to the signing of the 1999 Joint Declaration were focused on securing a guarantee of non-intervention in decisions on the status of Pirin Macedonia and its population. In view of Macedonia's constitutional concern for the fate of Macedonian minority communities under foreign sovereignty, Bulgaria insisted on a provision clarifying its non-application to Bulgaria. Bulgarian demands for such a provision were based on the precedent with Greece but in effect demonstrated political concern at official state level that Macedonia's constitution might be interpreted as a legal basis for intervention in Bulgaria's domestic affairs. The semantic link between territory and nation, pointed to above, is displayed in the very text of the Declaration. The provision guaranteeing the absence of any territorial demand immediately precedes the provision declaring the non-application of Macedonia's concern under Art.49 of its constitution. This was interpreted in Bulgaria as a withdrawal of any claim for the existence of a Macedonian minority: 'Skopje will not seek a Macedonian minority with us'.[128] Securing Macedonia's official confirmation that there were no territorial aspirations and no intentions to violate the unity and monolithic character of the Bulgarian national construction formed the basis of all future dialogue between the two states. The overall framework of Europe, which was referred to throughout, is evidence of its empowerment and the role it played in re-articulating Bulgaria's own vision of collective Self.

In Macedonia the link between territorial threat and national minority narratives was based on historical representations of Bulgaria as an occupant power.[129] These narratives had been upheld by key elements in the Macedonian identity construction (divided Macedonian land, dispersed Macedonian people) whose meaning had been defined against Bulgaria as the immediate foreign

---

128. Editorial headline, *Demokratsia* newspaper, 2 February 1999.

129. Parliament plenary session, 12 August 1992, 27; 27 October 1992, 80, etc.

Other. Bulgaria's act of recognition extending declarative support for the newly independent Macedonian state had not succeeded in dislocating the stories of occupation and aggression because of Bulgaria's ambiguous official position. Even though the new state had been recognised, the Bulgarian president had explicitly declared that recognition did not apply to the Macedonian nation (Zhelev, 2005). Within the discourse of Macedonian nationalism, therefore, recognition by Bulgaria had been interpreted as a tool for increasing Bulgarian influence and advancing Bulgarian aspirations on Macedonia. This interpretation of Bulgaria had not remained completely unchallenged[130] but it had been the most common one.[131] Bulgaria's failure to establish any meaningful institutional dialogue with Macedonia and its subsequent intransigence in the language dispute had reinforced this discursive configuration. This is evidenced by the absent or consistently negative reporting on Bulgaria in the Macedonian media.[132] In this sense the breakthrough in the language dispute was a positive outcome for transgressing the boundary of threatening Otherness in the simple fact that it permitted the initiation of inter-state dialogue with official Bulgaria. Placing the relationship between the two states on the plane of the pragmatic politics of cooperation allowed the opening up of Macedonia's discursive space for alternative narratives on Bulgaria.

As a result of the positive outcome of the language negotiations and in preparation for the Macedonian prime minister's official visit to Bulgaria, Macedonia requested military support in military equipment and weapons,[133] which Bulgaria granted. Among the list of cooperation initiatives and bilateral agreements (which included twenty-three items according to the official announcement of the Bulgarian Ministry of Foreign Affairs), a Bulgarian donation of 150 tanks and 142 artillery guns was formally announced. Against the condition of the Macedonian army at the time[134] the donation was evaluated in Macedonia as 'an exceptional gesture on behalf of the Bulgarian government' and 'the strongest proof of the existing trust between the two states'.[135] The signifiers of amity ('an exceptional gesture', 'existing trust') are a novelty in Macedonian narratives on Bulgaria.

---

130. Plenary session of the Macedonian parliament, 15 February 1992, 89, for a reference questioning the fact that Bulgaria's position was not reported as a positive outcome; ibid., 90, for an attempt to appeal to leave the past behind; ibid., 104–11 for a reference to Bulgaria as 'a friend', etc.

131. President Gligorov would not visit Bulgaria to avoid being called 'bugarash', Georgievski's visit to Sofia was regarded as 'highly suspicious' – see plenary session, 15 February 1992, 86–8.

132. For instance *Puls* newspaper (NIP *Nova Makedonija*) in their column dedicated to Bulgaria in the period 1992–6.

133. A standard request of the democratic Macedonian government in its contacts with NATO member states and in other contacts abroad, given that the retreat of the Yugoslav army left the republic in severe shortage of military equipment.

134. Four tanks in working condition, according to Georgievski at the press conference in Sofia, 22 February 1999, BTA Courier Service.

135. Ibid.

Unsurprisingly, they were questioned in the Macedonian parliament.[136] In defence of the policies of his government, the prime minister challenged the sedimentation of narratives constituting Bulgaria as a threat. Pointing to the link between the politics of the past and the interpretation of Bulgaria as the ultimate enemy, both in the communist regime of the federation and in the socialist government of the early transition period,[137] Georgievski attempted to demonstrate the political irrelevance of such interpretation and to discredit its logic. On this basis was his call for a change:

> We should once and for all discard this conspiracy theory that somebody should always attack us from Bulgaria. [...] Again and again we find ourselves in a situation when we are inventing problems with Bulgaria. It is a new problem every time. [...] Honestly, I do not understand this frustration of ours with regard to Bulgaria.[138]

Defining Macedonia's obsession with the threat from Bulgaria as the irrational expression of a bothered identity ('conspiracy theory', 'frustration'), the prime minister uncovers its 'invented' nature and denounces it. Against its irrationality he places rational considerations of classical realist national interest:

> If somebody gives you weapons in such quantities, [...] this, not least, proves that they are not planning military aggression against you. [...] An army that we have thought of all along as the enemy gives us weapons. What is the problem with that? [...] Is there greater security for us [than this]?[139]

Rhetorically demonstrating the lack of rationality and logic behind constituting Bulgaria as a threat in the context of the Bulgarian military donation, Georgievski successfully challenged the sedimentation of the narratives of animosity and opened up a discursive space for positive interpretations of Macedonia's relations with Bulgaria. Even though Macedonia's progress in the process of Europeanisation was still in its very early stages, European references were called upon to justify the relevance of such policy:

> I believe that we will be able to demonstrate what Europe wants from us [...] What we are doing now is the impossible, trying to reopen the document [Agenda 2000] and see whether we can be included somehow, by good will. [...] [T]he strategic interests of this state will remain the same [...] [guided] by the principles and rules of European democracy.[140]

---

136. In a hearing by the Macedonian president Gligorov who claims he had 'no knowledge of the donation', albeit he was Commander-in-Charge of the Macedonian army: see parliamentary session, 23 February 1999.
137. Parliamentary session, 23 February 1999, 14.
138. Ljubco Georgievski at the 12th plenary session, 23 February 1999: 15.
139. Ibid., 15.
140. Ibid., 16.

This discursive strategy is confirmed by the vice minister of foreign affairs and future president of Macedonia, Trajkovski:

> We have demonstrated the political will to overcome the past. The place of the past is in history, and we should be looking to the future. [...] We spoke to each other under the standards of Europe, I would like us to move from being on the periphery of Europe to becoming part of it.[141]

In line with the prime minister's rhetoric, Trajkovski repeated the association of antagonism with the past, thus confirming its irrelevance for the political present ('the place of the past is in history'). The signifiers of dialogue, understanding, good will ('spoke to each other', 'demonstrated the will') are, in contrast, associated with the future and its normative correctness ('we should'). By outlining the clear direction of this future (from the periphery to the heart of Europe), the vice minister indicated the desired change in Macedonia's identity: living up to 'the standards of Europe'. It is the ambition and appeal of European-ness that encouraged Macedonia to put the past behind it, together with the antagonisms that it had nourished.

National minorities and narrating nationhood

While taking the concern for the state's territorial integrity off the agenda of Bulgarian–Macedonian relations, the resumed dialogue between Bulgaria and Macedonia brought back to the fore antagonisms caused by divergent interpretations of nationhood in the narratives on minority communities at home and abroad. The central clash was predetermined by Bulgaria's insistence on a monolithic nation and Macedonia's comfortable accommodation of the idea of national minorities.

The incompatibility of the notion of national minority with the Bulgarian narration of nationhood was asserted at many levels. Even when ratifying the Council of Europe's Framework Convention for the Protection of National Minorities (7 May 1999), Bulgaria did so with the reservation that it had no national minorities.[142] Ratification was meant more as a gesture of goodwill and participation in common European processes rather than as an active legal framework for minority protection. This interpretation of nationhood was complemented by Bulgarian narratives on Macedonia, positioning it as an element of Bulgarian identity (ethnic, cultural, political, territorial, national). On the basis of it, Bulgaria expected a political relationship defined along the lines of 'brotherhood' (as systematic references to Macedonia as 'brothers' suggest) but also a clear order of the superiority of its own position. This interpretation made the issue of Macedonian minorities politically irrelevant and even

---

141. Boris Trajkovski, Sofia, 12 February 1999, BTA Courier Service.
142. See Bulgarian reservations, plus parliamentarian and jurist Lyuben Kornezov's special opinion of the 'legal absurdity' of the document: interview, *Duma* newspaper, 20 February 1999.

offensive. Macedonia's refusal to comply with it and acknowledge the element of commonality provoked Bulgaria's alienation and frustration, since reconstructing Macedonia as a foreign Other would also imply reconstructing its image of Self. As a consequence Bulgaria resorted to narratives of a prodigal brother, lost but still loved from afar.[143]

Macedonia, on the other hand, had positioned Bulgaria precisely as the constitutive Other in narrating its own story of difference. Together with the other antagonists of Macedonian Selfhood, Bulgaria was expected to either encroach upon or accept it, but was not permitted to participate in it. In the Macedonian interpretation of nationhood, the issue of minorities was not only politically relevant but indispensable to establishing any meaningful inter-state dialogue with Bulgaria. It could not be marginalised because its regulation indicated that the dialogue was being held from a position of equality: that of two distinct nations. Bulgaria's refusal to communicate on this basis and even acknowledge its relevance alienated Macedonia even further and helped reinforce the narrative construction of Bulgaria in terms of encroaching Otherness. This is why Macedonia explicitly rejected the 'brotherhood' narratives and insisted that the relationship was one of enmity, reflecting this in its position on national minorities at home and abroad.

Thus, the antagonisation of nationhood narratives had a serious impact on intra- and international relations in Bulgaria and Macedonia. The breakthrough in the language dispute did improve dialogue between the two states by placing their relations in the common realm of Europeanisation.[144] But it did not significantly alter narratives of nationhood determining the two states' positions on the minority issue. Their modification required concerted political effort and took time because they formed part of the history of the national Self. What the initiation of bilateral dialogue within the Europeanisation dynamic did was to distance the formulation of policy from interpretation of history.

The key sign of this change is the official rhetorical dissociation from historical narratives by ascribing their validity to the realm of the sciences, not politics. As early as the mid-1990s an improvement in the blocked relations was related to leaving the 'historical definition of national identity [to] the scientists'.[145] Around the time of negotiations on the Joint Declaration of 1999, the notion of Vergangenheitsbewälltigung designated the process as a success both domestically and internationally.[146] The imperatives of bilateral cooperation

---

143. 'In the end, we are brothers' –*Demokratsia* newspaper, and 'Seeing Macedonia is like meeting a loved relative whom you have expected for years', *Demokratsia* newspaper, 27 May 1992; 'Macedonia, our beautiful nostalgia', *Demokratsia* newspaper, 22 May 1992, etc.

144. Ivan Krastev, 'Bulgaria cut its "Macedonian" knot', interview for *Capital* newspaper, 13 February 1999.

145. Georgi Parvanov, interview for *Puls* newspaper, 26 April 1996.

146. Boris Trajkovski, Sofia, 12 February 1999, BTA Courier Service; Krasimir Karakachanov, interview in *Demokratsia* newspaper, 11 February 1999, Kostov and Georgievski at the press conference in Sofia, 22 February 1999, BTA Courier Service.

as an indicator of normalisation and, consequently, Europeanisation sidetracked concerns about history and took them off the immediate political agenda of inter-state dialogue.

Obviously, the deep sedimentation of narratives of nationhood did not permit their removal from the political rhetoric all together. They continued to be present in everyday politics even though they were no longer reflected in the official position of the state. In Bulgaria this was demonstrated in the political rhetoric surrounding the activities of various pro-Macedonian cultural and political organisations domestically. In Macedonia it was voiced in the concerns about surrendering the interests of the Macedonian nation by improving relations with Bulgaria. The text of the Joint Declaration limiting the Macedonian constitutional provision about care for minority communities abroad was interpreted as a limitation of one of the state's key responsibilities for protecting the national identity abroad:

> Macedonia is to enter a period of uncertainty [which is suggested by] the indications of renouncing the Macedonian language and the Macedonian minority in the Republic of Bulgaria, its statements of the factual non-existence of the Macedonian nation, etc.[147]

The attempt at resecuritisation ('a period of uncertainty') of the issues of language, minorities and nationhood in view of renewed relations with Bulgaria is indicative of the fluid character of the newly established frame for dialogue. Agreements with Bulgaria could still be interpreted as a threat to Macedonian national interests and identity.[148] These interpretations are related to the instability of Europe's normative power in Macedonia: the first tentative steps in the process of Europeanisation had not been sufficient to establish a stable institutional and political consensus on Europeanisation as the leading strategic goal of Macedonian politics:

> Should Macedonia have been so clever as to become Europe's experimental dough, a test zeppelin for somebody's questionable visions of reorganising international order?[149]

Putting in doubt the rationality of Macedonian policies in view of its compliance with European rules about international behaviour illustrated Macedonia's ambiguity about Europe. The suggested loss of identity ('experimental dough') and lack of a clear ethical trajectory ('a test zeppelin') indicated the most common avenues that this ambiguity took.

---

147. Plenary session, 12 February 1999.

148. 'Giving up our constitutional responsibilities', 'a step towards abandoning our compatriots in Bulgaria', 'a recognition that the Macedonian language is only a language under our constitution', Ilinka Mitreva, plenary session, 12 February 1999, 30.

149. Ibid.

But even though present in political discourse, these interpretations no longer appeared as the official position of the state. In its formal communication with Bulgaria, Macedonia adhered strictly to the rhetoric of Europeanisation, which opened and maintained a realm of commonality with Bulgaria. It is this discursive realm that enabled the initiation of inter-state dialogue. With the progress of the Europeanisation process in both states, commonality between the two states stabilised and expanded, which further marginalised conflictual interpretations as incompatible with it.

A similar dynamic is noticeable in Bulgaria where the empowerment of Europe was accelerated by Bulgaria's earlier progress in the Europeanisation process. Opposition to the proposed Bill for Regional Development in the Bulgarian parliament, in its section on trans-border cooperation between municipalities in Bulgaria and Macedonia, for example, was counter-attacked by a consistent argument in favour of European practices:

> We need to demonstrate that we are working for regional development so that Europe can look at us with fresh eyes;[150]

> the European Charter for Trans-border Cooperation, which we ratified: [...] this is how Europe has regulated this [field], [...] In Europe and in the normal world in general, things are being done this way;[151]

> We need to be in line with the European criteria.[152]

The vice prime minister reinforced the power of this line of argumentation by attaching it to the notion of 'national interest' and 'patriotism':

> I do not think that there exists a Bulgarian with national pride and patriotism who would be ashamed of what we are doing to open the borders with neighbouring states and turn them into an open door between us [...] and Macedonia.[153]

Emphasising the compatibility of the European norm with the notions of 'national pride and patriotism' was central in empowering Europe, particularly with regard to improving relations with Macedonia. The above statements illustrate how European references were utilised to transgress the constraints of national space and attach the notion of national interest to a realm of commonality that included Macedonia as an immediate Other.

---

150. Petar Mutafchiev, Democratic Left, plenary session, 5 March 1999.
151. Iliyan Popov, Union of Democratic Forces, plenary session, 5 March 1999.
152. Todor Kostadinov, plenary session, 5 March 1999.
153. Plenary session, 5 March 1999, Vice Prime Minister Evgeni Bakyrdzhiev in response to an enquiry from George Ganchev.

Narratives on national minorities, collective minority rights and political representation

Marginalising conflictual narratives of nationhood as pertaining to the realm of science and thus irrelevant to the political, however, proved more challenging when it came to the official state policy on minority status, minority protection and minority rights. Even though the official positions of the two states confirmed the political will to detach policies from mutually exclusive historical interpretations, they found it hard to reflect these positions in their domestic policies when faced with contentious minority demands. Against the background of progressing Europeanisation and narratives of good bilateral relations and cooperation, the minority issue was taken off the agenda of foreign policy. A turning point in this sense was the 1999 Joint Declaration, which confirmed that there was enough political will in the two states to overcome all sources of tension, including the ones related to the area of minority issues. Several of the text's provisions, among them renouncing the separatist appeals of public or private subjects, the attempts at intervention in the other state's domestic affairs, and negative propaganda, aimed to normalise this policy area.[154] Indeed, conflictual minority issues gradually ceased to appear as an object of official bilateral dialogue between Bulgaria and Macedonia. But they continued to plague discursive spaces of domestic politics in both states even after the Declaration.

Ultimately, conflict revolved around the issue of minorities' collective rights and political representation. In general, the two states had legitimate minority policies towards other minority groups and as a rule had granted them extensive minority protection. But they were reluctant to treat each other's minorities in the same way. In view of divergent historical interpretations of the national Other, these positions are unsurprising. But in the context of bilateral rapprochement they began to stand out as an aberration. Identifying various minority demands and the ways they were channelled in the two states reveals the mechanism of accommodation of minority narratives in the changing context of Europeanisation.

Shortly after the beginning of Bulgaria's transition the public presence of representatives of the Macedonian minority in Bulgaria was made known through various registered organisations and formations. They ranged from cultural and educational associations[155] to political parties. But while the organisation and functioning of the various cultural associations (through public activities, publications, etc.) was understood as part of the democratisation process, the registration of political parties was seen as more problematic. This was partly related to Bulgaria's legislative framework (the constitutional provision prohibiting the organisation of political parties along ethnic lines, the protection of the territorial integrity of the state and considerations of national security). Legislative considerations, however,

---

154. Text of the Joint Declaration, Art.11 and following provisions.

155. For example, the All-Bulgarian Union 'Macedonia', the Union of Macedonian Cultural and Educational Associations, and the Macedonian Scientific Institute.

were not decisive: there were ways to abide by them and still provide minority political representation, which is illustrated by the active participation of the party of the ethnic Turks in Bulgarian political life. What played a decisive role in the problematisation of Macedonian minority party representation in Bulgaria were political considerations. They were associated with the political taboo on discussions of separatism and distinct national identification, in view of the salience of the stories of territorial integrity and national unity in the narration of Bulgaria's national identity. This is demonstrated in the nuanced attitude towards the different Macedonian organisations.

Generally, Macedonian organisations in Bulgaria, and specifically political parties, can be divided in two groups: pro-Bulgarian and pro-Macedonian (see summary in Arsenova, 2001). The former claimed to represent the Macedonian minority as 'Bulgarians from the region of Macedonia and nothing else'.[156] In their view, 'recognising the Macedonian nation [...] is a juridical absurdity'.[157] The latter group claimed to represent the Macedonian minority in Bulgaria as part of the Macedonian nation in the Republic of Macedonia and in the rest of the Macedonian region. They wanted 'to unite all Macedonians from Aegean, Albanian, Vardar and Pirin Macedonia and their descendants living in Bulgaria'.[158] Unsurprisingly, the pro-Bulgarian group found it easier to make a permanent place for itself in the official Bulgarian political space. It was organised around the VMRO formation (one of the many who claimed ownership over the name) and declared its political presence as early as 1990. The majority of the demands it formulated under its programme were met almost immediately in the early 1990s,[159] among them to reopen the Macedonian Scientific Institute, to renew the activities of the Macedonian associations for culture and education, to restitute their property, etc.[160] In 1997 they even came to power as a coalition partner in the Kostov government of the United Democratic Forces. In the course of Europeanisation processes their active participation in formal politics forced them to adapt (Arsenova, 2001). On the one hand, they re-dressed their overt nationalist, and particularly anti-Macedonian, rhetoric in the guise of patriotism. They insisted that the Macedonian story remain unchanged in the children's schoolbooks.[161] On the other hand, they shifted the focus of their political efforts from the realm of

---

156. Valentin Kitanov, Executive Committee of VMRO–SMD (United Macedonian Revolutionary Organisation-Union of the Macedonian Associations) for *Trud* newspaper, 31 August 1993.
157. Stoyan Boyadzhiev, Chairman of VMRO–SDM for *Demokratsia* newspaper, 2 August 1994.
158. Art.1 of the Statute of VMRO–TMO (United Macedonian Revolutionary Organization – Traditional Macedonian Organization) Ilinden (independent) headed by George Solunski.
159. Programme Declaration of the Union of the Macedonian Cultural and Educational Associations published by BTA, 10 September 1990, BTA Courier Service.
160. The only one of their principal demands that could not be met was the return of the sarcophagus with the remains of the revolutionary Gotse Delchev, which are kept in Skopje: see Arsenova (2001).
161. Krasimir Karakachanov, 'Do not impinge on patriotism in the history textbooks', *24 Hours* newspaper, 1 December 1999.

bilateral relations (anti-Macedonianism in Macedonia) to the realm of domestic politics (pro-Macedonianism in Bulgaria), and their negative charge to positive. This is illustrated, for example, by abandoning their focus on confirming the 'actual' large numbers of ethnic Bulgarians in the Republic of Macedonia[162] in favour of concentrating on the Macedonian representation within the limits of Bulgaria.[163]

Accommodating the pro-Macedonian group of political parties in Bulgaria's legitimate political space proved more problematic, particularly in view of other antagonisms in Bulgarian–Macedonian bilateral relations in the 1990s. The more moderate formations among these groups, such as the VMRO – Traditional Macedonian Organisation Ilinden (led by George Solunski), were better tolerated. Their formal registration as political parties was facilitated by the explicit declaration that their organisation 'does not stake any territorial claims',[164] and does not aim to harm 'the territorial integrity of the state'.[165] The party never had any electoral significance due to the negligible number of its supporters and it did not attract any extraordinary political attention (due to its moderate programme), even though it existed for most of the 1990s. This is in contrast with the extreme pro-Macedonian political party United Macedonian Organisation (UMO) Ilinden (led by Yordan Kostadinov). It staked its claims for political relevance as early as 1990, declaring that it represented the 'numerous' Macedonian minority in Bulgaria. According to its articles of association and its programme, it aimed to 'unite all Macedonians in Bulgaria on a regional and cultural basis' and to achieve 'the recognition of the Macedonian minority in Bulgaria', as well as to work for the 'political development of Macedonia'.[166] And while these aims did not represent any unambiguous threat, the political rhetoric of its leaders made the party's extremist platform clear:

> You [Bulgaria] cut off Pirin Macedonia and annexed it. The other two parts of Macedonia you sold to the Serbs and the Greeks. You are separatists and your separatism needs to be corrected now.[167]

Its registration was, predictably, refused in subsequent court judgements of 1990 and 1991, where the courts found that the association's aims were 'directed against the unity of the nation', that it 'advocated national and ethnic hatred', and that it was 'dangerous for the territorial integrity of Bulgaria'.[168] It is interesting to

---

162. Karakachanov in *Standard* newspaper, 31 August 1993.
163. Karakachanov in *24 hours* newspaper, 23 September 1999.
164. Art.22 of the Statutes, Archive Ethno-sociology Archive of the Central Party Archive, Vol.4.
165. Platform Declaration of 14 November 1989, Ethno-sociology Archive of the Central Party Archive, Vol.4.
166. *Stankov and the United Macedonian Organization Ilinden v. Bulgaria*.
167. Yordan Kostadinov, interview for *Continent* newspaper, 25 April 1995.
168. *United Macedonian Organisation Ilinden–PIRIN and Others v. Bulgaria*.

note that, much like the Albanian minority in Macedonia, the pro-Macedonian activists in Bulgaria sought to capture the signifiers of Europe for the purposes of their own cause: 'Europe should unite Macedonia in the future so that there can be peace in the Balkans'.[169] Linking the unification of Macedonia with peace in the Balkans revealed a political agenda that was not necessarily compatible with Europeanisation processes. It is significant, nevertheless, that Europe was being utilised to counteract the majority's nationalist agendas (in a way similar to Albanian demands in Macedonia). In the context of hegemonic nationalism in the early years of transition, however, and in view of the political party's generally extremist rhetoric, the existence of such a formation was found inadmissible by the government, the law, and the general public. It did, however, acquire significant media presence, which notably politicised the issue of the Macedonian minority's political representation.

Unable to achieve legitimate political status, the organisation split in 1994 when the more moderate activists (around Ivan Singartiyski) founded their own party, UMO Ilinden–PIRIN. The activity of this organisation marked a peak in the politicisation of the issue of Macedonian minority representation in Bulgaria.[170] After amending its founding statutes, which the Sofia City Court[171] had found to be in conflict with Art.44 (2) of the constitution,[172] UMO Ilinden–PIRIN was formally registered as a political party in early 1999. Successful registration allowed it to run in the following local government elections and win two mayorship seats and three seats for municipal councillors in the Pirin Macedonia region.[173] This was significant, because it created the context for normalising the issue of Macedonian minority representation by attaching it to the processes of democratic representation. Against the general bilateral rapprochement between Bulgaria and Macedonia, initiated with the closure of the language dispute, this was an indication of political goodwill to implement the declared principles of amity in Bulgarian domestic politics. It was also in line with Bulgaria's progress in Europeanisation processes.

Seized by sixty-one members of parliament of various political backgrounds, however, Bulgaria's Constitutional Court issued a judgement in 2000, proclaiming the political party unconstitutional under Art.44(2) of the Bulgarian constitution. In its ruling, the court treated the UMO Ilinden–PIRIN party as a descendant of the extremist UMO Ilinden, and took into consideration not its official statutes but the activities of its leaders, including them under the umbrella of the banned party. Even though there was evidence for such argumentation, the suggestion that the final

---

169. Yordan Kostadinov, interview for *Continent* newspaper, 25 April 1995.
170. References to key public arguments by *Information Agency Focus News*, 25 July 2006, Archive Service.
171. The legal institution with jurisdiction over the registration of political parties in Bulgaria.
172. Prohibiting organisations whose activity is aimed against the sovereignty, territorial integrity and the unity of the nation, instigating ethnic or national hatred, etc.
173. In Gotsedelchevsko, according to BTA, 25 October 1999.

decision of the Court was influenced by political rather than juridical factors could not be avoided. Invoking Art.44(2) suggests a serious threat to national security. The actual political significance of the UMO Ilinden–PIRIN party, however, was negligible, as demonstrated in its electoral performance: it won 0.03 per cent of votes, which equalled approximately 2,500 people.[174] This, together with the fact that the party upheld a very moderate platform and maintained its activity within the limits of the law, indicated that there was little evidence of any actual threat to the national security of the state. The interpretation of conflict with Art.44(2) was based on discussion, (not on subversive action) on the territorial borders of the state:[175] a subject that was taboo in Bulgarian political and public space in view of the salience of the territorial integrity signifier of national identity. In fact, public debate on the existing territorial borders of a state should have been a legitimate subject of discussion in a democratic society and Bulgarian primary legislation provides for the possibility of changing them by a parliamentary decision for the sake of ratifying an international treaty.[176] Therefore, it was not so much legal but political argumentation that motivated the Constitutional Court's ban. Despite the partial marginalisation of explicitly nationalist political rhetoric and agendas in Bulgarian politics and public spheres, nationalist interpretations of key elements of national identity did apparently influence the constitutional judgement.

A sudden blow to the years of the democratic government's consistent effort to normalise bilateral relations with Macedonia, as well as an obstacle to Bulgaria's progress in the Europeanisation process, such a judgement can be best understood contextually. Around the beginning of the millennium progress towards Europeanisation had reached already visible dimensions. Europeanisation was present in the justification and interpretation of almost all politically significant decisions at state level and in rhetoric from the entire political spectrum. On the issue of minority rights, however, Europeanisation was notably ambivalent. Lacking a definitive reference point in its own legislation, the EU followed the lead of the Council of Europe, which produced a relevant international instrument only in the mid-1990s.[177] Controversial in its missing definition of the term 'national minority', the instrument was not even ratified by all EU member states at the time, or it was ratified with reservations (e.g. Germany and Luxembourg). Minority protection was not formally part of EU membership criteria (which was formulated in the early 1990s) even though

---

174. Momchil Milev, 'Theory of Macedonian conspiracy', *Capital* newspaper, 3 March 2000.

175. Based on a letter from Kiril Ivanov to the Open Society Institute in Bucharest, containing radical demands for separating Pirin Macedonia from Bulgaria. The letter reached the Court before one of the key deliberations and changed the direction of the debates. See *United Macedonian Organisation Ilinden-PIRIN and Others v. Bulgaria* (Application no. 59489/00); also Milev, 'Theory of Macedonian conspiracy', *Capital* newspaper, 3 March 2000.

176. Constitution of the Republic of Bulgaria, Art.5(4).

177. The 1992 European Charter for Regional and Minority Languages, the Framework Convention for the Protection of National Minorities (1994), and the system for protection developed under the ECHR, which set Europe's minimum standards of equality and non-discrimination.

indirectly, through the requirement for functioning democracy and the human rights provisions of the *acquis*, it had acquired significance in membership preparation and negotiation. So, predictably, the normative power of European references in the area of minority protection was unconvincing and this had been noted in public debates on the issue in both Bulgaria and Macedonia. Clashing with the meanings upheld by powerful nationalist interpretations, references to European norms and standards in the area inevitably faced resistance. In the immediate aftermath of war in Kosovo and escalating inter-ethnic tension in Macedonia, the question of recognising minority status and granting minority rights outside the already established Bulgarian model of ethnic accommodation became extremely problematic.

This context helps us to understand the decision to ban the political party of pro-Macedonian activists in Bulgaria, despite the marginalisation of nationalist narratives interpreting Macedonianism as a threat to Bulgaria's national identity and despite the empowerment of European narratives positioning Macedonia in the frame of amity and cooperation. Predictably, this provoked negative reactions from the Macedonian state. The Macedonian president expressed 'regret for the decision of the Bulgarian magistrates and hope that the Bulgarian authorities will be more careful in the future with regard to the delicate bilateral issues'.[178] The prime minister confirmed that 'the decision does not help the good bilateral relations'.[179] The foreign minister voiced doubt about Bulgaria's European future, 'because it does not respect minority rights'.[180] The Macedonian parliament reacted by adopting a declaration of support for the members of UMO Ilinden–PIRIN.[181] It is important to note, however, that these official Macedonian reactions, publicised immediately after the publication of the Bulgarian court's decision, did not have any further impact on bilateral relations. They were necessary in view of the media turmoil caused in Macedonian public space but at the official state level they had no further consequences. The official visit of the Bulgarian president two months later was expected as planned and the heads of state and government extended a 'cordial welcome'[182] to Stoyanov throughout his stay. More importantly, the Bulgarian president was also welcomed by the Macedonian media. Even the notoriously suspicious Bulgarian media noted the 'warm' reception.[183] At the formal press conference given by the two heads of state in Skopje the Bulgarian was indeed asked about the constitutional ban on UMO Ilinden–PIRIN but his response satisfied the audience. Stoyanov explained that the political party was banned because it called for a change in the state's territorial borders, which

---

178. Trajkovski, reported in *Capital* newspaper, 10 March 2000.
179. Georgievski, reported in *Capital* newspaper, 10 March 2000.
180. Dimitrov, reported in *Capital* newspaper, 10 March 2000.
181. Plenary session, 9 March 2000.
182. Editorial, Sasho Ordanoski, *Forum* journal, Skopje, 10 May 2000.
183. Aleksey Yurdanov, 'Macedonia Less Suspicious towards Bulgaria', editorial, *Capital* newspaper, 19 May 1999.

contradicted the constitution.[184] Nevertheless, the two presidents declared their accordance on a series of issues, which was confirmed in the signed treaties and agreements, and reiterated their goodwill to further develop bilateral cooperation, in view of European integration. In this sense the issue of the constitutional ban did not affect the manner in which talks were held, nor did it affect their outcome. This suggests that nationalist political agendas had already been discredited at official state level, even though they were still present in the domestic political space around minority issues.

In Macedonia the discursive dynamic around the issue of political representation of a pro-Bulgarian minority evolved in exactly the same fashion, despite Macedonian protests against the banning of pro-Macedonian political parties in Bulgaria. The political parties and organisations claiming to represent the Bulgarian minority were banned from official activity and registration. Several of the organisations acquired greater public significance, either because of their media presence or because of the publicity they achieved through alternative means. Among the political parties two have been more visible. The pro-Bulgarian VMRO–Tatkovinsko (led by Dimitar Tsarnomarov), one of the many organisations laying claims to the historical name of the Macedonian liberation movements, interpreted the state of Macedonia as a second state of the Bulgarian people and demanded that 'the borders of 1913 be erased'.[185] According to the statements of its members, the organisation had set up committees in 'almost all towns of the Republic of Macedonia'.[186] However, it was never officially registered. The Human Rights Party (of Iliya Ilievski) was the other pro-Bulgarian organisation that acquired visible public presence. Its leader claimed that it represented 'more than 200,000 Bulgarians [as] members'.[187] The party denied the distinct character of the Macedonian nation, claiming that it was Bulgarian,[188] and declared that Bulgarians in Macedonia were being 'assimilated and terrorised'[189] by the Skopje government, which was why it announced that it wanted 'Bulgaria to become homeland for Bulgarians in Macedonia'.[190] By the end of 1993 the party was officially prohibited as unconstitutional.[191] The court's argumentation referred to the activity of the party's leader, who threatened the territorial integrity and borders of the Macedonian state.[192]

---

184. Stoyanov and Trajkovski, press conference in Skopje, 19 May, BTA Courier Service.
185. Dimitar Tsarnomarov, *Makedoniya* newspaper, 18–25 April 1995.
186. Ibid.
187. Iliya Ilievski, *Novinar* newspaper, 2 November 1993.
188. *Trud* newspaper, 27 January 1994.
189. *Zemya* newspaper, 9 June 1993.
190. *Svoboden Narod* newspaper, 9 June 1993.
191. Constitutional Court decision of 9 December 1993.
192. Constitution of the Republic of Macedonia, Art.3. The same judicial position applied to Bulgaria.

In the context of the increased domestic instability of the early transition years and international uncertainty as a result of non-recognition, nationalist narratives of Macedonian identity prevented any interpretations of such public demands other than as threats to the national security of the Macedonian state. But even under the government of Georgievski in the late 1990s, which was notoriously 'pro-Bulgarian',[193] these organisations failed to establish any meaningful dialogue with the state or with the public. This suggests that they gradually lost political relevance. Indeed, a new descendent pro-Bulgarian organisation, the RADKO Association (led by Vladimir Paunkovski) did register formally in 2000.[194] Its political platform, however, was much more moderate than that of its predecessors. It called for 'cultural and spiritual unity' with Bulgaria but clearly avoided any territorial references.[195] Among its key goals was achieving equal status for the Bulgarian minority with that of all the other nationalities mentioned in the Macedonian constitution which represented a 'constitutive element' of the Macedonian nation. Consequently, the organisation also demanded that the Bulgarian language be one of the official languages in the Republic.[196] As in Bulgaria, however, judicial arguments gave way to political considerations. The seized Constitutional Court found that the organisation's platform and statutes were 'aimed at forceful change of the official state order, impeded the Macedonian people from freely expressing their national identity, and instigated national hatred and intolerance'. Clearly designating the pro-Bulgarian association's programme as a threat to Macedonian identity in the official position of the state was incompatible with its declared political will to advance bilateral trust and understanding. The situation bore significant similarities with the reaction to the registration of the pro-Macedonian political party in Bulgaria. However, in the Macedonian context it is important to emphasise that the court decision was taken amidst the ongoing civil conflict between the Macedonian majority and the Albanian minority,[197] which added utmost urgency to the matter, already framed in the discourse of national security. Obviously, in a situation of open conflict caused by extremist minority demands, the possibility of identical development along the lines of another majority–minority relationship was inadmissible. Again, as in Bulgaria, the judicial outcome was not transferred to the bilateral space of communication and did not affect Bulgarian–Macedonian relations in any harmful manner. As soon as the inter-ethnic conflict was over and the Macedonian state began to normalise its politics again, inter-state dialogue with Bulgaria was resumed with the early 2002 visit of the next Bulgarian president (Parvanov, in February 2002).

---

193. As accused by the Macedonian media and opposition, see *Capital* newspaper editorial, 12 May 2000.
194. From the Statutes of Incorporation of the RADKO Association-Ohrid. Available at http://web.archive.org/web/20120220044211/ http://www.radkomk.com/STATUT.htm (accessed 1 June 2015).
195. Ibid.
196. Ibid.
197. US Institute of Peace report on Macedonia, 2002.

It is important to note that in both Bulgaria and Macedonia the issue of recognising national minorities, when it came to Macedonian and Bulgarian minority groups respectively, was framed in a discourse that was slightly different from the discourse surrounding other national minority groups. While the terms 'Turkish minority' or 'Albanian minority' or 'Roma minority' had been established unambiguously to designate the respective communities, in the case of the Macedonian and Bulgarian minorities the denominator used was not that of nationality but of affiliation. Thus in Bulgaria one officially spoke of 'Macedonianists' while in Macedonia one spoke of 'Bulgarophiles'. In view of the sedimentation of divergent historical narratives excluding the Other as a constitutive element from the national identity construction, this is unsurprising. Even in the context of Europeanisation and European re-narration of the national stories, these divergent narratives are still present because they are part of the historical past. Europeanisation as a narrative has been predominantly focused on the political present and future, despite its more recent attempts to engage the past in an attempt to summon commonality. It came into being precisely because it enabled closure of the (conflictual) past. In this sense the story of Europeanisation is meant to shift the focus from the past to the possibilities of the present and future and, with time, to create new stories out of them. This helps understand why Bulgaria and Macedonia continued to speak in the categorisations of their nationalist pasts, where there could be no reconciliation between Self and Other. When it came to minorities, they simply had no different story to tell. What is significant, however, is that the two states no longer used conflictual categories in their official communications with each other and no longer allowed them to affect their bilateral relations. Articulated as an official position of the state, this was one of the key predicates for the marginalisation of minority related antagonisms from their immediate political agendas. In the long term, the depoliticisation of the issues could create an environment conductive to finding mutually acceptable solutions.

In collecting the national census data from the years 2001 (Bulgaria) and 2002 (Macedonia) both states provided the technical capability for their citizens to declare their ethnic and national identity as Macedonian or Bulgarian respectively. This is worth highlighting, since the structure of the previous censuses, particularly the first censuses from the post-communist period, had been questioned as prejudiced or manipulative in this regard. As a result of the change, 5,071 people in Bulgaria identified themselves as ethnically Macedonian[198] and 1,417 people in Macedonia identified themselves as of Bulgarian origin.[199] These numbers may seem insignificant, especially compared to the claims of the minority activists in both states for thousands of members of the respective minorities but they were largely confirmed in the 2011 census data from both states. But what is significant is that states officially provided the option to declare citizenship and

198. See http://www.nsi.bg/Census/Ethnos.htm (accessed 1 June 2015).
199. See http://makstat.stat.gov.mk/pxweb2007bazi/dialog/statfile18.asp (accessed 1 June 2015).

national and ethnic identity as separate categories. Despite the juridical bans on political party registration for minority organisations, the pro-Macedonian party in Bulgaria did have a chance to participate in local elections[200] and the return from its participation also confirmed the census data. In Macedonia pro-Bulgarian parties were not allowed into the electoral competition, so we have no basis of comparison there. But if the small numbers of the Macedonian and Bulgarian minorities in the two states should be questioned at all, it is worth considering as well how legitimate the claims of minorities' political representatives are, and whether minority rhetoric is not utilised for the advancement of other political agendas without either comparable representation or necessity among the minority communities. This suggestion raises concern not least because politicising narratives of national identity in a conflictual manner could have serious negative implications both for the normality of domestic politics and for the normality of bilateral relations. One way to neutralise such attempts would be to capture minority representation in the mechanisms and logic of democratic politics and gradually normalise the rhetoric of urgency surrounding it. What problematises this option in the context of Europeanisation is the fact that Europe itself is often ambivalent on it. Undecided between individual and collective protection and rights (Kymlicka, 1995), integration in Europe has so far managed to avoid taking a firm stance on minority representation, despite already established jurisdiction in the European Court on Human Rights on the matter (e.g. Gilbert, 2002). In this sense the Europeanisation of identity narratives on minorities is work in progress, in both the internal and the external realms of Europeanisation.

Europeanisation effects on identity narratives on national minorities

National minority issues in Bulgarian–Macedonian relations offer particularly difficult cases of Europeanisation of national identity narratives. The analysis above shows that bilateral antagonisms related to national minorities in the two states are linked to three problem areas (Table 5.3). One is the employment of minority stories in the securitisation of territorial integrity. Another is the incompatibility between minority narratives and majority identities in view of nationhood as the centre of the political community of the state. A third problem area is the normative ambiguity about granting collective minority rights and especially rights of collective political representation. An inability to find working solutions for these problem areas that both sides agree to is largely related to the policy vacuum in regulating national minorities at the supranational level. At the same time, ambiguities about the meaning of national minorities in EU politics do not stimulate political will to remove national minority issues from the scope of 'high politics' (defence, security, foreign policy). The embeddedness of the meaning of national minority into deeply sedimented historical narratives of identity is also a factor in modifying the narration of minorities to include Europe.

---

200. This happened in the period immediately following the establishment of the party, before it was banned.

Table 5.3: Narratives on national minorities in Bulgaria and Macedonia

State	Bulgaria	Macedonia
Meanings upheld by nationalism	Territorial threat	Territorial threat
	Incompatibility with narration of nationhood	Incompatibility with narration of nationhood
	Impossibility for political participation	Impossibility for political participation
Meanings upheld by Europeanisation	Taking minority narratives off the agenda of foreign and security policy through dissociation from the signifier of territory	Detaching narratives on Bulgaria from the positions of 'occupier' and 'aggressor'
	Distancing policy from history	Maintaining a realm of commonality
	Ambivalence between rhetoric and policy	Ambivalence between rhetoric and policy

It obstructs the decoupling of the narrative from historical interpretations and its attachment to the practicalities of the democratic process. Europeanisation effects on conflictual narratives of identity focused on the issue of national minorities are thus constrained by several factors, none of which has been consensually addressed within the EU. This means that nationalist interpretations of the meaning of national minorities and their place in the discursive pattern of national identity are much more difficult to modify through references to Europe. Current debates about inclusion and exclusion throughout the realm of integration testify, among other things, that Europe has not yet found a plausible solution to the clash between nationalist and European interpretations of national differences. At the same time, the exclusionary and divisive politics engendered by nationalist interpretations of minorities within the construction of national identity undermines the ability of nationalism to legitimise the discursive boundaries of political community in Europe. In the context of Bulgarian–Macedonian relations, this exclusionary potential created the impression of incompatibility with the idea of European integration. In this sense the alternative, European re-narration of the discursive element of national minorities, albeit non-consensual, offered a more plausible prospect of finding a legitimate solution to the place of national minorities. This was especially so against the background of European citizenship and the transformed functions of national borders in the EU. Bulgaria and Macedonia were by no means the only countries in the post-communist Europe at the time to struggle with finding a non-antagonistic formula for accommodating national minorities within their national identity constructions. The mere fact of this discursive struggle is evidence of the impact of Europeanisation. It also signifies a renewed search for legitimacy.

Conclusion: Comparing identity narratives of Otherness

Comparing modifications in narratives on minorities with those in narratives on recognition and language reveals important aspects of the discursive logic of re-narrating national identity with views of Europeanisation. In the first place, it demonstrates that, in time, European interpretations begin to acquire a taken-for-granted quality. Narratives telling the European story of recognition, for instance, appeared dominant during the late transition, despite the controversies that they raised around the actual time of recognition. They were no longer challenged by alternative interpretations. Nationalist interpretations of language also gradually ceased to appear in official state rhetoric, despite their deep sedimentation and greater popular appeal. By the time the issue of minorities had acquired more visible political dimensions, even the extremely salient nationalist interpretations of language were easily removable from formal inter-state dialogue. This suggests that European readings of national identity are stabilised in the course of advancing Europeanisation and have the potential to dislocate nationalist interpretations.

Second, the comparison reveals that articulating European meanings of central identity narratives becomes easier with time. With the progress of integration efforts by the two states, highly antagonistic interpretations became problematic owing to the simple fact that inter-state/inter-ethnonational conflictuality is normatively incompatible with the European project. The gradual empowerment of Europeanisation highlighted the incapacity of nationalism to uphold national identity in a manner adequate to the requirements of the process of preparation for membership negotiations. This emphasised the immediate relevance of Europeanisation to national politics.

Third, placing the three narrative groups of identity against each other and comparing the modifications that occurred in them in the course of Europeanisation reveals that some discursive elements are more difficult to modify than others. Nationalist narratives on minorities, for instance, did appear domestically at official state level even when other nationalist identity interpretations in Bulgarian–Macedonian relations had already been compromised. But they disappeared from official bilateral dialogue, which created the condition of possibility for their depoliticisation and eventual marginalisation in the public sphere. The meaning of minority representation, in particular, proved especially hard to modify in line within European narratives. This is related to historically established links between political representation and the legitimacy of political community centred around a nationalist vision of identity. The difficulty in modifying established interpretations of identity signals where the discursive omissions of Europeanisation are to be sought with regard to renegotiating collective belonging.

Overall, re-narrating national identity narratives of the Other in the course of preparation to join the integration project facilitated reconciliation along most lines of bilateral conflictuality and opened avenues for further rapprochement. Overcoming antagonisms significantly boosted the self-esteem function of national identity. At the same time, it enabled the inclusion of the Other in the discursive construction of national Self in a way that ensured continuity and credibility: by making Europe part of the identity construction. This radically modified the discursive boundaries of the national political community, thus adapting it to the imperatives of transnational politics. These outcomes visibly improved the legitimacy of the national political communities.

Chapter Six

Narrating National Identity within the Realm of Europe

Having established the dominant interpretations of identity narratives determining the position of Self and their possible implications for Bulgarian–Macedonian relations (Chapter Four), the analysis then followed three narrative groups maintaining bilateral conflictuality (Chapter Five). Identifying changes in their discursive narration with the progress of Europeanisation, the investigation established a visible trend towards reconciliation along most of the conflictual narratives. Enabling reconciliation changed the discursive position of Other along the axes of bilateral relations. The purpose of Chapter Six is to establish how this change fed back into the domestic discursive spaces. Focusing on the same discursive elements that upheld national identity at the beginning of transition, this chapter aims to identify modifications in their interpretation in the late transition, during the course of Europeanisation. It is meant to close the chronological timeframe of the period under study.

Bulgarian national identity narratives of Self towards the end of transition

Bulgaria was formally invited to begin its negotiations for EU membership at the very end of the old millennium (10 December 1999 at the Helsinki European Council). Initiating the negotiations made visible the reality of integration preparations in a very practical way. This helped the political imagining of Bulgaria's European prospects and greatly facilitated the empowerment of Europe as a normative force. The progress towards Europeanisation was briefly destabilised by the moment of disenchantment related to the 'lagging' (Gati, 1996) behind the Visegrad states in their progress towards full membership and the inclusion of the Baltic states in the earlier enlargement wave.[1] But Bulgaria quickly recovered its Euro-enthusiasm as efforts in the negotiation processes began to receive immediate feedback from the EU and access to pre-accession funds. The thorough reforms that the EU itself undertook in order to be able to cope with the future large-scale enlargement (European Council in Nice, 2000) also asserted the prospect of Bulgaria's membership as a tangible strategic goal.

---

1. The Baltic states were not among the immediate referents of the 1993 Copenhagen Council appeal to the 'associated member states' to join the Community, whereas Bulgaria was; see Asya Bocheva, 'Bulgaria in Brussels' waiting room: enlargement is still seen as concerning only Poland, Czech republic and Hungary', *Capital* newspaper, 2 June 2000; 'The day we missed the wave', *Capital* newspaper, 14 December 2002.

The rhetoric of Europeanisation offered alternative meanings to key political categories and began to appear on every level and every dimension of political life as a legitimising strategy providing the norm. The prospect of EU membership as the ultimate positive affirmation of Bulgaria's 'European-ness' provided European rhetoric with credibility. This determined the political relevance of the interpretations provided by Europeanisation to the meaning of statehood and nationhood, which inevitably clashed with traditionally dominant nationalist interpretations. The clash produced a modified pattern of national identity that was more compatible with the changing political contexts of transnational politics and Europeanisation. The new interpretations did not dramatically rearrange the discursive elements sustaining national identity. National community, territory and purpose continued to represent elements upholding key national identity narratives, as their function in the structure of the nation-state had been historically conditioned as essential. In this sense, Europeanisation could not break the supporting web of nationalism because of its indispensability to statehood. What it did was gradually marginalise nationalism's key interpretations of national identity by emphasising different dimensions, opening up new possibilities, and rethinking established rules. It thus managed to modify the contents of each of the central identity elements and ultimately transform the entire construct. In the course of Europeanisation, national identity appeared more positive, more inclusive, and less focused on the past. The following paragraphs highlight the key aspects of these discursive modifications.

Identity narratives of national community

The interpretation of the meaning of nationhood in terms of national unity had become so salient at the beginning of Bulgaria's transition because it contained a formula for preserving the national community's integrity in view of the inter-ethnic tensions that had marred the period. Towards the end of Bulgaria's transition the issue was no longer on the 'urgent' political agenda, so the idea of national unity ceased to form the centre of political debate and was no longer the central object of securitisation practices. Recurrently present in official rhetoric from the early years of transition as a panaceaic legitimisation strategy, towards 2005 it was only invoked in the specific minority–majority context that originally increased its salience, and mostly in terms of historical self-appraisal, not in view of everyday politics.[2] This opened the political space for alternative articulations of the meaning of nationhood. Europeanisation provided the most relevant alternatives.

Despite the continued validity of the constitutional prohibition of ethnic parties, for instance, which originated in the nationalistic idea of a monolithic nation and its political representation at the national level, the locus of

---

2. e.g. Lyutfi Mestan at the sitting of the National Committee for Celebrating Bulgaria's Accession to the EU, 8 November 2006.

party activity was no longer limited within the nation. Political parties were increasingly being interpreted not as national formations *per se*, but as members of larger, European political families. In a televised interview in one of the political weeklies, the prime minister discusses the reaction of the Bulgarian (centre-right) democratic formations to impending EU membership in comparison with the reactions of their European equivalent, the European People's Party.[3] In a different, printed interview, he clarifies the positions of his own party in a similar way:

> The Bulgarian Socialist Party [...] is a full member of the Party of European Socialists. This means that our ideology and policies should concur with the basic principles and values in the policies of parties in this family.[4]

Insisting on the normative imperatives ensuing from membership in the European political family ('our policies should concur'), the prime minister emphasised this aspect of belonging. Membership in the European political community invoked not only privileges, but also duties. Shifting the boundaries of political party representation from the national to the European space was one way in which nationalist interpretations of national political community boundaries were being challenged. The idea of national unity was marginalised to give way to alternative values, articulated at national level but linking the national to a community of nations.

Key among these values are the imperatives of cooperation and tolerance domestically, and of partnership and dialogue externally. In contrast with the nationalist interpretation of a monolithic nation as a highest value, the discourse of Europeanisation emphasises the centrality of difference and interprets it as a context of opportunity. Inter-ethnic and inter-religious differences and their successful accommodation acquire salience as a marker of civilisation. Among the main contributions that Bulgaria would make with its prospective bid for EU membership, the president highlighted precisely this:

> Bulgaria will bring to the EU its example of cooperation and tolerance between ethnicities and religions. Our model of ethno-political accommodation is not new. [...] Bulgaria can offer its European partners this experience, if you would allow me the immodesty.[5]

Implying a lack of modesty in offering this contribution, the statement indicated the great value that is placed on the model of tolerance and cooperation. The stark contrast between the way Bulgarian national identity had been articulated

---

3. Sergey Stanishev, prime minister of the Republic of Bulgaria, in an interview for the Bulgarian National Television's political analysis show *Panorama*, 29 September 2006.
4. Stanishev, *Trud* newspaper, 4 September 2006.
5. President Georgi Parvanov, 'Bulgaria at the doorstep of the EU', lecture at the Friedrich Ebert Foundation, 24 February 2006.

at the very beginning of transition and during the course of Europeanisation is visible on this point. The idea of ethnic tolerance was interpreted as an essential characteristic of Bulgaria's transition, even though the early post-communist years had been strained precisely by inter-ethnic tensions caused by intolerance:

> The ethnic aspects of Bulgaria's transition [cannot be] underestimated or unappreciated.[6]

> We have a great advantage. With all our defects, we kept ethnic peace and tolerance, which is our great achievement.[7]

Marginalising the idea of unity and emphasising the formula of national tolerance and cooperation, Bulgaria's national identity construction appeared much more inclusive when re-narrated taking Europe into account. This is demonstrated in the interpretation of external relations, where the values of tolerance and cooperation were translated into the imperatives of partnership and dialogue.

> Characterised by intensive contacts at the level of all institutions, [...] Bulgarian–Macedonian relations are European in the true sense of the word and are a good example for all nations and the whole region.[8]

> I have had more than 15 meetings with the president of Macedonia in the last four years. There is no other period in our history so full of intensive political contact at all levels with Macedonia, Serbia and Montenegro, and the rest of our neighbours.[9]

Interpreting bilateral and multilateral institutional dialogue as the European norm and claiming excellence in it ('good example', 'no other period in our history'), this rhetoric positioned Bulgarian national identity firmly within the realm of Europeanisation. It also revealed the stark contrast with the previous decade, when silence in bilateral relations was interpreted as defending national identity claims.

The opening up of Bulgaria's national identity to transcend the constraints of the nation-state is also visible in the new articulations of the notion of national interest. It was no longer formulated as referring strictly to the national space

---

6. Parvanov, 'Bulgaria's European integration: lessons and challenges', speech at the University for National and World Economy conference 'Bulgaria's road to Europe', National Palace of Culture, 10 November 2004.

7. Stanishev, Bulgarian National Television, Kanal 1, 'Media control' discussion with representatives of leading media, 25 March 2006.

8. Parvanov, interview for Macedonian Nation Radio, 4 November 2006.

9. Parvanov, 'Bulgaria: a stabilising factor in South-Eastern Europe', speech for the Association for South-Eastern Europe, 25 February 2006.

but was interpreted to include the well-being of immediate neighbour states, the region and Europe in general:

> advocacy for the interests of our neighbours [...] is part of our national interest. Having stable neighbours. It is our national interest that our neighbours have a clear European perspective.[10]

Such an interpretation of national interest is significant because it implies a responsibility for the immediate national Other(s), which was no longer governed by the antagonistic non-cooperative Self–Other dialectic within the nation-state. Responsibility for the well-being of the Other and awareness of the intertwinement with the well-being of the Self are indicative of a shift in the Self–Other boundary beyond state borders. They are indicative of a sense of belonging to a community of states, expressed in a politically pragmatic way: through the common interest. The reference to the 'European perspective' of the immediate neighbours and its significance for the stability of the region clearly indicates this community.

In general, the rhetoric of Europeanisation modified interpretations of the meaning of nationhood in a way that notably marginalised nationalist interpretations of unity and exclusivity. Emphasising different national values, offering different opportunities for political action and articulating the national interest in a different manner, Europeanisation interpreted the meaning of nationhood in a more open, more inclusive, and more proactive manner, which notably modified the contents of Bulgarian national identity towards the end of Bulgaria's transition period to give it more legitimacy in the new context.

Identity narratives of territory

Europeanisation's interpretation of the meaning of territory had a similar effect. Nationalism's emphasis on the notion of territorial integrity as a highest national value gradually gave way to different interpretations of national territory. Perceiving territorial space in its entirety as a central aspect of Bulgarian national identity had not been replaced by a more flexible territorial arrangement in the short span of a decade and a half. But this perception had significantly been de-politicised. Domestic inter-ethnic relations and cross-border international relations were no longer interpreted as a threat to the state's territorial integrity. This allowed the political relevance of this interpretation of territory to diminish. At the same time, improved domestic inter-ethnic relations and regional international relations had come to be recognised as a political resource for legitimacy and prestige. This enabled territory to be imagined no longer as a fortress against the Other(s) but as a bridge towards them.

This modification in meaning has been illustrated by the changed significance of borders. Political emphasis was no longer put on their maintenance as

---

10. Parvanov, 'Bulgaria: a stabilising factor in South-Eastern Europe'.

barriers (in terms of barbed wire fences, increased numbers of border guards, etc.). Quite to the contrary, concerted political effort was put in their being opened to the Other. Developing connecting railway and road infrastructure, establishing new commercial border control points, facilitating cross-border businesses, are some of the trends that testified to this change. They were all interpreted within the context of European integration and Europeanisation of the Balkans:

> [When] all Balkan states, without exception, have a clear European perspective, [...] I personally believe this will happen in the foreseeable future, the borders between different Balkan states [...] will lose their specific practical significance.[11]

On a different occasion, the opening of a new border checkpoint, the president appealed for continuing efforts 'for the true opening on both sides of the border'.[12] Interpreting the opening of borders as a benefit for the people and as an achievement for the state clearly demonstrates the contrast with earlier articulations of the significance of borders. Awareness of this change is confirmed in the reference to borders and border areas as 'doors' to Europe (ibid.). Rhetorically identifying the link between European integration and the decreased practical relevance of borders was an important political strategy. It aimed to emphasise the territorial commonality of European spaces as opposed to the separateness of national spaces. This facilitated the increased permeability of borders and put emphasis on their connecting (rather than separating) function.

One aspect of the interpretation of borders and their significance in Bulgarian politics still perpetuated the function of border maintenance but it was directly linked to Bulgaria's aspiration to belong to the common European space. It was related to Bulgaria's prospective role as the gatekeeper of EU's external border. In this sense Bulgaria was keen to demonstrate its capabilities in managing its borders even before it actually gained membership:

> Bulgaria already ambitiously and correctly fulfils its obligations as external border of the EU. [...] The reforms we are implementing [...] have had a direct effect on the common European space because security in united Europe is indivisible. [...] Bulgaria can contribute to that.[13]

Thus, in so far as borders continued to have political relevance, it was defined in terms of protecting the common European space from external threats. This interpretation demonstrates in practice the shift in the Self–Other dialectic from

---

11. Parvanov, summit on Balkan Economy and Tourism in Duras, Albania, 28 April 2006.
12. Parvanov, 'Elhovo becomes a door to Europe', speech during the president's visit to the municipality of Elhovo, 25 March 2006.
13. Parvanov, lecture on national security, National Palace of Culture, 23 June 2006.

the national to the supranational that the Europeanisation dynamic put into motion. The Other is a threat only as an outsider to the Community of Europe.

Translated into everyday politics, this awareness was also confirmed in the amendment of the constitutional provision prohibiting foreigners from land ownership rights in Bulgaria.[14] True, the enforcement of the new text was postponed (there was a transition period of seven years after accession) and subject to conditions.[15] But the fact that the sedimented quality of the constitutional arrangement had been successfully challenged by the demands of membership negotiations testified to the normative power of Europeanisation over nationalist interpretations of territory as exclusively national and indivisible. The normality with which the constitutional amendment was voted on and approved is illustrative of that:

> [amending the constitutional text on foreign ownership over land] is a natural change and we accept it. Giving up something we also receive a lot, as part of a political and economic community.[16]

Parliamentary debates on the change did not avoid references to preserving the traditions and independence of Bulgarian constitutionalism, but neither did they convincingly challenge the political priority of Europeanisation imperatives.[17] It is in this sense that nationalist interpretations of identity referring to the meaning of territory were marginalised in favour of interpretations of the national space as part of a larger, supranational community.

Identity narratives of purpose

Europeanisation also had a transformative effect on the contents of the element of national purpose. Sedimented interpretations embedded into the discourse of nationalism revolved around the idea of centrality in the Balkans and fluctuated between narratives of victimisation and paternalistic visions of purpose based on stories of past grandeur and tragic glory. As early as the first half of the 1990s European interpretations of national purpose began to affect the idea of general direction at state level. A decade later they hegemonically articulated the meanings of national purpose as inseparable from the discourse of Europeanisation.

One of the dominant narratives within the modified identity construction aimed to interpret Bulgaria's role in the Europeanisation project, not simply as

---

14. Amended Art.22, Para.2 in force from the enforcement date of Bulgaria's accession treaty.
15. Ownership is legalised for EU citizens only (not for foreign nationals); if they intend to settle in Bulgaria, see the Law on Land Ownership and Rights at http://www.lex.bg/laws/ldoc/2132550145 (accessed 1 June 2015).
16. Stanishev at the National Assembly, 348th session, 16 April 2004.
17. Meglena Kuneva, 'Constitutional amendment is expected by the EU', on *V Desetkata* (current affairs programme), BTV, 2 April 2006.

a beneficiary but as an active contributor who could add value to the community it aspired to join. The narrative served the dual purpose of a self-enhancement strategy (internally) and of a negotiation strategy (externally). Taken up at the highest political level – the head of state and government – the narrative of Bulgaria's value and contribution to Europe became increasingly salient during membership preparations:

> [W]e do not see EU membership as an opportunity just to receive funding [...]. So far, and even more from now on, Bulgaria will be an active factor of stability in South-Eastern Europe, a state implementing policies of good neighbourly relations, developing the cooperation model in all areas among the states in the region, a state that will be one of the key generators of peace, democratisation, effective market and social reforms.[18]

The narrative essentially told the common story of Bulgaria's transition: democracy, market liberalisation, social reform, preserving the ethnic peace at home and improving bilateral relations with neighbours in the region. What made it a unique story was its locus: against the background of the turbulent Western Balkans, Bulgaria's transition seemed remarkable in its normality:

> We have the self-confidence of being a factor of stability and peace in the whole region of South-Eastern Europe. Bulgaria will contribute to the EU its capital of excellent relations with its neighbours, [...] provide guarantee for the stability of the region, which the EU itself should seek.[19]

Pointing to the necessary dividends that Bulgaria could bring to the EU, the president effectively reversed the victimisation rhetoric to demonstrate how Europe depended on Bulgaria's role, rather than the other way around. This discursive strategy, though arguable in the validity of its claim, aimed to provide a credible positive role for the state in the wider context of Europeanisation, since its nationalist narratives of past glory had been left behind. It was this interpretation of purpose that ensured the normative power of Europeanisation in Bulgarian politics:

> Today the Republic of Bulgaria is the most advanced candidate state from the region in its negotiations for EU membership. This fact imposes on us additional duties in advancing the processes of integration in South-Eastern Europe.[20]

---

18. Stanishev, verbatim report from the public sitting of the European Integration Council chaired by the prime minister, 9 January 2006.
19. Parvanov, 'Bulgaria at the doorstep of the EU'.
20. Parvanov, 'Bulgaria's new regional role after NATO membership and prospective EU membership', lecture, National Palace of Culture, 12 May 2004.

Stabilising Bulgaria's place within the realm of Europeanisation, in turn, enabled the Europe narratives in the Balkans to be perpetuated, as Bulgaria's European interpretations of national purpose were closely linked to its position in the region:

> Bulgaria's EU membership will not only confirm our European identity. It will also send an important positive signal towards our neighbours about the irreversibility of the unification processes in Europe. [S]ecurity, stability and prosperity of South-Eastern Europe [are only possible] because of the region's prospects for EU membership.[21]

Interpreting Bulgarian narratives of national purpose within the Europeanisation dynamic provided Bulgaria with a credible positive role in the region and in Europe that was articulated in terms of 'setting an example' of peace, stability, prosperity.[22] Maintaining the credibility of this role posed certain imperatives on the state's foreign policy behaviour, which in effect promoted regional cooperation and international amity. In view of Bulgarian–Macedonian relations, this was an indicator of 'European-ness':

> Bulgaria has never had such good relations either with Macedonia or with the rest of the states in the region. There has been an ongoing dialogue [...] which had not been seen before in the centuries-long history of the region. Bulgarian–Macedonian relations set an example for [...] the future of the Balkans.[23]

In terms of solving the specific problems that had plagued Bulgarian–Macedonian relations, this interpretation of national purpose for Bulgaria in practice marginalised many of the points of conflictuality. Bulgaria insisted on maintaining a paternalistic tone in its dialogue with Macedonia.[24] Its paternalism, however, was now not based on the assumption of inequality but on the degree of Europeanisation. Bulgaria saw itself as an exporter of European experience and expertise,[25] and this was what determined its presumably more advantageous position. It is important to note that despite its paternalistic tone, Bulgaria's interpretation of bilateral relations had changed in one significant way. It no longer saw them within the brotherhood dialectic (implying the superiority of the 'older

---

21. Ibid.
22. Parvanov, interview for Macedonian National Radio, 4 November 2006.
23. Parvanov, 'Bulgaria's new regional role after NATO membership and prospective EU membership', lecture, National Palace of Culture, 12 May 2004.
24. Briefing by the spokesperson for the Ministry of Foreign Affairs, Dimitar Tsanchev, 26 July 2006.
25. Motif repeatedly occurring in the official bilateral communication in the period 2002–7 at the level of heads of state and heads of governments.

brother' over the 'younger brother'). Within Europeanisation discourse Macedonia was seen as a friend:

> We have achieved some serious progress and we are happy to share our experience with our Macedonian friends.[26]

> [W]ishing peace, stability and prosperity to our Macedonian friends.[27]

Given the high degree of conflictuality that the former interpretation had perpetuated, this change was significant.

Overall, the Europeanisation dynamic provided a positive interpretation of national purpose that in effect reduced national identity conflictuality. Its reading of Bulgarian national identity succeeded in articulating explicit nationalist interpretations as an aberration from normality. By emphasising the centrality of dialogue, cooperation and mutuality, the discursive change upheld the norm of European-ness and positioned conflictuality in contravention to this norm. Thus it increased the legitimacy of the national political community that had managed to improve bilateral relations and marginalise conflictual interpretations.

Modifications in the Macedonian national identity narratives of self

The Europeanisation dynamic in Macedonia took a different course owing to the different contexts structuring Macedonia's transition. Breaking up from the federation and declaring independence posed the need to achieve international recognition. On the one hand it delayed Macedonia's bid for a (re-)turn to Europe by disabling its capacity to participate in European politics until recognised by all EU members. On the other hand it made the transition process more cumbersome by adding a new dimension to it – the need to reaffirm statehood.

Macedonia's Balkan context also impeded the normative power of Europe because of the bilateral problems that it conditioned. Conflictuality in relations with Bulgaria was contained during the period under study. Other than numerous missed opportunities for increasing regional leverage, it did not involve serious impediments to Macedonia's path towards Europe, which was mostly in line with Bulgaria's declarative support for Europeanisation of the region. But conflictuality in relations with Serbia (then the Federal Republic of Yugoslavia and still under Milošević) revolved around a long-standing border dispute in the north-west of Macedonia (mostly but not exclusively along the border with Kosovo) which, together with the unrest in Kosovo and the large numbers of its refugees, temporarily destabilised peace in the republic. After the change of power in Serbia the dispute was officially resolved (at the beginning of 2001) but the instability it brought to the country exacerbated domestic inter-ethnic tensions, thus perpetuating micro-nationalisms and preventing progress in the

---

26. Parvanov, interview for Macedonian National Radio, 4 November 2006.
27. Parvanov, 'Ten years later', speech at the Macedonian parliament, Skopje, 27 February 2002.

Europeanisation processes.[28] Conflictuality in relations with Greece, in turn, also had very serious consequences for the empowerment of Europeanisation. Greek anxiety over Macedonia's national flag and the interpretation of its constitutional provisions (significantly, Art.49 of the Macedonian constitution) was mollified with the interim accord of 1995, which confirmed Greek recognition of Macedonian statehood and allowed Macedonia to formally initiate the process of its European integration. But Greek objections to the republic's constitutional name and the ensuing name dispute negotiations proved more intractable.[29] They delayed Macedonia's progress towards association negotiations and consequently, Macedonia's bid for full EU membership. But, most importantly, they diminished the normative power of Europe in Macedonia because of the EU's failure to exert pressure on Greece to reach an agreement. The fact that Greece instrumentalised its influence as an EU member for the purposes of the dispute in order to threaten Macedonia's future membership and hinder Macedonia's negotiations seriously compromised the European Community's standing among the Macedonian public. In effect it questioned the ability of European narratives to engage central discursive elements of national identity carried by the notion of 'Macedonianness' in the name of the republic. It thus challenged Europe's credible reading of Macedonian national identity.

Macedonia's Albanian context of minority–majority accommodation was another factor that distanced the republic from its European perspective and affected the normative power of Europe. Indirectly linked to unrest in Kosovo, Albanian insurgency groups in Macedonia brought the republic to a state of civil conflict for most of 2001. Marginalising the imperatives of everyday politics to give way to the urgent rhetoric of war and peace, the conflict exposed a serious inter-ethnic divide in the state. Reconciling domestic micro-nationalisms became a political priority, as they destabilised Macedonia's transition to democracy and postponed its active preparations for EU membership. EU's active role in brokering the peace agreement, however, kept Macedonia's European perspective in sight and reinstated the relevance of Europeanisation to Macedonian politics.[30]

So even though challenged by the specific Macedonian contexts invoking nationalist rhetoric on micro- and macro-levels, the empowerment of Europeanisation did not cease. On the contrary, in the first years of the new millennium it was seen as a strategic goal, and a wide political consensus maintained its domestic relevance. Macedonia's formal application for EU membership, submitted in 2004 (just before the enforcement of the Stabilisation and Association Agreement), was decided positively at the end of 2005, when Macedonia officially

---

28. Border Demarcation Agreement signed by Trajkovski and Kostunica, 23 February 2001, see Milenkovski and Talevki, 2001: appendix.

29. As confirmed publicly by Greece: http://www.umdiaspora.org/index.php?option=com_con tent&task=view&id=150&Itemid=76, also http://www.greekembassy.org/Embassy/content/ en/Article.aspx?offic =1&folder=24&article=18371 (both accessed 28 February 2013).

30. Ohrid Framework Agreement and the EU, see Bieber, 2008.

became a candidate state. In the course of empowering Europe and marginalising nationalist political agendas, Macedonian national identity began to be narrated in a much less conflictual and more inclusive manner.

Identity narratives of nationhood

At the beginning of its transition Macedonia attempted to interpret the state community as organised around the notion of national tolerance. This interpretation was meant to reconcile the long-standing Macedonian aspiration for an independent national state with the political impossibility of establishing the new state along ethno-national lines. In view of the domestic deterioration of inter-ethnic relations, the salience of this interpretation dramatically increased precisely because of the absence of tolerance. It signified what the state community desperately needed in order to preserve its integrity. The centrality of the discursive element of nationhood interpreted in terms of national tolerance is evident, in the first place, in frequent and formulaic references to it as the solution of exacerbating inter-ethnic tensions:

> Everybody in Macedonia [...] should know that the success of ethnic extremism [...] means the end of peace and stability in the region. [...] This is a deadly blow to inter-ethnic relations. It can, in a very short time, turn the tolerance that took years to build up into destructive hatred.[31]

Securitising tolerance as a highest value ('took years to build') was achieved by establishing a discursive opposition between it and the obvious pernicious consequences of hatred (qualified as 'destructive'). This opposition was reinforced by announcing the incompatibility of the rhetorical antonym of tolerance – ethnic extremism – with peace and stability. Expanding the negative impact of abandoning national tolerance beyond the borders of the national space to include the 'region' emphasised in a dramatic manner its central importance as a signifier of national identity. It determined both the domestic stability of the community (its absence is 'a deadly blow to inter-ethnic relations') and the international standing of the state as a key actor in the region.

The significance of the discursive element of nationhood interpreted in terms of national tolerance is also evident in the post-conflict political rationalisation of civil unrest. The conflict was explained exclusively as an attempt to surrender this key signifier of 'Macedonian-ness':

> The insurgents skilfully used some still open issues and stereotypes and shook the backbone of Macedonian stability, culture and history – inter-ethnic tolerance – to bring the state to the brink of inter-ethnic war.[32]

---

31. Trajkovski, parliamentary address, 6 March 2001.
32. Trajkovski, parliamentary address, 21 December 2001.

A repeated emphasis on tolerance as a core identity marker rearticulated the Macedonian state community in terms of what it lacked, revealing the centrality of the discursive element. Ascribing the insurgency to the contingent instrumentalisation of simple 'open issues' and 'stereotypes' and not to deeper underlying problems in the construction of the state was an attempt to diminish its political relevance and re-establish normality. Reference to the intertwining of inter-ethnic tolerance and the 'backbone' of 'Macedonian-ness' reinforced this rhetorical attempt. The established chain of equivalence between notions of stability, culture and history also served this purpose. While the salience of culture and history in the construction of Macedonian national identity was undisputed domestically, that of stability was not. Positioning stability on a par with culture and history was an act of identity constitution that reaffirmed the discursive centrality of tolerance.

The idea of national tolerance continued to be increasingly salient not only in the immediate post-conflict period but throughout the first decade of the new millennium. This had to do with national reconciliation imperatives and the construction of a legitimate collective identity at the state level. Upon its return to power in 2006, the democratic party appealed precisely to such imperatives. The new prime minister declared his government's priority as 'leading Macedonia forward, in coexistence, tolerance and understanding'.[33]

The salience of this interpretation of Macedonian national identity was upheld by the stronger emphasis placed on inter-ethnic 'dialogue', 'good inter-ethnic relations'[34] and overcoming inter-ethnic 'divisions'.[35] Lending credibility to these notions logically put forward the necessity of articulating the state community along not national but civic lines:

> We need to send a message that Macedonia is a civic community committed to tolerance and coexistence. We have shown that we know our way in nurturing our [...] traditional tolerance, developing democracy, respecting human rights and transitioning to market economy.[36]

Awareness that the community of the state should be organised along civic lines was a major change from the uncertainty articulated at the beginning of Macedonian independent statehood. Connecting civic identity with the idea of tolerance and the key requirements of the transition (functioning democracy, human rights, market economy) enabled Macedonia to reclaim its Europeanness: 'Macedonia develops and supports the multi-culturality of its society within the framework of the [...] civic character of the state'.[37] The salience of the

---

33. Gruevski, *Utrinski* newspaper, 30 October 2006.
34. Trajkovski, parliamentary address, 6 March 2001.
35. Gruevski, *Utrinski* newspaper, 30 October 2006.
36. Trajkovski, parliamentary address, 6 March 2001.
37. Trajkovski, parliamentary address, 21 December 2001.

idea of national tolerance and its significance for the success of the transition ultimately served the purpose of advancing preparations for European integration as Macedonia's strategic goal in the transition. It attempted to prove that the state had managed inter-ethnic unrest and left it behind, and was ready to be included in the common European processes. This was how it was related to the Europeanisation empowerment discourse:

> In the end, we are all trying to join the European family, where we belong, with dignity.[38]
>
> Our duty is to overcome inter-ethnic [...] divisions and demonstrate that Macedonia is ready to take its due place in Europe.[39]
>
> Macedonia's determination on European integration [...] has been a key element of its policies from the very start as a consensus among all political parties.[40]
>
> We are working to meet specific standards from our European agenda.[41]

The repeated claim that Macedonia belonged to the European 'family' and had its 'due place' there, the reference to preparation for integration as a 'key element' of Macedonian politics, the suggestion that Macedonia's bid for EU integration constituted a clear 'European agenda', demonstrated that Europeanisation was being consistently empowered at official state level. The appeal for 'duty', the claim for 'determination' and 'consensus', the notion of 'dignity' revealed elements of the political will that maintained gradual empowerment.

Attaching the interpretation of national tolerance to the discursive element of the nation and discursively linking it to the meaning of Europe ultimately produced a less conflictual national identity construct at state level. It emphasised Macedonian identity as 'open to the world',[42] and to life with 'Others'.[43] In bilateral relations with Bulgaria this was illustrated in the gradual normalisation of political rhetoric on Otherness. In terms of majority–minority relations it led to the gradual de-tabooisation of the idea of a Bulgarian minority, even if not to formal recognition of such. While at the beginning of the transition Bulgarians were never listed by the majority as one of the numerous 'nationalities' inhabiting Macedonia,[44] towards the mid-2000s occasional references to ethnic Bulgarians

---

38. Trajkovski, parliamentary address, 6 March 2001.
39. Trajkovski, parliamentary address, 21 December 2001.
40. Ljubisha Georgievski, speaker of parliament, 3rd plenary session, 7 September 2006.
41. Buckovski, 2nd plenary session, 26 August 2006.
42. Trajkovski, parliamentary address, 21 December 2001.
43. Ibid.
44. When they were mentioned, it was by Albanian minority representatives.

living in the state became a relatively safe political choice.[45] This was significant, given the inevitable anti-Bulgarianism of Macedonian identity construction since the first years of Macedonian statehood. Uncovering the mechanism that would stabilise the idea of national tolerance as central to Macedonia's national identity in view of Europeanisation addressed this modification.

Identity narratives of territory

As with the discursive element of identity described in the previous section, the interpretation of national territory was closely linked to the specific context of Macedonia's transition. In the first years of independence and in view of the imperatives of launching the statehood project, Macedonian identity politics revolved around the idea of belonging to Macedonia as homeland and, consequently, around the centrality of the Macedonian denominator in domestic affairs. In the context of overcoming international isolation and inter-ethnic division, these interpretations were gradually marginalised to give way to less antagonistic identity narratives. In order to stabilise Macedonia's regional standing and to make progress in Macedonia's European integration aspirations, Macedonia needed to send clear messages about its commitment to respecting the Balkan territorial status quo. Most significantly this implied a guarantee of non-intervention in the domestic affairs of neighbouring states in view of minority status promotion. The imperative of improving relations with neighbours led to providing such guarantees in bilateral state communication with Greece (the interpretation of Art.49 of the constitution in the Interim Accords of 1995 with Greece) and Bulgaria (the provision in the same tone in the Joint Declaration of 1999 with Bulgaria). Retreating from the vision of maintaining active links with adjacent parts of geographical Macedonia notably decreased the external conflictuality of Macedonian national identity. It shifted the focus on the sovereign territory of Macedonia at the time, marginalising historical narratives of belonging, and re-interpreted Macedonian national territory in terms of completeness and integrity.

The dynamic of bridging domestic inter-ethnic divides upheld a similar interpretation of territory. Problems along the north-western border and the Albanian insurgency put Macedonia's territorial integrity under actual threat. With the prospect of having to surrender sovereignty over part of the state territory to Kosovo or to profoundly transform the form of statehood to acknowledge internal divisions as autonomous territories or federation, Macedonian politics swiftly turned to securitising territorial integrity as a priority. The suggestion that Macedonian statehood could renounce unitarism and devolve into a federation was interpreted as the worst-case scenario. It was articulated through the ideas of 'fission' and 'breakdown'.[46] Unitarism, on the other hand, was articulated in terms

---

45. See parliamentary session, 26 October 2006.
46. Radmila Shekerinska, 2nd parliamentary session, 26 August 2006.

of 'security' and 'stability'.[47] Securitising the form of statehood was reinforced by another rhetorical strategy. Official Macedonian rhetoric consistently linked unitary statehood to the individual as a referent object of security. It was repeatedly suggested that surrendering unitarism would have a serious negative impact on the 'peace and serenity of all citizens of the Republic of Macedonia',[48] on the 'serenity of every household' and on the 'tranquillity of our children'.[49] By directly engaging the individual in the cause of defending unitary statehood and territorial integrity, Macedonian politics definitively articulated them as central in the national identity of the state.

In view of Macedonia's long-awaited and quite recent independent statehood, the increased salience of territorial integrity and unitarism is unsurprising. Preserving the integrity and the unitary form of the state, however, posed the imperative of national reconciliation. Successfully accommodating the demands of the Albanian political representation for fair participation in the statehood project demanded shifting the focus on 'Macedonian-ness' as a central element of state identity and emphasising instead togetherness and participation (Trajkovski, Buckovski, Gruevski). Such an interpretation of state identity concurred with the meaning of Europe in Macedonian politics. This ensured its salience in the course of Europeanisation. The significance of borders, for instance, was visibly transformed in this sense. Despite the insistence on their fixedness, borders were rearticulated in the context of national reconciliation and Europeanisation as open and transparent:

> At a time when all European borders are falling, [ethnic extremists] want to erect new, ethnic borders. [This] demand for ethnically pure territories is motivated by [...] racism and hatred.[50]

Renouncing ethnic divisions in the state, the president uncovered the incompatibility of 'bordering' Macedonia with the European orientation and the integration processes in Europe: 'The only option that we stand behind is European and transparent borders in the region'.[51] This declaration was sustainably maintained in the advancement of Macedonia's transition. In the context of border control and border management as a prerequisite for EU candidacy, the legislative framework on the subject was determined in a view to European standards[52] and the permeability of borders for 'people, goods, and capital' (and impermeability for criminality): '[The aim is to] ensure European standards and the conditions for having ever more open borders'.[53]

---

47. Buckovski, 2nd parliamentary session, 26 August 2006.
48. Trajkovski, 71st plenary session, 6 March 2001.
49. Ibid.
50. Trajkovski, parliamentary address, 21 December 2001.
51. Trajkovski, 71st plenary session, 6 March 2001.
52. Discussion, section on border police in the bill on police, 6th plenary session, 26 October 2006.
53. Ljubisha Georgievski, 3rd plenary session, 7 September 2006.

The idea of openness towards the outside world was a significant transformation in the interpretation of Macedonian national identity. In stark contrast with the nationalist interpretations of besieged territory from the early years of independence, Macedonia now articulated its statehood as open to immediate national Other(s). This is evident in the way the neighbours were positioned in terms of Macedonia's strategic future:

> In its aspiration for EU membership [...] Macedonia will soon be fortunate in having two neighbours, Greece and Bulgaria, who are EU members and should be able to help us to realise our objective, on which the political parties and the citizens of this state are in consensus.[54]

The rhetoric of bilateral partnership and mutual assistance in preparations for EU membership had been an indispensable element of Bulgarian–Macedonian inter-state communication since 1999. Its appearance in Macedonia's domestic discursive space had been less frequent. Referring to Greece in terms of 'good fortune' had been even rarer. This is why the modification of the interpretation of borders as an opportunity to connect rather than to divide was novel. It suggested a decrease in the conflictuality of external projections of Macedonian national identity.

Identity narratives of purpose

Modified interpretations of the discursive element of national purpose also open up Macedonian national identity towards the Other(s). Nationalist rhetoric of victimisation and vindication through independent statehood, characteristic of the early transition, placed the political emphasis on the realisation of the Self. The project of independence was meant to assert Macedonian national identity as a legitimate state. In contrast, the rhetoric of the late transition, already guided by the strategic goal of European integration, interpreted Macedonian identity through its role in the region. In this sense the articulation of national purpose included the immediate Other(s) in a non-antagonistic manner, as participants in the regional community of states. Having achieved independent statehood and having preserved the integrity of the new state, Macedonia turned to Europe as a way to stabilise the fundament of its statehood project. European integration offered a model of non-national governance which the post-Ohrid Macedonian state could subscribe to.[55]

In order to articulate this inherent compatibility, Macedonian politics had to marginalise internal conflictuality and emphasise stability and predictability (often constructed as a 'predictable partner' in the rhetoric of the prime minister).

---

54. Vesna Janevska, 6th plenary session, 26 October 2006.
55. This idea is more frequently voiced by the Albanian political representation, see for instance Azis Polozhani during the 12th parliamentary session, 9 November 2006.

Thus, like in Bulgaria, the interpretation of national purpose began to focus on Macedonia's role as a key to the stability of the region.

> Macedonia acquired broad international support for its policies and reaffirmed itself as a pivot of stability in the region.[...] Destabilising Macedonia will challenge the new climate and legitimate aspirations for peaceful and prosperous Balkans.[56]

At the level of head of government, this interpretation remained a central theme in the articulation of national purpose. Upon his stepping in office, the new Macedonian prime minister from the right was advised by his predecessor from the left to 'continue building the image of Macedonia as a factor of stability and a regional leader'.[57] Announcing Macedonia's regional standing as a factual confirmation of identity-building rhetoric ('continue building the image of [...] a regional leader') served the purpose of increasing its credibility. This discursive strategy was applied consistently in the period in order to essentialise the assumption of leadership: 'Never has Macedonia been as respected as now because we have a stance, we have an active policy, we have an active position [on Kosovo]'.[58]

Articulating Macedonian national identity in the region in terms of agency also increased the credibility of the particular interpretation of purpose. This wass in contrast with the passivity of the victimisation narratives since the beginning of transition. Macedonia's leadership positioned the state as a master of its own destiny. This interpretation was emancipatory and optimistic – it was oriented towards the future:

> Everything is in our hands. We should try to see not what the international community can do for us [but what we can do for ourselves]. We are members of the international community. We have the chance but time does not wait – the decision of the European Union will not wait.[59]

Already an EU candidate state, Macedonia asserted its interpretation of national purpose in a forward manner and in optimistic terms. Positioning itself as a full member of the international community, the republic demonstrated detachment from the frustrations of the past. Historically antagonistic relations were now interpreted as opportunities. Albania, Greece and Bulgaria were seen as a bridge towards realising Macedonia's European aspiration:

> [The new government] should promptly establish contacts with both Berisha and Stanishev; it should also try again with Karamanlis, perhaps to better ends.[60]

---

56. Trajkovski, 6 March 2001.
57. Buckovski, directed at Gruevski in his address in parliament, 26 August 2006.
58. Ibid.
59. Ibid.
60. Ibid.

Seeing the prime ministers of neighbouring states in terms of pragmatic politics and not as adversaries, despite the various degrees of conflictuality that still strained bilateral relations, was an indication of the transformation in interpretation of the national purpose. Macedonian national identity had been determined by its European orientation, so nationalist interpretations should have been transcended. It was this articulation of purpose that enabled the marginalisation of conflictual interpretations of the Macedonian national identity construction.

In view of this modification, the uniqueness of Macedonian identity was determined in positive terms. The historical myths of uniqueness gave way to a new mythologisation of Macedonia's regional standing. It was centred around the story of 'the most successful fairytale on the Balkans' and the 'small regional miracle'.[61] What enabled the upholding of these new myths was Macedonia's claim to having preserved the peace.[62] Against the background of war-torn Kosovo, and previously Serbia, Croatia, Bosnia, this claim sounded credible. Even though not entirely correct, it allowed the re-narration of Macedonian identity as unique and positive. In this narrative, the 2001 inter-ethnic turmoil was retold not as a 'conflict' but as a 'crisis situation, resolved politically'.[63] The incompatibility of ethno-political conflict with the discourse of Europeanisation determined this narrative turn.

The modified interpretation of national purpose in the late Macedonian transition is closely linked to Macedonia's strategic objective of European integration. The imperative of making sense of the most recent event in the chronology of the Macedonian state – inter-ethnic conflict – in view of Macedonia's European aspirations produced a more open, more optimistic, and less nationalistic interpretation of national purpose. Unlike Bulgaria, where the aspiration for integration came with the inertia of the 'refolutions' (Garton Ash, 1989) in the rest of Central and South-Eastern Europe, Macedonia turned to Europe after the first wave of applicant states had launched their negotiations. This had to do with the delay in achieving recognition. In the meanwhile, it was caught in the turmoil of inter-ethnic tension, which seriously destabilised its statehood project from within. While attempting to restore stability, Macedonia's leadership cultivated an awareness that the painful process of reconstituting statehood and transcending nationalist interpretations of national identity were meant to reform the state as truly European. In this sense, European incentives in the form of declarations of support[64] or visa liberalisation agreements (as expected by Macedonia by the end of 2006) significantly reinforced the normative power of Europeanisation in Macedonia. Failure to provide such incentives, on the other hand, promised to affect the credibility of the European reading of Macedonian identity.

---

61. In the words of the prime minister Buckovski in parliament, 26 August 2006.
62. Ljubisha Georgievski, parliamentary address, 7 September 2006.
63. Ibid.
64. Such as the declarations from Germany: *Deutsche Welle* quoting Angela Merkel's declaration of support: 'Germany is very interested in the successful outcome of Macedonia's application', 17 October 2006.

Comparing modifications in identity narratives of Self

As demonstrated above, modifications in national identity patterns and transformations of national identity narratives in the two states are linked to understanding the contingent political contexts that shaped them. Contexts were very different in Bulgaria and Macedonia, and so were the national identity patterns they produced. Despite the often similar interpretations of identity elements, the discursive positions of national Self differed significantly (Table 6.1). The different relations established between the various discursive elements in the two identity constructions reproduced different outcomes. The notion of territorial integrity, for instance, appeared as a central interpretation of the meaning of national territory at the beginning of Bulgaria's transition and towards the late Macedonian transition. Its implications, however, were very different in the two cases. While in Bulgaria territorial integrity was upheld as a reference in nationalist rhetoric, in Macedonia it signified Europeanisation and detachment from nationalism. A similar dynamic is detectable in the changed interpretations of nationhood (in terms of 'unity' and 'tolerance') and national purpose (in terms of 'centrality' and 'contribution'). This observation confirms the validity of the assumption that the specific content of the identity-discursive elements is contingent and historically bound. This assumption points to the direct dependency of national identity narratives on the political and sees identity change as a function of that. From this perspective national identity change is not only conceivable, it is inevitable in a changed discursive context. The empowerment of Europeanisation invoked such a change.

What enabled this outcome in both Bulgaria and Macedonia was placing strategic priority on inclusion in the dynamic of European integration and the subsequent empowerment of Europeanisation. In this context nationalist readings of identity lost relevance and credibility as conflictual, determined by the past and failing to provide an optimistic vision of national Self. Embarking upon the road to Europe, the two states rearticulated their national identities so as to that position them as participants in a supranational community of states. This challenged the constraining power of nation-state borders and offered national identity a significantly wider and more inclusive discursive space. The position of constitutive Otherness shifted from the immediate national Other(s) to the projected borders of the community. In view of this repositioning, the salience of certain interpretations of identity which had been centred around difference, such as the notion of national unity, the narrative of vindication and the encapsulating role of state borders, gradually decreased. It was substituted by more emphasis on commonality and tolerance, and accentuating inclusive dimensions of difference. Accommodated within the dynamics of Europeanisation, national identity narratives appeared less antagonistic, more optimistic and more positive. The credibility of this interpretation and its self-enhancing function stabilised the process of Europeanisation. This in turn enhanced the legitimacy of the political community, which had managed this outcome.

Table 6.1: Changed patterns of national identity: Bulgaria and Macedonia

State community	National identity narratives of Self		
	Nation	**Territory**	**Purpose**
Bulgaria	National unity: • ethnic→ national→ European political parties • increased salience of 'national' values such as good neighbourly relations, cooperation, trust • redefinition of the 'national interest' to include well-being of neighbours, the region and Europe.	Territorial integrity: • decreased salience of national borders as a barrier • increased salience of borders as a 'door' to Europe • negotiability of the Constitution • selling land to foreigners.	Centrality in the Balkans: • contribution • stability factor • exporter of stability • dialogue • example • renegotiation of the brothers/ friends relationship with Macedonia.
Macedonia	National tolerance: • increased salience of the signifier of tolerance as the pivot of Macedonian stability • civic community, emphasis on dialogue, good inter-ethnic relations, overcoming inter-ethnic divisions • openness to the world	Territorial belonging: • territorial integrity • unitary state • gradual detachment from the notion of 'severed whole' • relaxation of the insistence on 'Macedonian-ness' in domestic politics • borders: 　- transparent and European, but 　- fixed and unchanging	Victimisation narrative: • Sovereignty • the most successful fairy-tale • key to stability in the region • maintaining peace

Chapter Seven

Conclusion: Legitimacy and the Europeanisation of National Identities

The functions of national identity in the political community and the dynamics of identity change have entertained political scientists of all persuasions. Particularly in the context of European integration and Europeanisation, these themes have been an object of special interest. This is related to the prolific strand of research in the Europeanisation literature investigating the emergence of a common European identity that compares, competes with or supplements national identity. Studying national identity in Europe together with European identity and in comparison to it has been suggested by other central themes in the Europeanisation literature: the problems of legitimacy and the crisis of confidence that have characterised EU politics of the past decade. But investigating the theme of European identity together with national identity may have diverted attention from the effects of Europeanisation on national identity in terms of legitimacy and support for integration. Focusing instead on national identity and understanding how national identity transforms and evolves in the context of European integration promises to tell us much more about the common basis of belonging in Europe, about the legitimacy of political community and about the reasons for supporting integration through its times of crisis.

This book has studied the Europeanisation of national identity from the perspective of national politics and identification with the political community of the nation-state. It has explored the modifications introduced into the narration of national identity with the progress of external Europeanisation and the consequences thereof. The book contends that narrating national identity in view of Europe modifies the boundaries of political community and radically changes the normative basis of belonging. If a political will for Europeanisation is at hand, the process of identity re-narration can enhance the legitimacy of both political community in the context of European integration and integration itself.

The changes that the discursive construction of national identity undergoes within the realm of Europeanisation enable the inclusion of national Others, as integration establishes a basis of commonality that transcends national borders and arrests the dynamic of Othering that they traditionally perpetuate. National identity is thus re-narrated in a less antagonistic, reconciliatory manner that helps manage and overcome identity-based conflictuality. We have explored this dynamic along the lines of bilateral relations between two states and their respective minorities but its mechanisms in other inter-group configurations (e.g. conflictuality with regard to various national Others) could be just as promising. The ability to manage identity-based antagonisms and enable cooperation between national Others is an important aspect of the political community's legitimacy in an increasingly transnational world. National identity narrated within the context of Europeanisation seems to facilitate this ability in national political communities. This is the first proposition that the book has argued.

At the same time, re-narrating identity to make it compatible with the normative foundation of European integration and with the process of Europeanisation has engaged European meanings into the national stories. The process has significantly impacted the way national political community has been imagined and the way it has behaved politically. Aligning the national stories with Europeanisation has highlighted the immediate relevance of integration to national politics, thus bridging the gap between integration and its publics that can be found at the heart of the EU's legitimacy problem. In the golden years of integration these outcomes were linked to the legitimacy derived from the positive output of economic prosperity, welfare and redistribution policies, as well as that of democracy, rule of law and human rights protection. Particularly in the context of Europeanisation in the former communist space, this output-based legitimacy boost has played an important role in re-imagining the national stories of Self in a positive, self-enhancing and optimistic manner. This was the specific context this book explored. Even in the context of economic crisis and austerity, however, national identity narrated in view of Europe has engaged the national political community as a participant in the unique political project of ensuring a common and peaceful future for Europe. In times of crisis, the integration project can thus lend its unique participation-based legitimacy, which is becoming increasingly relevant in an interdependent and globalised Europe. Narrating national identity in view of European integration and its normative basis highlights the benefits of Europeanisation and its relevance to national politics. It can, therefore, be a useful tool in boosting support for integration. This is the second proposition this book has put forward.

The Europeanisation of national identities has thus emerged as a central theme in the study of both the legitimacy of national political communities in Europe and the legitimacy of European integration and the EU. This is what invites concerted analytical attention to understand the discursive logic and mechanisms of this dynamic. The current book is but a modest attempt in that direction. It has set out to demonstrate that the Europeanisation of national identity modified the boundaries of political community, which transformed the basis of belonging and exclusion. The modifications have had a horizontal and a vertical dimension. Along the horizontal dimension, Europeanisation halted the dynamics of Othering along national borders and established a basis of commonality, thus enabling the reconciliation of mutually exclusive and antagonistic national stories, and the inclusion of national Others into the political community of the state. Along the vertical dimension, the dynamics of Europeanisation have enabled the inclusion of key European references into the national stories of Self, which made them perpetually relevant to the national. Unlike identification with Europe and a common European identity, which seems to display an unclear correlation with support for integration, making Europeanisation part of the national stories has increased the relevance of integration as it has taken it down to the level of national politics, contestation and mobilisation and integrated it as a discursive element within the national identity construction. The result has been a horizontal and vertical modification of the boundaries of political community that radically transformed the basis of belonging and exclusion. The criteria for membership in the national community, exclusionary, antagonistic and anchored in the past, were thus adapted to enable commonality with national Others and to include participation it the project of integration as an element in the national stories. In this sense, then, the national political communities that this book studied within the realm of Europeanisation have become politically less 'national' and normatively less nationalist. In the interconnected, multicultural and transnational world of European politics, this should be a welcome development. By adapting national political communities in Europe to these political contexts, the Europeanisation of national identities has ultimately lent them legitimacy to continue to represent their publics beyond the traditional national criterion of membership. Both national politics and European politics should benefit from that.

Beyond the studied cases, however, and in the context of economic crisis and fast-paced societal change involving closed contact with national difference, the normative power of integration and its rationale are meeting rising resistance from traditional forms of political community. These are based on historically dominant narratives of national identity upheld within the logic of nationalism as exclusive, anchored in the past and disabling full-fledged engagement of national Others. As the organisational structure and logic of national and international politics has remained the nation-state, in spite of pooling sovereignty in a series of areas, the logic of nationalism has remained relevant to the interpretations of belonging, interest, responsibility and purpose. In this sense nationalism emerges as the normative adversary of Europeanisation in imagining political community in Europe. Nationalism's interpretations of the national stories compete directly with the stories of community articulated within the realm of Europeanisation and in view of integration. The outcome of the discursive clash that this competition predicates should determine the kind of political community that better suits European politics. But this outcome is ultimately a matter of political choice and political will. The significant implications of each discursive option suggest why a better understanding of the logic and mechanisms of this dynamic is needed. This book has compared the relevance, appeal and mobilising power of identity narratives told within the logic of nationalism (before Europeanisation) and after joining the dynamic of Europeanisation in order to ascertain their consequences for the legitimacy of political community and of integration in two states. From the narrow basis of this small story, the book has explored questions that relate to many big stories of European politics, such as the future relevance of integration and the basis of belonging within the European nation-state.

Methodology

The analysis was carried out on the basis of a comparative case study over two states: Bulgaria and Macedonia. The task was to explore national identity and its meanings as they were narrated and renegotiated in the public sphere, spun between governments and the recipients of governance. This macro-focus was meant to capture the integrative power of national identity narratives in view of the entativity of political community, avoiding at the same time the myriads of personal forms of identification with the community that a micro-level would have had to engage with. Also, the macro-level offered a way to link interpretations of national identity with specific state behaviour, whereas that link would have been much more indirect at the micro-level. Furthermore, the macro-level appeared as the locus where elite interpretations of identity met sedimented popular interpretations. In this sense the macro-level revealed the potential for change contained within the compromise between elite and popular visions of political community and belonging. It thus promised a good perspective on the discursive mechanisms of identity change, which were the object of this investigation.

The book explored the Europeanisation of national identity within the external dynamic of Europeanisation. This topical and methodological choice was determined by the unique opportunity offered by the context of EU enlargement of capturing the discursive clash between nationalism and Europeanisation on interpretations of national identity. This dynamic would not have been as visible in the realm of the EU proper as the struggle between Europeanisation and nationalism occurred there in a different discursive context. On the one hand, the legitimacy of nationalism in interpreting national identity had traditionally been much more subtle and indirect in view of the historical circumstances of the Second World War and the role of nationalism in it. Even today, when explicit nationalist agendas have reappeared across Europe, they are still ascribed to extreme formations and are not normalised as legitimate political rhetoric. The former communist space displayed openly nationalist state rhetoric much more visibly and thus offered a more feasible research context. On the other hand, the impact of Europeanisation seems more difficult to capture because of the long-term structuring effects of integration and its institutions and practices, as well as the normalising effects of discussions on the role of integration. The context of EU enlargement into the post-communist space thus served as a 'clean slate' in terms of capturing the discursive clash between nationalism and Europeanisation in interpreting national identity. In many ways this clash resembled the early years of the European project and pointed to the underlying normative power of European integration and its original *raison d'être*. What complements the methodological suitability of this context to the object of this investigation is also the initial relative isolation of the post-communist public sphere from discussions on European integration, as well as the clear starting point of such discussions occupying the public sphere. These factors help capture and identify the effects of Europeanisation on the narration of national identity.

From the realm of post-communism and in the context of EU enlargement, the investigation turned to the Balkan region. This analytical choice was prompted, again, by the visibility of national identity renegotiation in the Balkans, but also by the presumably heightened antagonistic potential of national identity there. The region is widely seen as the European exception in terms of the relevance of nationalism to politics and in terms of the appeal of Europeanisation from the viewpoint of pragmatic calculations of interest. The book attempted to challenge both assumptions. On the one hand, it set out to demonstrate the banality of the mechanisms of engaging national identity narratives for the purposes of popular mobilisation and political action. Numerous similarities could be found between this dynamic in the Balkans and politics anywhere else in Europe. On the other hand, the context of enlargement to the Balkans was useful in highlighting the process of engaging with European integration a public that positioned itself exclusively within the realm of the national space and its stories. Investigating this discursive dynamic from the Balkans was meant to support two assumptions that have not been widely accepted within the study of Europeanisation. First, external Europeanisation should not be taken for granted: it is not a calculable outcome of offering the privilege of membership and pursuing a predictable stick-and-carrots conditionality agenda. Much as it depends on the credibility of the membership perspective, external Europeanisation is bound by compatibility with national identity constructions and dominant visions of political community. In fact, external Europeanisation cannot be fully understood outside identity politics. Second, the process of renegotiating national identity to make it compatible with Europeanisation is central to maintaining the relevance of European integration in national politics. This dynamic has been quite visible in the external context where Europeanisation had to be negotiated anew. But its applicability to the internal strand of Europeanisation appears just as critical in view of the current crisis of confidence in the EU. If understood fully, this dynamic could address many of the uncertainties that integration currently has to deal with in terms of legitimacy deficit and lack of popular support.

Of all the Balkan states that were (and are) lined up for EU membership, Bulgaria and Macedonia were selected because of the peculiar identity-based conflict that marked their complex relationship. Joining the process of Europeanisation seemed to have tilted this conflict towards reconciliation, which suggested that the impact of Europeanisation on national identity narrated in the antagonistic, exclusive and deterministic manner dictated by nationalism could be quite significant. With the renewed relevance to European politics of what has been termed post-liberal nationalism, understanding the impact of Europeanisation on national identity in terms of reconciliation, and overcoming conflictuality become pressing. Choosing Bulgaria and Macedonia as case studies thus reflects a search for comparability, as the conflict that marked Bulgarian–Macedonian relations could well relate to many other latent 'cold' conflicts that strain identity politics in Europe.

This choice was also analytically justified in view of the conceptual framework of this book. National identity was conceptualised as a discursive construction that emerged from the dialectic of positioning the Self against and in relation to the Other(s). Within this conceptualisation identity cannot be fully understood without its constitutive Other(s). Bulgarian–Macedonian relations seemed to form such a central axis of Othering in the national identity constructions in the two states because of the specific historical circumstances that had shaped the relationship. Isolating this axis and focusing the investigation on it thus enabled a reasonable balance between feasibility and detail. Focusing on one state only would have been insufficient in view of exploring the discursive positions of Self and Other in specific state behaviour. Selecting more than two states, on the other hand, would have significantly complicated the task of incorporating the identity-building dynamic into a methodologically viable research design. This is what suggested working with these two states only. Studying national identity narratives that sustained their bilateral relations formed the empirical part of the book.

The investigation looked at the most salient stories told about the nation and its subjects in the context of Bulgarian–Macedonian relations, and selected six narrative groups that were identifiable in both states. They also formed, predictably, part of most national identity constructs: stories about nationhood, territory, purpose, statehood, language, minorities. Despite the very specific local contexts in which these narrative groups uphold national identity, their almost universal presence in the construction of the nation points to the basis of comparability and inference from the conclusions of this investigation. Applying a methodological hybrid of discourse and contents analysis in conjunction with historical and foreign policy analysis, the investigation attempted to break down the selected narratives into their constitutive discursive elements. It identified their structuring centres – territory, language, minority, etc. – and aimed to capture the dynamic of fixing their meanings. Unsurprisingly, changing political contexts, actors and imperatives seemed to affect the process of re-narration. Identifying these was thus the analytical starting point of deconstructing the narratives.

Focusing on one discursive element at different points in time, the investigation followed the Self–Other dialectic that eventually produced the meaning of identity. Comparing meanings upheld at different points in time during the progress of Europeanisation allowed for an understanding of the modification that the discursive realm of integration had introduced into the narration of identity. The process of empowering Europe began during the post-communist transition. The analysed points in time were selected within its timeframe. The selection was guided by the increased political salience of certain discursive elements from the national identity narratives. Articulating the meaning of language in the national story, for instance, was more intensive during the so-called language dispute between Bulgaria and Macedonia. Looking at interpretations of language when the dispute began and after its resolution revealed different subject positions linked to changed discursive contexts. Highlighting the discursive dynamics of subject repositioning pointed to the mechanisms of identity change in the process of empowering Europeanisation. To be able to draw valid conclusions about these mechanisms, the investigation followed the dynamic of subject repositioning

Legitimacy and European national identities | 179

around six key discursive elements from the national identity constructs. To be able to fully grasp the implications of this dynamic, it traced variations in interpretation both within and across the narrative unit. Identifying differences in the interpretation of the analysed elements pointed to modifications in the national identity narratives. These modifications revealed how imagining the political community had changed in the course of Europeanisation.

Discursive logic of identity change

Inevitably, Europeanisation's ability to articulate alternative meanings to the central elements sustaining the national narratives depended on the structural features of the changing discursive contexts that characterised the transitions in the two studied states. A variety of factors, both domestic and external, influenced the progress of the transition and the pace of the process of Europeanisation in the two states. Tracing the interpretation of similar elements in the discursive patterns of identity diachronically in the two states demonstrated that variations were linked to the formal progress of integration. The meaning of national territory, for example, transformed significantly with the advance of membership negotiations in Bulgaria. The idea of a closely guarded territory whose integrity was to be protected at any cost was gradually replaced with a vision of open borders and the aspiration to guard a much larger territorial space: Europe. In Macedonia, the interpretation of national territory as part of a severed whole was gradually marginalised to emphasise the legitimacy of the territorial status quo of the time and to protect it. Very different in themselves, the variations in the national narratives in both states ultimately upheld a less antagonistic national identity story in terms of internal and external Others. The formal progress of integration, however, took a different course in the two states. This, in its turn, was linked to a combination of domestic and international factors, which included the political configuration in power, the modalities of majority–minority accommodation, the problems arising from the regional setting (Figure 7.1). These factors ultimately determined the political consensus on Europe, as well as the specific incentives provided by Europe to stimulate such consensus. Where the domestic political outcomes did not favour immediate progress in the integration process, the relevance of Europeanisation's reading of national identity decreased. Comparing the two states under study here, the problem of Macedonia's international legal subjectivity impeded by Greek non-recognition stands out as one such outcome. Significantly slowing down Macedonia's integration efforts, it reduced the political relevance of integration and reinforced the discursive power of nationalist interpretations of identity. The prolonged stay in office by former communists in Bulgaria, compromising the legitimacy of the post-communist transition, stands out as another example of such a domestic outcome. Impeding successful reforms, it prevented progress towards membership negotiation and decreased the political relevance of Europeanisation. As soon as membership negotiations began after a domestic change of government, the process of Europeanisation began to stabilise and could produce more relevant readings of national identity narratives.

180 | Between Nationalism and Europeanisation

Figure 7.1: Discursive logic of the Europeanisation of national identity narratives

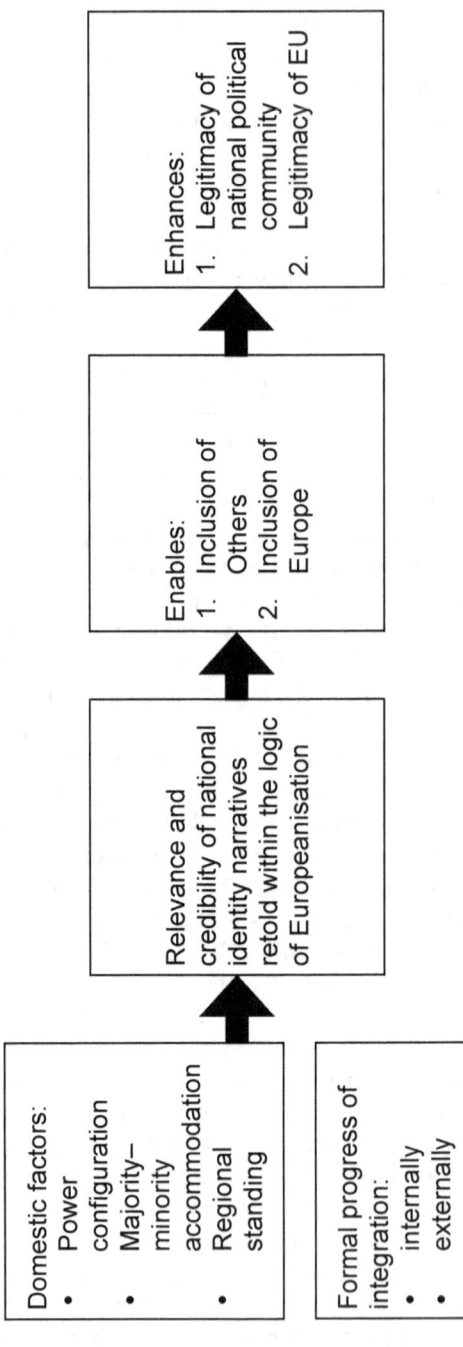

The increased relevance and credibility of European interpretations of national identity narratives conditioned by these specific contexts produced modifications in the discursive construction of national identity. The limit of belonging no longer followed strictly national lines but began to point to a political community with much more open, inclusive and flexible boundaries. The modifications enabled the inclusion of national Other(s) and of Europe as elements in the discursive construction of national Self. As a result, the political community of the state appeared much more adequate and suitable to the changed realities of transnational politics and integration in Europe. This enhanced its legitimacy. At the same time, the inclusion of European references in the national stories 'internalised' integration within the realm of national politics, made it part of domestic political mobilisation and contestation, and thus enhanced the legitimacy of the EU itself.

The discursive logic of this dynamic was followed synchronically in the two states in the interpretations of the same discursive elements structuring bilateral relations. Identifying variations in the interpretation of their meanings in Bulgaria and in Macedonia enabled these variations to be checked against the progress of Europeanisation in the two states. Where political consensus on the relevance and appropriateness of Europeanisation failed – in the context of other domestic problems taking priority or of staggering integration efforts – nationalist interpretations resumed their salience and reproduced antagonisms in bilateral relations. Detached from the discourse of Europeanisation, Bulgaria's recognition of Macedonian statehood, for instance, was interpreted as a national threat in both Bulgaria and Macedonia. With the opening up of national spaces towards the integration processes in Europe, however, this interpretation was marginalised to give way to constructive interpretations of the act of recognition. But while in Bulgaria this happened almost immediately with the first steps towards Europeanisation, Macedonia had to wait in isolation before it could initiate interstate dialogue with European states. The remarkable domestic silence on Bulgaria's presumably amicable act of recognition testifies to this discursive vacuum. Against its background, the only interpretations of it were provided by the discourse of nationalism, which asserted its hegemonic presence in Macedonian politics.

A very similar discursive dynamics characterised interpretations of language at different stages of the language dispute. At the very beginning of Europeanisation in the region, language was interpreted as a central element of the national identity construction and compromises with it were seen as an immediate identity threat. With the gradual empowerment of Europeanisation, helped most significantly by the election of democratic governments in both states, European interpretation of culture as a field of commonality and mutual complementation affected the salience of language as an identity element and facilitated the resolution of the language dispute. European readings of national identity enabled reconciliation, enhancing the legitimacy of the national identity stories as the pivot of political community and stabilising the discursive power of Europeanisation which upheld them. This outcome was observed despite the divergent interpretations of the identity narratives in the specific national contexts. Subscribing to the discourse of Europeanisation resulted in different, often even contradictory, meanings attached to one and the same discursive element in the two states. But the implications of these meanings in the way the political community was being seen were generally quite similar: less antagonism along national lines, more relevance for the integration project.

Despite the accelerated progress of integration and the visible salience of Europeanisation, however, the relevance of European interpretations remained low around certain discursive elements. Determining the subject positions of Self and Other around the discursive element of minorities proved particularly resistant to the meanings upheld by Europeanisation. Tracing variations both within and across this narrative unit (in the narratives of nationhood and in the narratives on mutual recognition of minorities, respectively) confirmed this finding. The weakness of Europeanisation rhetoric around this discursive element not so much contradicted the discursive dynamic confirmed in the reading of all the other elements, as pointed back to the assumption from which the investigation started. Europeanisation needs to be able to compete with nationalist interpretations of national identity because European integration occurs within the constraints of the nation-state whose normative foundation is sustained by the logic of nationalism. The historical precedence of nationalism in interpreting the national stories makes it difficult for Europeanisation to modify some of the most sedimented interpretations. Establishing credible European readings of national identity in the narratives studied in the two states is empirically linked to nationalist interpretations being marginalised and the normative power of Europeanisation being reinforced. On the contrary, where elite rhetoric does not succeed in providing credible alternative interpretations of national identity within the logic of Europeanisation, the political relevance of nationalism is increased. Nationalism's deterministic and non-flexible interpretations of the political community's borders, the basis for belonging within it, and vision of its future, are incompatible with the logic of integration. In the context of nationalist rhetoric the process of Europeanisation appears as an encroachment on the sovereignty of the political community of the nation-state. This seriously compromises the normative power of the EU and its legitimacy, which feeds back into the realm of national politics by stabilising traditional interpretations of political community within the logic of nationalism.

It is obvious from these observations that the discursive struggle between different interpretations of national identity has a direct impact on the way the political community of the state is imagined. Nationalist rhetoric sustains a vision of political community centred around nationhood, dependent upon history, ambiguous about fully integrating national Other(s), and maintaining the boundary of national difference as a matter of national survival. Such political community contains a high conflictual potential in view of national Otherness, which compromises its legitimacy in a transnational globalising world, and is suspicious of Europeanisation as an encroachment on its sovereignty, independence, and sense of Self. Europeanisation rhetoric, on the other hand, envisages a political community that establishes a basis of commonality between national Others, is willing to overcome history and historic antagonisms for the benefit of a common future, transforms the function of national borders as connecting rather than separating European nations, and pushes the boundary of difference beyond national spaces to the outer limit of the realm of Europeanisation. Imagined within the logic of Europeanisation, political community appears as much more open and receptive of national Otherness, less antagonistic towards historic adversaries, and more engaged with the progress of Europeanisation. The normative power of Europeanisation supports the self-esteem boosting function of national identity narrated within this logic, and helps maintain a positive and optimistic vision of political community. The internalisation of European references into the national identity construction, in turn, increases the relevance of integration in national politics, thus enhancing the legitimacy of the Europeanisation process. The outcome of the discursive struggle between competing interpretations of national identity thus emerges as central to the future of the national political community and to the future of the EU.

Research contribution

This book has argued that national identity is a central element within the discursive spaces of national political communities and of Europeanisation. The interpretation of the meaning of national identity has important consequences for the boundaries of political community and directly affects its legitimacy. It also affects the legitimacy of the Europeanisation process and the supranational governance it sustains by engaging national politics with it. Thinking about narratives of identity in those terms is significant because it addresses in a challenging way many of the central debates in the study of European politics. The discussion on an emerging European identity and how it relates to national identity and to support for integration, for example, has traditionally explored the way European identity and national identity compare, and how identification with Europe (rather than with the nation) generates (or does not) support for integration. This book suggests that such an analytical focus might not be the most productive. National identity and European identity are neither mutually exclusive nor necessarily antagonistic. But a comparison between the two reveals little about legitimacy and support for integration simply because European identity cannot compete with the historical precedence of national identity in mobilising support for the political community and its projects. Looking instead into the effects of Europeanisation on national identity can be much more productive. It suggests that the legitimacy of integration is linked to national identity much more than to the emerging European identity, and that support for integration much depends on how credibly national identity is engaged with Europe and how effectively it internalises European references as discursive elements of the national identity construction itself.

The study of the normative power of Europeanisation and the external role of the European project as an agent of change, another important discussion in the Europeanisation literature, can also be seen in a new light. Identity politics is crucial to successful outcomes of external integration. Successful engagement of the national identity stories with the logic of Europeanisation and its normative foundations can determine the type of change Europeanisation can induce. Such a claim goes against mainstream approaches that analyse external Europeanisation in terms of integration's economic benefits (presumed as given despite the crisis riddling the EU), the impact of political conditionality (despite the ambiguous sustainability of change invoked through the conditionality process), or the effect of a range of domestic structures (an approach that ultimately essentialises domestic contexts and defies the ability of Europeanisation to induce change).

Understanding the relevance of nationalism to European politics is another way in which this book challenged established frameworks. The tradition of studying nationalism as an extreme phenomenon peripheral to Europe has not helped identify the structuring impact of nationalism on resistance to integration both externally and internally. Untangling the interpretations upheld by nationalist narratives and pointing to their consequences for state behaviour and political mobilisation has revealed a discursive dynamic that is not region-specific but context specific. It is also identifiable in the context of normal politics – not extreme, hot conflict situations. In this sense, the relevance of nationalism and its related phenomena to the entire realm of Europeanisation – and not just the periphery – needs to be fully understood. This is particularly important in terms of rising identity-based antagonisms, intolerance of Otherness, xenophobia and racism in European politics. That Europeanisation contains the potential to arrest identity-based conflictuality, if pursued to that end, is an important aspect of the integration project that has been overlooked in the current context of rising nationalist populism. This book has aimed to emphasise that, rather than being the problem, the process of integration might be the solution to identity-based antagonisms and nationalism embedded within the structure of modern politics. Its reconciliatory potential needs to be further investigated and understood.

Exploring the impact of Europeanisation on national identities and the consequences thereof on the specific regional viewpoint of this book also challenges the established methodological bifurcation in the Europeanisation literature between internal and external strands. External Europeanisation is often studied as a one-directional dynamic of norm transfer and conditionality, whereas internal Europeanisation is more often than not examined as a two-directional dynamic of negotiation and deliberation. It is important to overcome this methodological bifurcation in order to understand the negotiation and deliberation dynamics that shape the process of external Europeanisation and feed back into the realm of the EU. It is obvious that enlargement has significantly changed perceptions and practices of integration. Understanding how the meaning of Europe has been negotiated and deliberated during the process of enlargement is but the first step to understanding that change.

The specific regional focus of this book aimed to contribute to an understudied tenet of Balkan politics. Bulgaria and Macedonia have not attracted significant academic interest compared to other Balkan states because of their relative stability as compared to the (rest of the) Western Balkans. Bulgarian–Macedonian relations, in particular, have been even more understudied. They were discussed extensively in the respective national academic communities during the time of the totalitarian state. These discussions, outdated and tainted by the ideological struggles of the time, at present fail to provide an accurate idea of the complex layers of conflictuality that strain regional relations, or an accurate understanding of their political implications. In view of Macedonia's pending EU negotiations and the persisting strain on Bulgarian–Macedonian relations (Nancheva and Koneska, 2015), it is important to understand the mechanisms of bilateral tensions.

Finally, the book has strived to contribute methodologically to the study of national identity in Europe and to the study of national identity change within Europeanisation in particular. Its unique theoretical and meta-theoretical framework, combining reflectivist strands from several academic (sub-)disciplines whose mainstreams are widely rationalist. International relations theory, area studies and cultural-political geography, European studies and nationalism studies have each in their own way approached national identity and attempted to explain its political relevance. Constrained by the limitations of their rationalist epistemologies and by their own disciplinary agendas, however, their accounts have been challenged on many grounds: level of analysis, area focus, ontological assumptions. Looking at national identity from a multidisciplinary perspective allows for the incorporation of various theoretical approaches (securitisation theory, normative theories of Europeanisation, critical approaches to studying nationalism), various levels of analysis (seeing the macro-level not as a system or state level but as embedded in both the international and the domestic contexts), various qualitative methods (comparative analysis over a small number of cases carried out on the basis of discourse and contents analysis and historical and foreign policy analysis). The discursive approach to the study of national identity change, in particular, opens up compelling new ways of understanding the implications of identity narration on the boundaries and legitimacy of political community in Europe.

What next?

Pointing to this exciting research agenda, this book has aimed to make its contribution by framing a much-repeated concept – national identity – in an original research context and analysing it in a novel and challenging way. It has sought to answer the questions it posed. At the same time, it has opened new questions that remain to be answered. One concerns the mechanisms of maintaining the reconciliatory effects of Europeanisation along the axes of Bulgarian–Macedonian relations once the dynamics of the relationship had changed. Radically repositioning the national subjects with regard to the process of integration, Bulgaria's EU accession significantly affected the re-narration of identity and bilateral relations. The consequences of this need to be studied in the changed dynamic of Othering across the external EU border. Identity-based antagonisms with another, longer-standing, EU member – Greece – also beckon more attention to the effects of Europeanisation on identity narration that occurs along the lines of member/candidate-member relations. This is particularly important because both members and candidate members are engaged with the Europeanisation process and do have an impact on its course. At the same time, identity-based conflictuality within and across member states needs further investigation in view of the propositions made in this book.

Linked to this is another question that beckons further research. The modalities of accommodating difference in the various contexts of identity-based antagonisms that riddle the realm of Europeanisation have been referred to in this book through a common denominator – post-liberal nationalism. These phenomena, however, display significant peculiarities in the various contexts, even though they are all linked to the discursive narration of identity in view of Other(s). They need to be studied in greater detail, as the Europeanisation dynamic engages the subjects and objects of such antagonisms in very different ways: the *problématique* of the asylum framework and Europeanisation, of minority regimes in the EU, of anti-racism policies, of the securitisation of migration in the EU all invite focused, analytical inquiry.

Finally, this book has argued at length that the impact of Europeanisation on the narration of national identities has directly affected the legitimacy of the political communities they signified and referred to. This concerns both the national political community and the supranational community with which national communities engage. If this is truly so, as this book has argued, then the Europeanisation of national identities should be directly linked to attitudes and support for European integration. That link needs to be studied separately from both a qualitative and a quantitative perspective in order to be fully understood. How it functions and whether it can be modified appears, perhaps, as the biggest story that remains to be told about Europeanisation.

Bibliography

Agger, B. (1991) 'Critical theory, poststructuralism, postmodernism: their sociological relevance', *Annual Review of Sociology*, 17, 105–31.
Anderson, B. (1983, 1991) *Imagined Communities*, London: Verso.
Angelov, V. (2004) *The Macedonian Question in Bulgarian–Yugoslavian Relations*, Sofia: University St Kliment Ohridski.
Arsenova, D. (2001) 'Ethno-centric formations in Bulgaria and Macedonia: an object of inter-state consensus', *Challenges of Transition*, Sofia: Archive Bulgaria–Macedonia, available at http://www.balkans21.org/arhiv/dolores6.htm (accessed 1 June 2015).
Aykaç, C. E. (2011) 'What space for migrant voices in European anti-racism', in G. Delanty, R. Wodak and P. Jones (eds) *Identity, Belonging and Migration*, Liverpool: Liverpool University Press: 120–34.
Bach, M., Lahusen, C. and Vobruba, G. (eds) (2006) *Europe in Motion: Social Dynamics and Political Institutions in an Enlarging Europe*, Berlin: edition sigma.
Barnard, F (1967) *Herder's Social and Political Thought*, Oxford: Clarendon Press.
Baylis, J., Smith, S. and Owens, P. (eds) (2011) *The Globalization of World Politics: An Introduction to International Relations*, Oxford: Oxford University Press.
Berov, I. (1999) 'United Europe, the barbarians and civilization', *Demokratsia* newspaper, 2 February.
Bhabha, H. K. (ed.) (1990) *Nation and Narration*, London: Routledge.
Bhavnani, K.-K. and Phoenix, A. (1994) 'Shifting identities, shifting racisms: an introduction', *Feminism and Psychology*, 4, 5–18.
Bieber, F. (2008) 'Conclusions: the Ohrid Framework Agreement after 7 years', in F. Bieber (ed.) *Power-Sharing and the Implementation of the Ohrid Framework Agreement*, Skopje: Friedrich Ebert Stiftung: 207–11.
Billig, M. (1995) *Banal Nationalism*, Sage: London.
Bloom, W. (1990) *Personal Identity, National Identity and International Relations*, New York: Cambridge University Press.
Breuilly, J. (1982) *Nationalism and the State*, Manchester: Manchester University Press.
— (2014) 'Nationalism and the Balkans', in Rutar, S. (ed.) *Beyond the Balkans: Towards an Inclusive History of Southeastern Europe*, Wien, Zürich, Berlin: Lit: 29–47.
Brubaker, R. (1994) 'Rethinking nationhood: nation as institutionalized form, practical category, contingent event', *Contention*, 4(1), 3–14.

— (1999) 'The Manichean myth: rethinking the distinction between "civic" and "ethnic" nationalism', in H. Kriesi, A. Wimmer, K. Armingeon and H. Siegrist (eds) *Nation and National Identity: The European Experience in Perspective*, Zürich: Ruegger: 55–71.

Brubaker, R. and Cooper, F. (2000) 'Beyond identity', *Theory and Society*, 29(1), 1–47.

Bruter, M. (2004) 'Civic and cultural components of a European identity: a pilot model of measurement of citizens' levels of European identity', in R. Herrmann, T. Risse and M. M. Brewer (eds) *Transnational Identities*, Boulder: Rowman & Littlefield.

— (2005) *Citizens of Europe? The Emergence of a Mass European Identity*, Basingstoke: Palgrave Macmillan.

— (2008) 'Legitimacy, Euroscepticism and identity in the European Union – problems of measurement, modelling and paradoxical patterns of influence', *Journal of Contemporary European Research*, 4(4), 273–85.

Buecker, N. (2006) 'Returning to where? Images of "Europe" and support for the process of EU integration in Poland', in I. P. Karolewski and V. Kaina (eds) *European Identity: Theoretical Perspectives and Empirical Insights*, Münster: LIT Verlag: 265–95.

Bulgarian Academy of Sciences (1999) *History of Bulgaria*, Volume 8, Sofia: GALICO.

Bulgarian National Anthem (Национален химн на България – 'Мила Родино'; музика и текст – Цветан Радославов, 1885 г. Приет – 1964 г.), National anthem of Bulgaria : 'Mila Rodino'; music and lyrics by Tsvetan Radoslavov, 1885. Adopted in 1964.

Burgess, P. (2002) 'What's so European about the European Union? Legitimacy between institution and identity', *European Journal of Social Theory* 5(4), 467–81.

Burke, P. (1980) 'The self: measurement requirements from an interactionist perspective', *Social Psychology Quarterly*, 43, 18–29.

Calhoun, C. (1997) *Nationalism*, Buckingham: Open University Press.

Campbell, D. (1998a) *National Deconstruction: Violence, Identity and Justice*, Minneapolis: University of Minnesota Press.

— (1998b) *Writing Security: United States Foreign Policy and the Politics of Identity*, Minneapolis: University of Minnesota Press.

Caporaso, J. A. and Kim, M.-H. (2009) 'The dual nature of European identity: subjective awareness and coherence', *Journal of European Public Policy*, 16(1), 19–42.

Castano, E. and Dechesne, M. (2005) 'On defeating death: group reification and social identification as strategies for transcendence', in W. Stroebe and M. Hewstone (eds), *European Review of Social Psychology*, Chichester, England: Wiley, pp. 221–255.

Cerutti, F. and Lucarelli, S. (2008) *The Search for a European Identity: Values, Policies and Legitimacy of the European Union*, Oxon: Routledge.

Checkel, J. (2001) 'Why comply? Social learning and European identity change', *International Organization*, 55(3), 553–88.
— (2005) 'Getting socialized to build bridges: constructivism and rational choice, Europe and the nation state' (with M. Zuern), *International Organization*, 59(4).
Checkel, J. and Katzenstein, P. J. (eds) (2009) *European Identity*, Cambridge University Press.
Choueiri, Y. (2000) *Arab Nationalism: A History. Nation and State in the Arab World*, Basingstoke: Palgrave.
Correll, J. and Park, B. (2005) A model of the ingroup as social resource', *Personality and Social Psychology Review*, 9, 341–59.
Cowles, M. G., Caporaso, J. A. and Risse-Kappen, T. (eds) (2001) *Transforming Europe: Europeanisation and Domestic Change*, Ithaca, NY: Cornell University Press.
Cox, R. (1993) 'Gramsci, hegemony and international relations: an essay in method', in S. Gill (ed.) *Gramsci, Historical Materialism and International Relations*, Cambridge: Cambridge University Press: 49–66.
Craiutu, A. (1995) 'A dilemma of dual identity: the democratic alliance of Hungarians in Romania,' *East European Constitutional Review*, 4(2) (Spring), 43–9.
Danforth, L. (1993) 'Claims to Macedonian identity: the Macedonian Question and the breakup of Yugoslavia', *Anthropology Today*, 9(4), 3–10.
Daskalovski, Ž. (2004) *The Macedonian Conflict of 2001: Problems of Democratic Consolidation*, Libertas Paper 56.
Deets, S. (2006) 'Reimagining the boundaries of the nation: politics and the development of ideas on minority rights', *East European Politics and Societies*, 20(3): 419–66.
Deflem, M. and Pampel, F. C. (1996) 'The myth of postnational identity: popular support for European unification', *Social Forces*, 75(1), 119–43.
Delanty, G. and O'Mahony, P. (2002) *Nationalism and Social Theory*, London: Sage.
Delanty, G., Wodak, R. and Jones, P. (2011) *Identity, Belonging and Migration*, Liverpool University Press.
Derrida, J. (1982) *Margins of Philosophy* (translated by A. Bass), Chicago: University of Chicago Press.
Deutsch, F. (2006) 'Legitimacy and identity in the European Union: empirical findings from the old member states', in I. P. Karolewski and V. Kaina (eds) *European Identity: Theoretical Perspectives and Empirical Insights*, Münster.: LIT Verlag: 149–78.
Deutsch, K. (1942) 'International affairs: the trend of European nationalism – the language aspect', *American Political Science Review*, 36(3), 533–41.
— (1954) *Political Community at the International Level*, Sandy, UT: Aardvark Global.
Diez, T., Manners, I. Whitman, R. G. (2011)'The changing nature of international institutions in Europe: the challenge of the European Union', *Journal of European Integration*, 33 (2), 117–38.

Díez Medrano, J. and Gutiérrez, P. (2001) 'Nested identities: national and European identity in Spain', in *Ethnic and Racial Studies*, 24(5), 753–78.
Di Palma, G. (2013) *The Modern State Subverted: Risk and the Deconstruction of Solidarity*, Colchester: ECPR Press.
Dragnev, D. (1998) *The Skopje Icon Blazhe Koneski: Macedonian Linguist or Serbian Political Worker?* Sofia, Macedonian Scientific Institute.
Elster, J. (ed.) (1996) *The Roundtable Talks and the Breakdown of Communism*, Chicago: University of Chicago Press.
Eriksen, E. O. (2005) 'An emerging European public sphere', *European Journal of Social Theory*, 8(3), 341–63.
Fairclough, N. (1992) *Discourse and Social Change*, Cambridge: Polity Press.
Favell, A. (2008) 'The new face of east–west migration', *Journal of Ethnic and Migration Studies*, 34(5), 701–16.
Featherstone, K. and Kazamias, G. (2001) *Europeanisation and the Southern Periphery*, London: Frank Cass.
Featherstone, K. and Radaelli, C. (eds) (2003) *The Politics of Europeanisation*, Oxford: Oxford University Press.
Fichte, J. G. (2009) *Addresses to the German Nation*, Cambridge: Cambridge University Press.
Fierke, K. M. and Wiener, A. (1999) 'Constructing institutional interests: EU and NATO enlargement', *Journal of European Public Policy*, 6, 721–42.
Finnemore, M. and Sikkink, K. (1998) 'International norm dynamics and political change', *International Organization*, 50(4), 887–917.
Fligstein, N., Polyakova, A. and Sandholtz, W. (2012) 'European integration, nationalism and European identity', *Journal of Common Market Studies*, 50(1), 106–122.
Flockhart, T. (2006) '"Complex socialization": a framework for the study of state socialization', *European Journal of International Relations*, 12(1), 89–111.
Føllesdal, A. (2006) 'The legitimacy deficits of the European Union', *Journal of Political Philosophy*, 14(4), 441–68.
Foret, F. (2009) 'Symbolic dimensions of EU legitimization', *Media, Culture and Society*, 31(2), 313–24.
— (2010) 'European political rituals: a challenging tradition in the making', *International Political Anthropology*, 3(1), 55–77.
Foret, F. and Rittelmeyer, Y.-S. (eds) (2014) *The European Council and European Governance: The Commanding Heights of the EU*, London: Routledge.
Foucault, M. (2002) *Archaeology of Knowledge*, London: Routledge.
Franklin, M. N. and Van der Eijk, C. (1996) 'The problem: representation and democracy in the European Union', in C. van der Eijk and M. N. Franklin (eds) *Choosing Europe? The European Electorate and National Politics in the Face of Union*, Ann Arbor: University of Michigan Press: 3–10.
Freeman, G. (1995) 'Modes of immigration in liberal democratic states', in *International Migration Review*, 29(4), 881–902.

Fuchs, D., Magni-Berton, R. and Roger, A. (2009) 'Euroscepticism', in *Images of Europe Among Mass Publics and Political Elites*, Opladen and Farmington Hills: Barbara Budrich.

Galbreath, D. and McEvoy, J. (2012) 'European organizations and minority rights in Europe: on transforming the securitization dynamic', *Security Dialogue*, 43(3), 267–84.

Ganev, V. (2004) 'History, politics, and the constitution: ethnic conflict and constitutional adjudication in postcommunist Bulgaria', *Slavic Review*, 63(1), 66–89.

Garton Ash, T. (1989) 'Revolution in Hungary and Poland', in *New York Review of Books*, 17 August.

Gati, C. (1996) 'If not democracy, what? Leaders, laggards and losers in the postcommunist world', in M. Mandelbaum (ed.) *Post-Communism Four Perspectives*, Washington, DC: Council on Foreign Relations.

Gellner, E. (1983) *Nations and Nationalism*, Oxford, Blackwell.

Georgievski, L. (2007) 'Facing truth' (С лице към истината: есета) Sofia: Balkani.

Gerring, J. (2004) 'What is a case study and what is it good for?' *American Political Science Review*, 98(2), 341–54, 343.

Glenny, M. (2000) *The Balkans: 1804–1999: Nationalism, War and the Great Powers*, London: Granta.

Gotsev, D. (1981) *National Liberation Struggles in Macedonia 1912–1915*, Sofia: Bulgarian Academy of Sciences. In Bulgarian.

Guiannakos, S. (2001) 'Bulgaria's Macedonian dilemma', *Journal of Southern Europe and the Balkans*, 3(2), 153–70.

Habermas, J. (1998) *The Inclusion of the Other: Studies in Political Theory*, Cambridge, MA: MIT Press.

Habermas, J. and Derrida, J. (2003) 'February 15, or what binds Europeans together: a plea for a common foreign policy, beginning in the core of Europe', *Constellations*, 10(3), 291–7.

Hanauer, D. I. (2011) 'Non-place identity: Britain's response to migration in the age of supermodernity', in G. Delanty, R. Wodak and P. Jones (eds) *Identity, Belonging and Migration*, Liverpool: Liverpool University Press: 198–218.

Hansen, L. and Wæver, O. (2002) *European Integration and National Identity: The Challenge of the Nordic States*, London: Routledge.

Hayes, C. (1931) *The Historical Evolution of Modern Nationalism*, New York: R. R. Smith.

Herrmann, R. and Brewer, M. B. (2004) 'Identities and institutions: becoming European in the EU', in R. K. Herrmann, T. Risse and M. B. Brewer (eds) *Transnational Identities: Becoming European in the EU*, Lanham.:Rowman & Littlefield: 1–22.

Hix, S. (2005) 'Neither a preference-outlier nor a unitary actor: institutional reform preferences of the European Parliament', *Comparative European Politics*, 3(2), 131–54.

Hobsbawm, E. (1990) *Nations and Nationalism since 1780*, Cambridge: Cambridge University Press.
Hoffmann, S. (1966) 'Obstinate or obsolete? The fate of the nation state and the case of Western Europe', *Daedalus*, 95, 862–915.
Hogg, M. and Abrams, D. (1988) *Social Identifications*, London: Routledge.
Hooghe, L. (2007) 'What drives Euroskepticism? Party-Public cueing, ideology and strategic opportunity', *European Union Politics*, 8(1), 5–12.
Hooghe, L. and Marks, G. (2005) 'Calculation, community and cues: public opinion on European Integration', *European Union Politics*, 6(4), 419–43.
— (2007) 'Sources of Euroscepticism', *Acta Politica*, 42(2–3), 119–27.
— (2009) 'A postfunctionalist theory of European integration: from permissive consensus to constraining dissensus', *British Journal of Political Science*, 39(1), 1–23.
Hopf, T. (2002) *Social Construction of Foreign Policy: Identities and Foreign Policies, Moscow, 1955 and 1999*, Ithaca, NY: Cornell University Press.
Höpken, W. (1997) 'From religious identity to ethnic mobilisation: the Turks of Bulgaria before, under and since communism', in H. Poulton and S. Taji-Farouki (eds) *Muslim Identity and the Balkan State*, London: Hurst, pp. 54–81.
Howarth, D. R. and Torfing, J. (2005) *Discourse Theory in European Politics*, Palgrave Macmillan.
Hristov, A. (1971) Creating the *Macedonian State (1893–1945)*, Belgrade: Contemporary Administration. In Serbian.
Ingebritsen, C. and Larson, S. (1997) 'Interest and identity: Finland, Norway and European Union', *Cooperation and Conflict*, 32, 207–22.
Joppke, C. (1998) 'Why liberal states accept unwanted immigration', *World Politics*, 50(2), 266–93.
Jovanović, M. (2005) 'Recognizing minority identities through collective rights', *Human Rights Quarterly*, 27(3), 625–51.
Kaina, V. (2006) 'European identity, legitimacy, and trust: conceptual considerations and perspectives on empirical research', in I. P. Karolewski and V. Kaina (eds) *European Identity: Theoretical Perspectives and Empirical Insights*, Münster: LIT Verlag pp. 113–46.
— (2009) *Wir in Europa: Kollektive Identität und Demokratie in der Europäischen Union*, Wiesbaden: VS Verlag für Sozialwissenschaften.
Kaina, V. and Karolewski, I. P. (2009) 'EU governance and European identity', *Living Reviews in European Governance*, 4(2), available at http://www.livingreviews.org/lreg-2009-2 (accessed 1 June 2015).
Karolewski, I. P. and Kaina, V. (2006) *European Identity: Theoretical Perspectives and Empirical Insights*, Münster: LIT Verlag.
— (eds) (2012) *Civic Resources and the Future of the European Union*, Oxon: Routledge.

Karolewski, I. P. and Suszycki, A. M. (eds) (2010) *Multiplicity of Nationalism in Contemporary Europe*, Plymouth: Lexington Books.
— (2011) *The Nation and Nationalism in Europe: An Introduction*, Edinburgh University Press.
Kedourie, E. (1993) *Nationalism*, Oxford: Blackwell.
Kohn, H. (1955) *Nationalism: Its Meaning and History*, Princeton: D. Van Nostrand.
Kolishevski, L. (1981) *Aspects of the Macedonian Question*, Belgrade: People's Book. In Serbian.
Koneski, B. (1982) *Grammar of the Macedonian Literary Language*, Skopje: Kultura, 1982.
Kopper, Á. (2006) 'Anchoring at the Western shore: the European identity of Hungarians at the wake of European accession', in I. P. Karolewski and V. Kaina (eds) *European Identity: Theoretical Perspectives and Empirical Insights*, Münster: LIT Verlag pp. 297.
Krastev, I. (2004) *Shifting Obsession: Three Essays on the Politics of Anticorruption*, Cambridge: Cambridge University Press.
Kymlicka, W. (1995) *Multicultural Citizenship: A Liberal Theory of Minority Rights*, Oxford: Oxford University Press.
Lalkov, M. (1995) *Rulers of Bulgaria*, Sofia: Kibea Publishing. In Bulgarian at http://www.historyfiles.co.uk/FeaturesEurope/EasternBulgaria_Kubrat.htm (accessed 1 June 2015).
Lavenex, S. (2002) 'EU enlargement and the challenge of policy transfer: the case of refugee policy', *Journal of Ethnic and Migration Studies*, 28(4), 701–21.
Lindberg, L. N. and Scheingold, S. A. (1970) *Europe's Would-be Polity: Patterns of Change in the European Community*, Englewood Cliffs: Prentice-Hall.
Linklater, A. (1998) *The Transformation of Political Community: Ethical Foundations of the Post-Westphalian Era*, Cambridge: Polity Press.
Lyotard, J.-F. (1984) *The Postmodern Condition: A Report on Knowledge*, Minneapolis: University of Minnesota Press.
Manners, I. (2002) 'Normative power Europe: a contradiction in terms?' *Journal of Common Market Studies*, 40: 235–58. doi: 10.1111/1468-5965.00353.
— (2011) 'The European Union's normative power: critical perspectives and perspectives on the critical', in R. Whitman (ed.), *Normative Power Europe: Empirical and Theoretical Perspectives*, Basingstoke: Palgrave Macmillan: 226–47 (Palgrave Studies in European Union Politics).
Marcussen, M., Risse, T., Engelmann-Martin, D., Knopf, H.-J. and Roscher, K. (1999) 'Constructing Europe: the evolution of French, British and German nation-state identities', *Journal of European Public Policy*, 6(4), 614–33.
Mastropaolo, A. (2012) 'Is democracy a lost cause? Paradoxes of an imperfect invention', Colchester: ECPR Press.
Melone, A. (1994) 'Bulgaria's national roundtable talks and the politics of accommodation', *International Political Science Review*, 15(3), 257–73.

Milenkovski, M. and Talevki J. (2001) 'Delineation of the state border between the Republic of Macedonia and the Federal Republic of Yugoslavia', *iBRU Boundary and Security Bulletin* (Summer 2001), appendix (Border Demarcation Agreement signed by Trajkovski and Kostunica on 23 February 2001).

Miller, D. (1995) *On Nationality*, Oxford: Clarendon Press.

Mitrany, D. (1966) *A Working Peace System*, 4th edition, Chicago: Quadrangle Books.

Mole, R. (ed.) (2007) *Discursive Constructions of Identity in European Politics*, Basingstoke: Palgrave Macmillan.

Moravcsik, A. (1998) *The Choice for Europe: Social Purpose and State Power from Messina to Maastricht*, Ithaca, NY: Cornell University Press.

Motyl, A. (2002) 'Imagined communities, rational choosers, invented ethnies', *Comparative Politics*, 34(2), 233–50.

Mouffe, C. (2000) *The Democratic Paradox*, London: Verso.

— (2007) *On the Political*, London: Routledge.

Nancheva, N. (2007) 'What are norms good for? Ethnic minorities on Bulgaria's way to Europe', *Journal of Communist Studies and Transition Politics*, 23(3): 371–95.

Nancheva, N. with C. Koneska (2015) 'Europeanisation without Europe: the curious case of Bulgarian–Macedonian relations', in *European Politics and Society*. doi: 10.1080/23745118.2014.996325.

Neumann, I. (1992) 'Identity and security', *Journal of Peace Research*, 29(2), 221–6.

Noutcheva, G. and Bechev, D. (2008) 'The successful laggards: Bulgaria and Romania's accession to the EU', in *East European Politics & Societies*, 22(1), 114–44.

Olsen, J. (2002) 'The many faces of Europeanisation', *Journal of Common Market Studies*, 40(5), 921–52.

Özkırımlı, U. (2000) *Theories of Nationalism: A Critical Introduction*, Oxford: Palgrave.

— 2005 *Contemporary Debates on Nationalism: A Critical Engagement*, Oxford: Palgrave.

Paleshtuski, K. (1983) *The Macedonian Question in Bourgeois Yugoslavia 1918–1941, Sofia*: Bulgarian Academy of Sciences. In Bulgarian.

Panagiotou, R. (2008) 'FYRoM's transition: on the Road to Europe?' *Journal of Southern Europe and the Balkans*, 10(1), 47–64.

Perry, D. (1988) *The Politics of Terror: Macedonian Revolutionary Movements, 1893–1903*, Durham, NC: Duke University Press.

Petroska-Beska, V. and Najcavska, M. (2004) *Macedonia: Understanding History, Preventing Future Conflict*, Washington, DC: United States Institute of Peace.

Pichler, F. (2008) 'European identities from below: meanings of identification with Europe', *Perspectives on European Politics and Society*, 9(4), 411–30.

Popova, K. and Hajdinjak, M. (eds) (2006) *Forced Ethnic Migrations on the Balkans: Consequences and Rebuilding of Societies*, Sofia: International Center for Minority Studies and Intercultural Relations.

Poulton, H. and Taji-Farouki (eds) (1997) *Muslim Identity and the Balkan State*, London: Hurst.

Ragaru, N. (2008) *Macedonia: Between Ohrid and Brussels*, Cahiers de Chaillot: 41–60.

Renan, E. (1982) "What is a nation?", text of a conference delivered at the Sorbonne on 11 March 1882, in E. Renan, *Qu'est-ce qu'une nation?* (translated by E. Rundell), Paris: Presses-Pocket.

Risse, T. (2001) 'A European identity? Europeanization and the evolution of nation-state identities', in M. G. Cowles, J. Caporaso and T. Risse (eds) *Transforming Europe: Europeanization and Domestic Change*, Ithaca, NY: Cornell University Press pp. 203–4.

— (2010) *A Community of Europeans? Transnational Identities and Public Spheres*, Ithaca, NY: Cornell University Press.

— (2012) 'Identity matters: exploring the ambivalence of EU foreign policy', *Global Policy*, 3, 87–95. doi: 10.1111/1758-5899.12019.

— (2014) 'No demos? Identities and public spheres in the Euro crisis', *Journal of Common Market Studies*, 50(1), 106–22.

Roller, E. and Sloat, A. (2002) 'The impact of Europeanisation on regional governance: a study of Catalonia and Scotland', *Public Policy and Administration*, 17(2), 17–68.

Roudometof, V. (2002) *Collective Memory, National Identity, and Ethnic Conflict: Greece, Bulgaria, and the Macedonian Question*, Westport, CT: Praeger.

Rousseau, J.-J. (1895 [1762]) *The Social Contract* (translated by H. J. Tozer), London: Swan Sonnenschein.

Rumelili, B. (2004) 'Constructing identity and relating to difference: understanding the EU's mode of differentiation', *Review of International Studies*, 30(1), 27–47.

Rutar, S. (ed.) (2014) *Beyond the Balkans: Towards an Inclusive History of Southeastern Europe*, Wien, Zürich, Berlin: Lit.

Schimmelfennig, F. (2000) 'International socialization in the new Europe: rational action in an institutional environment', *European Journal of International Relations* 6(1), 109–39.

— (2001) 'The community trap: liberal norms, rhetorical action, and the eastern enlargement of the EU', *International Organization*, 55(1), 47–80.

Schimmelfennig, F. and Sedelmeier, U. (eds) (2005a) *The Europeanisation of Central and Eastern Europe*, Ithaca, NY: Cornell University Press.

— (2005b) *The Politics of EU Enlargement: Theoretical Approaches*, London: Routledge.

Schlesinger, P. (1999) 'Changing spaces of political communication: the case of the European Union', *Political Communication*, 16, 263–79.

Schöpflin, G. (2000) *Nations, Identity and Power*, London: Hurst.
Sedelmeier, U. (2011) 'Europeanisation in New Member and Candidate States' *Living Reviews in European Governance*, 6(11), available at: http://www.livingreviews.org/lreg-2011-1 (accessed 11 November 2014).
— (2012) 'Is Europeanisation through conditionality sustainable?: Lock-in of institutional change after EU accession', in *West European Politics*, 35(1), 20–38.
Shotter, J. and Gergen, K. (eds) (1989) *Texts of Identity*, London: Sage.
Sifft, S., Brüggemann, M., Kleinen-V. Königlsöw, K., Peters, B. and Wimmel, A. (2007) 'Segmented Europeanisation: exploring the legitimacy of the EU from a public discourse perspective', *Journal of Common Market Studies*, 45(1), 127–55.
Smith, A. (1992) 'National identity and the idea of European unity', *International Affairs*, 68(1), 55–76.
Snyder, L. (1968) *The New Nationalism*, New Jersey: Transaction Publishers.
Stankov, V. (2003) *Bulgarian Literary Language in the Revival: Scientific Facts and Pseudo-Scientific Arguments*, Sofia: Macedonian Scientific Institute,.
Stoyanov, V. (1998) *The Turkish Population in Bulgaria between the Poles of Ethnopolitics*, Sofia: LIK. In Bulgarian.
Stråth, B. (2002) 'A European identity: to the historical limits of a concept', *European Journal of Social Theory*, 5(4), 387–401.
— (2011) 'Belonging and European identity', in G. Delanty, R. Wodak and P. Jones (eds) *Identity, Belonging and Migration*, Liverpool: Liverpool University Press, pp. 21–38.
Suszycki, A. M. (2006) 'European identity in Sweden', in I. P. Karolewsk and V. Kain (eds) *European Identity: Theoretical Perspectives and Empirical Insights*, Münster: LIT Verlag: 179–207.
Tajfel, H. (ed.) (1981) *Human Groups and Social Categories*, Cambridge: Cambridge University Press.
Talev, D. (2002) *Zhelezniat Svetilnik*, Sofia: Zahariy Stoyanov. In Bulgarian.
Taylor, D. and Moghaddam, F. (1994) *Theories of Intergroup Relations*, Westport, CT: Praeger.
Taylor, P. (2008) *The End of European Integration: Anti-Europeanism Examined*, London/New York: Routledge.
Thomassen, J. (ed.) (2009) *The Legitimacy of the EU after Enlargement*, Oxford: OUP.
Todorova, M. (1997) *Imagining the Balkans*, Oxford: Oxford University Press.
— (2005) 'The trap of backwardness: modernity, temporality and the study of Eastern European nationalism', *Slavic Review*, 64(1), 140–64.
Toggenburg, G. (2000) 'A rough orientation through a delicate relationship: the European Union's endeavours for (its) minorities', *European Integration Online Papers* 4(16), available at http://eiop.or.at/eiop/texte/2000-016a.htm (accessed 1 June 2015).

Torfing, J. (2005) 'Discourse theory: achievements, arguments and challenges', in D. Howarth and J. Torfing, *Discourse Theory in European Politics: Identity, Policy and Governance*, Basingstoke: Palgrave Macmillan.
Triandafyllidou, A., Wodak, R. and Krzyżanowski, M. (2009) *The European Public Sphere and the the Media: Europe in Crisis*, Basingstoke: Palgrave.
Tröbst, S. (1983) *Die bulgarisch-jugoslawische Kontroverse um Makedonien 1967–1982*, München: R. Oldenbourg. In German.
Tyulekov, D. (2007) *Political Myth for the 'Macedonian Minority' in Bulgaria*, Blagoevgrad: Macedonian Scientific Institute.
Wodak, R. (2011) '"Us" and "them": inclusion and exclusion – discrimination via discourse', in G. Delanty, R. Wodak and P. Jones (eds) *Identity, Belonging and Migration*, Liverpool: Liverpool University Press pp. 54–78.
Wodak, R., de Cillia, R., Reisigl, M. and Liebhart, K. (1999) *The Discursive Construction of National Identity*, Edinburgh: Edinburgh University Press.
Zhelev, Z. (2005) *In Spite of It All: My Political Biography*, Sofia: Kolibri. In Bulgarian.

Institutional archives

Bulgarian National Institute of Statistics. Census data available at http://www.nsi.bg/Census/Ethnos.htm (accessed 1 June 2015).
Embassy of the Hellenic Republic in Washington, DC. Electronic Archive available at http://www.greekembassy.org/Embassy/content/en/Article.aspx?office=1&folder=24&article=18371 (accessed 28 February 2013).
European Commission in Sofia: Information Centre. Available at http://ec.europa.eu/bulgaria/abc/pre_accession/history_relations/eu-political-relations_bg.htm (accessed 1 June 2015).
European Council Summits since 1985. Available at http://www.europarl.europa.eu/summits/ (accessed 1 June 2015).
Government of the Republic of Bulgaria: Information Service. Some electronic contents available at http://old.government.bg/cgi-bin/e-cms/vis/vis.pl?s=001&p=s_0008&g= (accessed 1 June 2015).
Government of the Republic of Macedonia: Media Service. Limited electronic contents at http://www.vlada.mk/?language=mk (accessed 1 June 2015).
Macedonian National Institute of Statistics. Census data available at http://makstat.stat.gov.mk/pxweb2007bazi/dialog/statfile18.asp (accessed 1 June 2015).
Ministry of Foreign Affairs of Bulgaria: Public Information Section. Briefing Archive available at http://www.mfa.bg/bg/news/category/4 (accessed 1 June 2015).
Ministry of Foreign Affairs of Macedonia: Press Centre. Electronic Archive at http://mfa.neotel.net.mk/default1.aspx?ItemID=324 (accessed 28 February 2013).

National Roundtable Talks, Bulgaria, 3 January–14 May: unabridged verbatim reports. Available at http://www.omda.bg/public/bulg/k_masa/2901/1.htm (accessed 1 June 2015).
Parliament of the Republic of Bulgaria. Full Electronic Archive available online at http://www.parliament.bg/bg/plenaryst (accessed 1 June 2015).
Parliament of the Republic of Macedonia. Full Electronic Archive available online at http://www.sobranie.mk/ext/sessions.aspx?Id=8440FB6B-A4144-7499-2705-CB070CE4997 (accessed 28 February 2013).
President of Bulgaria: Press Centre. Electronic archive available at http://www.president.bg/news_archive.php?from=news&type=3 (accessed 1 June 2015).
President of Macedonia: Media Centre. Some electronic content available at http://www.president.gov.mk/mk/20110-61-70-95-50-7/20110-90-31-13-65-9.html (accessed 28 February 2013).
The History of the European Union. Available at http://www.europa.eu/about-eu/eu-history/index_en.htm (accessed 1 June 2015).
United States Institute of Peace: 'Macedonia: Understanding history, preventing future conflict'. Available at http://www.usip.org/publications/macedonia-understanding-history-preventing-future-conflict (accessed 1 June 2015).
United States National Archives and Records Administration: President Woodrow Wilson's Fourteen Points, 1918. Document available electronically at http://www.ourdocuments.gov/doc.php?flash=true&doc=62 (accessed 1 June 2015).

Media sources

Bulgarian newspaper archives from the period 1991–2007. *24 Hours, Capital, Continent, Demokratsia, Duma, Makedoniya, Novinar, Otechestven Vestnik, Standard, Svoboden Narod, Trud, Zemya*.
Bulgarian Telegraph Agency (BTA), Courier Service.
Information Agency Focus News, Archive Service.
Macedonian newspaper archives from the period 1991–2007. *Dnevnik, Forum, Kapital, Makfax, Nova Makedonija, Puls, Utrinski, Vecher*.

Legal texts and international treaties

Bulgarian Law on Land Ownership and Land Ownership Rights, 1991. Available at http://www.lex.bg/laws/ldoc/2132550145 (accessed 1 June 2015).
Constitution of the Republic of Bulgaria, 1991. Available at http://www.parliament.bg/en/const (accessed 1 June 2015).
Constitution of the People's Republic of Bulgaria, 1971. Available at http://www.parliament.bg/bg/19 (accessed 1 June 2015).
Constitution of the Republic of Macedonia, 1991. Available at http://www.sobranie.mk/ustav-na-rm.nspx (accessed 1 June 2015).

Council of Europe, Framework Convention for the Protection of National Minorities, List of Declarations made with respect to Treaty No.157. Available at http://conventions.coe.int/Treaty/Commun/ListeDeclarations. asp?CL=ENG&NT=157&VL=1 (accessed 1 June 2015).
European Communities and European Union Founding Treaties, EU Law. Available at http://eur-lex.europa.eu/en/treaties/index.htm#founding (accessed 1 June 2015).
European Court of Human Rights, *Stankov and the United Macedonian Organisation Ilinden v. Bulgaria*, nos 29221/95 and 29225/95, §§ 10–14, ECHR 2001–IX.
European Court of Human Rights, *United Macedonian Organisation Ilinden – PIRIN and Others v. Bulgaria* (Application no. 59489/00).
Joint Declaration of the Prime Minister of the Republic of Bulgaria and the Prime Minister of the Republic of Macedonia, 1999. Available in the English language at http://www.bcci.bg/bulgarian/events/decl_mac_en.htm (accessed 1 June 2015).

Political party documents

Platform Declaration of the United Macedonian Revolutionary Organization – Traditional Macedonian Organization Ilinden led by Georgi Solunski, 14 November 1989, Ethno-sociology Archive of the Central Party Archive, Vol.4.
Statutes of Incorporation of the RADKO Association-Ohrid. Available at http://www.crwflags.com/fotw/flags/mk_radko.html (accessed 1 June 2015).
Statutes of United Macedonian Revolutionary Organization – Traditional Macedonian Organization Ilinden led by Georgi Solunski, Archive Ethno-Sociology of the Central Party Archive, Vol.4.
United Macedonian Diaspora. Electronic Archive available at http://www.umdiaspora.org/index.php?option=com_content&task=view&id=150&Itemid=76 (accessed 28 February 2013).

Index

Albania-Macedonia relations 55, 74, 168
  see also under Macedonia

Balkans 6–7, 140, 158, 177, 184
  academic study of 10, 177
  Europeanisation, appeal of in 156, 177
  and peace/stability 63, 69, 85, 88, 89, 94, 96, 119, 140
  nationalist analysis of 6, 10, 33, 157, 177
  see also Bulgaria; Macedonia
Bosnia 169
Bulgaria
  academic analyses of 7, 184–5
  Berlin Treaty (1878) 62
  Bulgarian Socialist Party 50, 95 n.40, 98, 153
  Club of the Repressed 58
  communism, fall in (1989) 42
  democratic transition in 48, 49–51, 56, 80, 93–9, 106–7, 158, 179
    and appeal for national unity 57–8
    democratic collapse 1992 109
    and market economics 107
    nationalist narratives during 56–65, 99
    and territorial integrity 59–60
  EU accession process 7, 8, 12, 95, 97–9, 114, 151–2, 185
    Association Agreement (1993) 98
    Council membership 95, 96
    as 'laggard' in 7, 151
    and Macedonia position 114, 116
    2007 joining 42
  Europeanisation of 8–9, 49–51, 75, 93–9, *105*, 107, 122–3, 136, 141, 151–8, 169–71, 185
    borders, changed significance of 155–7, 170, *171*, 179
    as communist counter-discourse 93–4, 97, 122
    and ethnic tolerance 153–4
    and meaning of territory 155–7, 179
    national identity, construction of 1, 8–9, 49, 50–1, 105, 107, 123, 152, 154, 157–8, *171*
    national interest, new meaning of 119, 154–5, *171*
    and national purpose 157–60
    nationalism, instrumentalisation of 36, 49–51
    nationhood, new meaning of 152, 155
    return to Europe narrative 63–4, 78, 90, 94–5, 98, 107
    see also Bulgarian-Macedonian relations
  Macedonia, cultural view of 54, 59, 62, 109, 112, 114–15, 127, 129
    as 'brothers' 59, 83–4, 133, 134, 159–60, *171*
    language commonality claim in 109, 112, 113, 120
    narrative of loss in 64, 77–8, 82, 94, 109, 115, 117
    repositioning of 117–18, 119, 122, 159–60, *171*

Macedonian statehood recognition 41–2, *46*, 63, 74, 76, 80, 81–8, 90, 93, *105*, 108–14, 117, 129, 159–60
  Badinter Commission, role in 82–3
  Bulgaria as 'malevolent Other' in 85–6, 87, 90
  'Europe' position of 83, 89, 117, 121, 159–60
  as foreign policy issue 89–90, 114, 122
  issue rhetoric in 42, 54, 76, 80–1, 83–5
  language dispute in 108–14, 115–18, 120, 130
  1991 referendum, effect in 81–2
  notion of patronage in 84–5, 86, 107, 109, 110, 111
  socialists' position on 122
  see also Bulgarian-Macedonian relations
minority recognition in 53, 58–9, 64, 76, *77*, 127, 129–33
  ethnic accommodation model in 127, 142
  Europeanisation effect on 140, 141, 153–4, *171*
  Framework Convention (1999) 133
  nationhood narrative in 133
  and 'Otherness' 64, 127, 134
  Pirin Macedonia issue 61, 69, 76, 88–9, 91, 129–30, 138, 140
  and trans-border co-operation 136
minority parties in 137–46, 152–3
  judiciary rulings in 42, 140
  registration and banning of 41, 58–9, 137–8, 139–41, 142–3, 144, 146
  Macedonian pro/anti groups 137, 138–46

UMO/ Ilinden-PIRIN 139, 140–1, 142–3
VMRO 138, 139
nationalist narratives 49–51, 55, 76, *77*, *105*, 152
  democracy/nationalism opposition 49–50
  of geographical centrality 61–3, 64
  minority accommodation in 50–1, 129–33
  nation v. people appeals 50
  of national unity 50–1, 57–8, 60, 64, 76, *77*, *105*, 138, 152, 153, 170, *171*
  orientation to the past in 64–5
  and party legitimation 51
  Self/Other dimension in 59, 60, 62, 64, 155, 157, 170–1
  of territorial integrity 59–61, 64, 76, *77*, 138, 141, 155, 170, 179
  of victimisation 62, 77–8, 157, 158
Turkish minority in 49, 50, 59, 127, 129
  assimilation of (1980s) 49, 50, 51
  autonomy, issue of 59–60, 89
  democratic mobilisation of 49
  Movement for Rights and Freedoms 59
  political party of 138
Bulgarian-Macedonian relations
  academic analyses of 7, 184–5
  identity-based conflict in 8, 16, 36, 44–6, 75, 78, *105*, 177, 185
  Europeanisation effect on 105–6, 159–60, 177, 185
  and logic of nationalism 36, 44, 78, 79, 88, *105*, 110
  identity narratives analysis 38–46, 104–49, 176–86
  'critical juncture' in 43
  discursive construction elements in 44, 177–8, 181

Europeanisation effect on 39, 40, 44–5, 75, 79, 92, 104–49, 159–60, 170–1, 178–9, 185
  methodology/data in 40–6, 177–9
  and nationalist discourse 44, 75–6
  research design 44–5, 46, 176
  Self/Other dialectic in 38, 39–40, 42, 43, 44, *45*, *46*, 59, 76, 79, 80, 170–1, 178, 179, 181, 185
  timeframe used in 42–3, *46*, 151, 178
  see also identity narratives
Joint Declaration (1999) 120–1, 130, 135, 137, 165
  language formula in 120–1, 134
  minority provision in 130, 134, 137
language disagreement between 7, 8, 36, 40, 41, 79, 106, 107–25, 126, 130, 140, 178, 181
  centrality to identity of 109–10, 181
  change of government incentive in 116, 121
  commonality issues in 108, 109, 110, 111, 120, 181
  Europeanisation, effect of on 8–9, 10, 106, 114, 117–20, 124–8, 178, 181–2
  friendship/Europe equivalence in 118
  historical/political separation in 121, 125–6, 135
  and Macedonian distinctness 110, 111
  narratives used in 43, 44, *46*, 110–18, *125*, 126–8, 181–2
  national interest narrative in 116, 119
  1994 diplomatic deadlock 108–9, 110, 111, 116

Otherness, interpretations in 107–8, 124, 126, 127
reconciliation narratives in 116–18
minority recognition between 40, 41, 42, *46*, 61, 79, 88, 127–49, 182
  appeal to European criteria in 133, 136, 141, 142, 147, 149, 182
  Bulgarian 'threat' narrative in 130–2, 134, 142
  census declarations 145–6
  commonality, development in 136, 181
  language negotiations, effect on 131, 134
  military donations (Bulgarian) effect on 131–2
  minority party bans 41, 58–9, 137–8, 139–41, 142–3, 144, 146
  narratives used in 40, 42, 43, 44, *46*, 76, *105*, 127, 128–33, *147*, 148–9
  nation/territory link in 128, 129–33
  nationalist vision of identity in 148–9
  nationhood interpretations in 133–4, 137, 146
  Self/Other positions in 134, 136, 137, 148–9, 182
reconciliation in 10, 11, 16, 44, 79, 107, 116–18, 148, 177
  bilateral partnership rhetoric 167
  commonality, increase in 136, 181
  and identity re-narration 16, 79, 81, 107, 126, 148–9, 159–60, 185
  inclusive, imagining in 79
  and political community boundaries 45, 79

role of stability (Bulgaria) use in 118–19, 126, 158–9, *171*
tolerance, use of notion (Macedonia) 161–5, *171*
statehood recognition 40, 41–2, *46*, 79–88, 181
  anti-Bulgarian rhetoric in 85–8, 90–1
  defiance/paternalism rhetoric in 80, 84–6, 159
  European signifier effect on 81, 83, 90, 92
  narratives used in 40, 41–2, 43, 44, *46*, 79–88, *105*
  national minorities issue in 88–9, 91
  nationhood contestation in 88–9
  as political hegemony struggle 92
  Self-Other distancing in 81, 85, 88, 105–6
  see also Bulgaria; Macedonia
Council of Europe 30
  Framework Convention for the Protection of National Minorities 41, 141 n.177
Croatia 169

EU legitimacy 9, 13, 16, 20 n.1, 21, 173, 174, 177
  and Constitutional Treaty 31
  and nationalism 182
  and re-narration of identity 174, 181
European Charter for Trans-border Cooperation 136
European Convention of Human Rights 41
European Court of Human Rights 41, 43, 146
  and minority representation 146
European identity 3, 20–2, 34, 173, 175, 183
  analysis/measurement of 21–2, 31, 183
  commonality features of 17–18
  and national identity 183
  as post-national 3, 17, 18
  as a project 32
  as supranational political 21, 34
  see also political community
European integration 1, 2–3, 4–5, 18, 31, 173
  and citizenship 18
  in economic crisis context 174, 175, 184
  and logic of nationalism 175
  minority rights, attention to 146
  national identity, cognitive effect of 23–4, 29, 183
  and nationalism 2–3, 147, 182, 184
  popular support, decrease of 4–5, 15, 177
  and post-communist states 6, 28, 29, 32–3
  supranational community view of 4, 5, 15, 17–18, 32
  supranational institutions of 18
  transformative potential of 32, 35
  and rhetoric of benefits 35
Europeanisation 1, 8–9, 16–17, 30–1, 173–5, 181–3
  academic study of 28–9, 30–1, 33–4
  definitions, use of 30–1
  notion of change in 30–1
  rationalist vs reflectivist theories 28–9
  of national identities 3, 9, 10–13, 16, 20, 28–9, 31–2, 33–4, 35, 36, 48–9, 173–4, 176, 177, 181–3
  and conflict reconciliation 12, 16, 17, 35, 45, 173, 177, 184, 186
  legitimacy effect on 20, 30, 32, 34, 35, 45, 49, 173–4
  re-narration of 10, 11, 16, 36, 173, 174
  Self/Other dynamics, effect on 173–5, 181, 182, 184
  vertical/horizontal dimensions of 9, 45, 174–5
  see also identity narratives

national impact of 3, 4, 10, 32–4, 174, 181–2
  on identity narratives 3, 4, 5, 10, 11, 16, 33, 45, 173, 178, *180*, 181–3
  on nationalist agendas 32–34, 45, 182
  normative and institutional 33, 174, 182, 183
  as process/agent of change 30–1, 183–4
  political community, change of 3, 5, 6, 8, 11, 18–20, 34, 35, 45, 173, 174, 179, 181, 182–3, 186
  commonality, notion of in 18, 173, 175, 182
  legitimisation effect in 20, 30, 32, 34, 35, 36–7, 173–4, 181, 183, 186
  supranational institutions in 18, 28
  see also under Bulgaria; Macedonia
Euroscepticism 6

globalisation 2, 182
Greece-Macedonia relations 54, 69, 74, 75, 87, 90, 93, 103, 161, 165, 167, 168, 179, 185
  and economic blockade 103, 107
  EU's reaction to 102, 161
  name dispute 69, 70, 80, 86, 87, 101, 161
  and UN recognition 103

identity
  concept of 20, 22
  and contingency 25
  role of language/discourse in 25, 186
  see also European identity; national identity
identity change 11, 12, 22, 24, 43, 46, 173
  conceptualisations of 28–9
  'critical junctures' in 22, 43
  discursive mechanisms of 39, 176

identity narratives 5, 10, 15, 17, 29, 30, 36–8, 48–9
  difference, construction of 37, 38
  discursive elements of 37–8, 39–40, 49, 179, 183
  inside/outside distinction in 15, 23, 38
  political community, role in 36, 37, 38
  and nation-state legitimacy 15, 17, 38
  and narrative reconstruction 37
  Self-Other distinction 15, 23, 25, 38, 39–40, 49
  discursive elements of 40
  see also Bulgarian-Macedonian relations analysis; under national identity

Kosovo 142, 160, 166, 168

Macedonia
  Albanian minority recognition in 53–4, 65, 66–7, 70, 93, 100, 101, 102, 103, *105*, 124, 127–8, 140, 144, 166
    European rhetoric, use by 100, 101, 124, 140
    referendum blockade by 93
    and 2001 conflict 161
  Bulgarian Macedonians 127, 128, 139
    identity politics of 42, 61, 164–5
    party ban of 41, 143
    protection denied to 128
  Declaration of Independence (1991) 42, *46*
  democratic transition in 48, 51–5, 80, 103, 106–7, 161
    communists' return to power 103, 106
    and international recognition 80
    and market economics 107

nationalist narratives during
65–75
rise in nationalism in 51, 78
EU accession process 2, 8, 42–3,
99–104, 123, 134, 161–2
application (2004) in 161–2
and Greek conflict 161, 179
and Serb border 160–1, 165
Europeanisation in 75, 99–104,
105, 107, 123–4, 136, 160–71,
181
Bulgaria position change 124–5,
166, 167, 181
EU incentives/support (2006)
169
and EU statehood recognition
101–2, 105–6, 107, 123, 160,
169
logic of nationalism in 99, 100,
102, 105, 106, 181
national purpose articulation
167–9
and political division 123–4
territory, re-interpretation of
165–8, 170, 179
tolerance, salience of notion in
163–5, 170, *171*
identity narratives analysis 41–2,
53–4, 65–75, 102–3, *105*, 107,
170–1
language as central to 108–14,
170
and minority recognition 53, 54,
65–8, 73–4, *171*
Self/Other dialectic in 42, 53,
54, 68, 74, 77, 78, 104, 105–6,
164, 167, 170, *171*
inter-ethnic conflict in 7, 52, 65–8,
73–4, 104, 105, 106, 142, 161–6
and Albanian exclusion 53–4
border significance, change in
166–7, 170
Europeanisation, effect on
166–7, 169

nationalist discourse in 36, 42,
52, 54, 65–8
re-narration as resolved 'crisis'
169
territorial narrative, effect on 71,
165–7, 170
tolerance, discursive use of
162–5
2001 civil conflict 104, 161, 169
minority parties in 41, 143–4
Human Rights Party 143
RADKO Association 144
registration ban on 41, 143
VMRO-Tatkovinsko 143
minority recognition in 53, 65–7,
75, 127–8, 140, 142
national tolerance formula of
128, 162–4
and territorial threat narratives
130–1
nationalist narratives in 51–2, *105*,
107, 112, 169, 170
country name significance in
69–71, 75, 76, *77*
external/internal others in 52
and independence project 52, 53
nation/state correlation in 53
of national tolerance 65–8, 74,
76, 88, 162–5
of territorial belonging 68–71,
76, *77*, 88, 165, *171*
of victimisation 71–4, *77*, 86,
171
national identity, construction of 1,
8–9, 65–75, 163, 169, 170–1
Europeanisation effect on 8–9,
10, 104, 162, 169, 170–1
and inter-ethnic hostility 55, 169,
171
language distinctness claims in
110, 111
re-narration of 169, 170, *171*
stability/culture positioning in
163, 166, 168, *171*

statehood recognition 41–2, *46*, 52–3, 65, 67, 72–4, *77*, 80–8, 101–4, *105*, 167
  anti-Bulgarian rhetoric 85–6, 124, 125
  civic imperatives in 67–8, 75, *77*, *105*, 163–4, *171*
  EU reservation and recognition 93, 101, 104, 167
  Greece, negotiations with 103–4
  language link in 108, 109–10, 112
  and minority inclusion 54, 67, 87
  as 'national liberation' 73
  nationalist rhetoric in 52–3, 72, 80, 88
  1991 referendum on 81
  victimisation discourse in 72–3, 74, *77*, 78, 167, 168, *171*
  vindication, notion of in 72, 74, *77*, 78, 88, 167
  see also under Greece
  UN membership (1993) 102, 103
  name dispute in 103
migration/asylum 2, 15, 29, 186
  intra-EU 35
  national effects on 31

nation, concept/definition of 20, 22, 24
national identity 1, 3, 10–13, 15, 22–6, 33, 36, 173
  analysis of 10–13, 21–6, 185–6
    in European politics 22, 23–4, 25, 33–4, 173, 184
    reflectivist approach 10, 11, 23, 27, 28, 29–30
    Self-Other dialectic in 12, 178
  construction of 1, 5, 11, 15, 18, 27–8, 37, 178
    commonality claims in 18
    contingency/contextuality in 29
    discursive struggles/mechanisms in 4–6, 27–8, 29–30, 37, 39, 49, 184
  elites, role in 4, 5, 29, 40
  language, role in 110, 112
  see also under identity narratives
  and collective memory 24
  and cosmopolitanism 3
  definitions of 22–3, 177–8
  exclusionary rhetoric/attitudes in 18–19
  measurement of 21
  and minorities 146–7
    historical narratives of 146–7
  narratives used in *see* identity narratives
  and political community 22, 23, 183
  identification, role in 24, 39
  political functions of 17, 23–6, 39
    antagonistic potential in 25
    cognitive effects 23–4
    on collective action 24–5
    state legitimising role in 17, 23, 24, 25, 39
    territoriality element in 23
  see also European identity; identity change
nationalism 1, 15, 19, 26–8, 176, 184
  academic study of 1, 11, 26–8, 33–4, 184
    in post-communist Europe 2, 4–8, 25–6, 28–9, 33–4
  conceptualisations of 26
    antagonistic potential in 26, 27, 186
    modernist view of 27
    postmodernist approaches to 25–6
  European history of 26–7, 34, 176
  hegemonic role of 27, 28, 29
  national identity, function of in 23, 25–6, 176
  negative consequences of 3, 26
  'post-liberal' 18, 19, 31, 33, 34, 177, 186
  see also under Europeanisation; national identity
Norway 2

OSCE 30

PHARE programme 103–4
political community 5, 6, 7, 9, 12–13, 17–19, 176
  concept of 17, 35
  and Europeanisation 3, 5, 6, 8, 11, 18, 35, 174
  imagining/narratives of 5, 7, 9, 174
    elites, role in 5
  legitimation of 1, 11
  and national identity 1, 5, 15, 19, 35, 182
  nationalist vision of 5, 6, 8
  as sovereign state 4
  as supranational 5, 17
populism 184
post-communist states 2, 4–8, 8, 25, 28, 29, 32–3, 176
  academic analysis of 2, 4–8, 25–6, 28–9, 33–4, 176
    frame of nationalism in 6, 26, 33–4, 176
    identity politics, focus in 2
    see also national identity
  democratic transition in 47–8
    as a 'critical juncture' 48
    EU membership as goal of in 48–9
    and nationalist rhetoric 48, 55–6
  Europeanisation effects of 2, 4–7, 22, 28–9, 33, 78, 174, 176
    on national identity 2, 5–6, 8, 25–6, 49, 176
    on nationalism 33, 47, 56, 176
    'return to Europe' frame 36, 78, 90
    on Self/Other narratives 48–9, 174
    see also Europeanisation

  identity-based conflict in 9, 29, 33, 56
  transition process in 25, 33
    and nationalism 2, 4, 6, 25–6, 33
    see also Bulgaria; Macedonia
racism 2, 9, 18, 184
  'syncretic racism' 18
  'xeno-racism' 18
Romania 7

securitisation theory 16
Serbia 90, 160
  and Macedonian relations 55, 160, 169
  UN embargo 107
Soviet Union 47
state, the
  and identity narration 1, 3, 25, 34, 37–8
    discursive elements of 37–8
    inside/outside distinction in 15
    Self/Other distinction in 15, 25
    see also identity narratives
  and nationalism 4, 25
  and popular sovereignty 4
  transnational challenge to 31–2
  see also national identity; political community

transnational democracy (Habermas) 17
Turkey 89

xenophobia 2, 184

Yugoslav federation 47, 72, 80, 90
  Macedonian involvement in 72

www.ingramcontent.com/pod-product-compliance
Lightning Source LLC
Chambersburg PA
CBHW071355290426
44108CB00014B/1554